JANE AUSTEN'S
ART OF MEMORY

JANE AUSTEN'S ART OF MEMORY

JOCELYN HARRIS

Associate Professor in English, University of Otago

The right of the
University of Cambridge
to print and sell
all manner of books
was granted by
Henry VIII in 1534.
The University has printed
and published continuously
since 1584.

CAMBRIDGE UNIVERSITY PRESS

Cambridge

New York   Port Chester

Melbourne   Sydney

Published by the Press Syndicate of the University of Cambridge
The Pitt Building, Trumpington Street, Cambridge CB2 1RP
40 West 20th Street, New York, NY 10011, USA
10 Stamford Road, Oakleigh, Melbourne 3166, Australia

First published 1989

Printed in Great Britain at
the University Press, Cambridge

British Library cataloguing in publication data
Harris, Jocelyn
Jane Austen's art of memory
1. Fiction in English. Austen, Jane, 1775–
1817 — Critical studies
I. Title
823'.7

Library of Congress cataloguing in publication data
Harris, Jocelyn.
Jane Austen's art of memory / Jocelyn Harris.
p.   cm.
Bibliography.
Includes index.
ISBN 0-521-36391-8
1. Austen, Jane, 1775–1817 — Knowledge — Literature. 2. Austen,
Jane, 1775–1817 — Books and reading.   3. Influence (Literary,
artistic, etc.) 4. Memory in literature. 5. Allusions. I. Title.
PR4038.L5H37   1989
823'.7 — dc 19   89-502   CIP

ISBN 0 521 36391 8

823.7
A 933 L ha

WG

For Margot and Angus Ross

Contents

Preface

Jane Austen read very extensively in history and *belles-lettres*, and her memory was extremely tenacious.[1] Her invention sprang largely from books, for in the English classics that were once women's liberal education, Jane Austen found languages to write with. I here set her books against other books to show how memory gives origins to art, and without claiming to have discovered everything, explore how her mind might have worked.

Jane Austen uses 'allusions' and 'influences' neither by chance nor merely for embellishment. *Northanger Abbey* for instance, far from being the slightest of her novels, dramatises Locke to display a method and a manifesto. This, the first of her longer works to be completed in 1803, seems virtually unaffected by Richardson, whom she had satirised ruthlessly in the juvenilia. The 1804 publication of his *Correspondence* may have revived her respect for a favourite author, because difficult critical cruxes in *Sense and Sensibility* disappear if Jane Austen built her book on *Pamela*, *Clarissa*, and *Grandison*, and if she was prompted by the *Correspondence* to revise her novel in the 'lost years' 1805–9, as I shall argue. *Sense and Sensibility* contains particularly nice contrasts between some scenes she fully reworked from Richardson and Milton, and others she hardly assimilated at all. *Pride and Prejudice* demonstrates the dazzling variety of ways in which she rewrote *Grandison*, along with glances towards *Pamela* and *Much Ado about Nothing*. *Mansfield Park* calls upon *Grandison* yet again to develop Richardson's Miltonic hints into the important scene in the wilderness. It shows what she can do, essentially, with a change of key. By contrast, *A Midsummer Night's Dream* more thoroughly diffuses all of *Emma*, as Chaucer's Wife of Bath does *Persuasion*. By this stage the literary-critical impulse of her Richardson-based books dissolves for the most part into a method more open, confident, and free. Although her differences are at least as important as her similarities, books do seem thus to have provided her beginnings. And if Jane Austen invigorated herself by reading Chaucer, Shakespeare, Locke, Milton, Pope, Richardson, Fielding, and Coleridge, she only did as they all did when she made them new and when she made them hers.

Some people will resist the idea. One early critic, Richard Simpson, wrote 'If she had no personal help from her contemporaries, she cannot be said to have derived much from books', and A. Walton Litz decided recently that while 'her novels are filled with literary references, many of them are either trivial or misleading, and conventional source studies ... show how little vital background is uncovered by an investigation of these allusions'.[2] But I am not the first to try and catch her in the act of greatness[3] by guessing where she began. Q. D. Leavis names the early works as a major source, though R. W. Chapman and B. C. Southam do not agree; Mary Lascelles argues that she used conventions similar to Fanny Burney's; Clara Thomson shows that Maria Edgeworth influenced her in ways that Marilyn Butler calls 'anti-jacobin'; Kenneth Moler and Frank Bradbrook uncover a host of allusions to other books; Henrietta Ten Harmsel sees her drawing on a diffused network of conventions; Peter L. De Rose looks to Samuel Johnson; and Juliet McMaster argues for Shakespeare. Alvin Metcalfe, Jan Fergus, and Gerard Barker perceive the special importance of *Grandison*. Alistair Duckworth places her in the conservative tradition, while Margaret Kirkham sets her among eighteenth-century feminist debates.[4] These critics assume as I do, that to know her reading is to understand her better.

Susan Gilbert and Sandra Gubar, drawing on Frank Kermode's and Harold Bloom's Freudian paradigms about the necessary 'anxiety' of writers confronted by the burden of the past, sketch a Jane Austen who resists male-dominated art. Dale Spender endows her with a matriarchal novelistic inheritance, and Jane Spencer explores thematic links with female forerunners.[5] I myself believe that Jane Austen took what she wanted from anywhere, not just from women, and not just from fiction either, and that her memory energised her art in a manner far more coherent even than 'intertextuality'. In spite of Freud and his followers, I detect no trace of anxiety in her, for to paraphrase

Dryden on Jonson, she 'invades Authors like a Monarch, and what would be theft in other Poets, is only victory in her' (*Of Dramatick Poesie*, p. 90). Every detail of my argument may not strike others as forcefully as it did me, but I hope that the accumulation of detail will. In any case, we flatter ourselves to think we know more than she did, for if we know even part of it, we are doing pretty well.

What, as Jane Austen said in echo of Harriet Byron, am I to do with my gratitude? I am grateful to Pat Brückmann, John Burrows, Marilyn Butler, Margaret Dalziel, Ian Donaldson, Margaret Anne Doody, Alistair Duckworth, E. E. Duncan-Jones, David Erdman, Catherine Fitzgerald, Colin Gibson, David Gilson, John Hardy, Lenore Harty, David Hoeniger, Park Honan, Jonathan Lamb, Mary Lascelles, D. C. Measham, the late Ellen Moers, Michael Neill, Ruth Perry, Clive Probyn, Claude Rawson, Barry Roth, Juliet Sheen, George Starr, Janet Todd, Howard Weinbrot, my editor Kevin Taylor, and my copy-editor Andrea Smith. Anaig Fenby, Lynnsay Francis, Michael Hamel, John Jackson, Jane Jones, and Mary Sullivan were expert friends, while John, James, and Lison Harris simply made everything possible.

1

Northanger Abbey

Jane Austen was surely teasing when in her 'Advertisement' she called *Northanger Abbey* a 'little work'. On the face of it, this story, like so many stories, like so many of Jane Austen's stories, tells of a young girl's entrance into the world, her achievement of some kind of intellectual maturity, and her marriage to a man entirely suitable for her. The tale seems slight, parodic,[1] of interest only to females, and therefore to be dismissed as trivial. For some, only the facility and accuracy save the day. It is well done, certainly, but was it worth doing at all?

But the tale may be told another way, like this. Catherine Morland, though ignorant, and assailed by corrupt companions and corrupting reading, develops her own powers of understanding at Bath. Free from the biases of traditional education, she courageously tests her hypothesis that General Tilney is a murderer. She picks her way through falsehood and hypocrisy until she proves herself rational, able to know true from false. Her pursuit after happiness, the proper aim of any reasonable being, is fulfilled in the perfect felicity of her marriage. This book shows a mind educating itself through innate powers.

If this sounds familiar, it is, for *Northanger Abbey* is, I believe, a close realisation of ideas from John Locke's *Essay Concerning Human Understanding*, while Catherine's education derives from his influential treatise.[2] *Northanger Abbey*'s words and phrases often resemble Locke's as I shall show,[3] and though only a novel, its aim may be as serious as his, to explore how one may take 'a Survey of our own Understandings, examine our own Powers, and see to what Things they were adapted' (I.i.7). To exercise our reason, says Locke, is to praise the God who gave it, and this is what Catherine Morland, as a reasonable Christian, does.

It would be remarkable if Jane Austen knew nothing of Locke, whose *Essay* was the most influential book of the eighteenth century, except for the Bible. The posthumously published addition *On the Conduct of the Understanding* (1706) and *Some Thoughts Concerning Education* (1693) were several times reprinted in the eighteenth century. What made Locke's philosophy of mind so very agreeable to a wide variety of people, especially women, must have been its assurance that everyone could develop powers of understanding. Locke's thesis that everyone started equal, his argument that everyone should be educated at home as girls had always been, and his preference for English and virtue over classical languages, all obviously appealed to those denied an education for reasons of class or sex. Locke's emphasis on individual perception rather than on blind submission to received opinion must make him at least partially responsible for the sudden upsurge of feminism in the eighteenth century.

Intelligent women in particular could have seen how to take responsibility for themselves. The pioneering feminist Mary Astell, Mrs Catherine Cockburn, and Locke's patron Lady Damaris Masham all commented on Locke. Richardson, that middle-class autodidact, found Locke sympathetic for the same reasons as the women did. Pamela comments at length on Locke's *Education* (VI. 258–315), and part of an important debate about learning and languages in *Sir Charles Grandison* depends upon it.[4] Even Mrs Fitzpatrick claimed to have read *Human Understanding* in *Tom Jones* (XI. vii), and Dorothea Brooke would marry Casaubon because he reminded her of Locke. Whether Jane Austen met Locke at one remove, or whether she read him for herself we do not know. What does matter is to see how systematically and intelligently she 'translates' him in *Northanger Abbey*.

Catherine Morland's education

Jane Austen presents an image of successful education with a mischievous hint, like Locke's, that she is stepping out of line. Where he addresses those who 'dare venture to consult their own Reason, in the Education of their Children, rather than wholly to rely upon Old Custom' (§ 216), Jane Austen flouts not only romantic but educational conventions to speak in the first chapter of Catherine Morland's 'extraordinary' abilities, or nonsensically of the fact that 'she could never learn or understand any thing before she was taught'. (Johnson wrote similarly in his life of Milton that 'nobody can be taught faster than he can learn'.) Catherine's failure to become a fashionable female is described as 'profligacy', and yet strange and unaccountable as it seems, she turns out well. Her busy mother's tolerant neglect together with her own determined choices make up in fact an educational programme exactly like that prescribed by Locke to more deliberate parents. All the benefits result that he had hoped for, her escape from the corruptions of education, and her engaging readiness to learn.[5]

Jane Austen describes Catherine's early years with speed and precision. 'Fond of all boys' plays', preferring 'cricket, base ball, riding on horseback, and running about the country' to the conventional pursuits of girls (13, 15),[6] Catherine fulfils Locke's opening recommendation for a healthy mind in a healthy body. She always will. When Henry advises more frequent exercise, and objects that her love for a hyacinth is 'rather domestic' – like Locke's complaint that painting is 'a sedentary Recreation' (§ 203) – she replies firmly, 'but I do not want any such pursuit to get me out of doors. The pleasure of walking and breathing fresh air is enough for me, and in fine weather I am out more than half my time. – Mamma says, I am never within' (174). So too Locke had recommended that the more girls are in the air, 'the stronger and healthier they will be; and the nearer they come to the Hardships of their Brothers in their Education, the greater Advantage will they receive from it all the remaining Part of their Lives' (§ 9). Catherine is plain, with a thin and awkward figure, but to Locke 'plain and rough Nature left to it self, is much better than an Artificial Ungracefulness' (§ 66.2). She does grow to be '*almost* pretty' (15) as Locke had promised. 'Never trouble your self about those Faults in them, which you know Age will cure', he says reassuringly (§ 67). Her healthy body is assisted as much by the good constitution of her mother (13) as by the fact that she is usually a sound sleeper: 'nothing is more to be indulged Children than *Sleep* ... nothing contributing more to the Growth and Health of Children than *Sleep*', says Locke (§ 21).

Her mother's benign neglect, for 'her time was so much occupied in lying-in and teaching the little ones, that her elder daughters were inevitably left to shift for themselves' (15), conforms to Locke's advice that children 'for all their innocent Folly, Playing and *Childish Actions, are to be left perfectly free and unrestrained*' (§ 63). Catherine, writes Jane Austen, was noisy and wild, hated confinement and cleanliness, and loved nothing so well in the world as rolling down the green slope at the back of the house (14). Nor does Mrs Morland force an education upon her daughter unsuitable to youth. If Catherine is 'often inattentive, and occasionally stupid' (14), Locke knew that 'Inadvertency, forgetfulness, unsteadiness, and wandring of Thought, are the natural Faults of Childhood' (§ 167). Locke recommends Aesop's Fables (§ 156); Mrs Morland chooses for Catherine an appropriate one from Gay, about a naive hare betrayed by friends. But the fact that her daughter takes three months to learn it confirms the truth of Locke's observation that learning by heart is time and pains mis-spent (§ 175). His repeated recommendation that learning should never 'be made a Burthen to [children], or imposed on them as a *Task*' if they are not to take an aversion to it (§ 73.1) is implicitly accepted by Mrs Morland, who once Catherine's enthusiasm for music evaporates, 'did not insist on her daughters being accomplished in spite of incapacity or distaste, [and] allowed her to leave off' (14). Locke maintains that music 'wastes so much of a young Man's time, to gain but a moderate Skill in it ... Our short Lives will not serve us for the attainment of all things' (§ 197). Elsewhere in her novels Jane Austen portrays this female accomplishment as a trap. Marianne Dashwood's sensibility is dangerously heightened by her musical powers, Mary Bennet's musical earnestness turns her into a public guy, Janet Fairfax's proficiency drives her to the slave-trade of governessing, and Anne Elliot plays that other people may dance. Elizabeth Bennet, however, plays only to amuse herself, and Emma Woodhouse, queen of Highbury, will never practise.

Locke is equally kindly about that other female accomplishment, drawing. 'Ill Painting is one of the worst things in the World; and to attain a tolerable degree of Skill in it, requires too much ... Time' (§ 203). Catherine's taste for drawing is 'not superior', and as her look-alike houses and trees, hens and chickens show, she has 'no notion of drawing' (14, 16). Mrs Morland does not press her. Where the genius for drawing is wanting, says Locke, 'it is better to let him pass [it] by quietly, than to vex him about [it] to no purpose: And therefore in this, as in all other things not absolutely necessary, the Rule holds, *Nihil invitâ Minervâ*' (§ 161).

If Locke recommends the memorising of 'Wise and Useful Sentences' for their 'future Life' (§ 176), Catherine in a delightful inversion learns 'those quotations which are so serviceable and so soothing in the vicissitudes of [heroines'] eventful lives' (15). But otherwise the result is everything that Locke predicts. Catherine has neither a bad heart nor a bad temper, and is very kind to the little ones; 'Vertue, and a well-temper'd Soul is to be preferr'd to any sort of *Learning* or *Language*', says Locke, so 'teach him betimes to love, and be *good natur'd* to others' (§§ 177, 139). She is seldom stubborn, and stubbornness is rare under Locke's regime; she is rarely tyrannical, a vice that Locke warns parents against (§§ 78, 109). Most important of all, she never lies, a habit of which he says 'a Child should be brought up in the greatest abhorrence ... imaginable' (§ 131).

Such is Catherine when she leaves her father's house, promisingly ignorant and eager to learn. As Henry says she is 'a very close questioner' (151), often curious. Curiosity in children, says Locke, 'is but an Appetite after Knowledge ... the great Instrument Nature has provided, to remove that Ignorance they were born with; and which, without this busie *Inquisitiveness*, will make them dull and useless Creatures'. The tutor's task, then, is to answer all questions however ignorant. Children may 'modestly put in their Question as Learners' (§§ 118, 145), and Catherine does so during Henry's lecture on the picturesque taste. She is 'so hopeful a scholar' that Henry is delighted with her progress. Jane Austen's comments on the attractions of imbecility, or ignorance, in females (111) recalls Richardson's pedant Walden, who enjoys instructing an ignorant and humble woman (*Grandison*, I. 70).

But Henry is not always an ideal tutor for Catherine. He condescendingly accuses his sister of being stupid, that is, not rational, about the very shocking thing to come out of London, and raillies her and Catherine in a whole string of epistomological words:

Come, shall I make you understand each other or leave you to puzzle out an explanation as you can? No – I will be noble. I will prove myself

a man, no less by the generosity of my soul than the clearness of my head.
I have no patience with such of my sex as disdain to let themselves
sometimes down to the comprehension of yours. Perhaps the abilities
of women are neither sound nor acute – neither vigorous nor keen.
Perhaps they want observation, discernment, judgment, fire, genius, and
wit.   (112)

Catherine grows grave, and Eleanor rebukes him. 'And now,
Henry … that you have made us understand each other, you may
as well make Miss Morland understand yourself – unless you
mean to have her think you intolerably rude to your sister, and
a great brute in your opinion of women in general' (113). To Locke
a 'brute', a beast, is not-human, not employing one's God-given
and uniquely human powers (IV.xvii.1),[7] so that Henry by
calling his sister 'stupid' and 'simpleton' proves himself to be so.
Because he is not in a sober mood, Eleanor excuses his frivolous
riposte, lifted straight from Sir Charles Grandison (III. 246–7),
that he does indeed 'think very highly of the understanding of all
the women in the world – especially of those – whoever they
may be – with whom I happen to be in company' (113–14).
Catherine, who loves Henry, believes he can never be wrong, but
Locke, writing sternly of education as 'so nice and tickle a
business, wherein a little slip may spoil all', advises that any
wrong turn may leave upon the mind of those made uneasy by
it 'the lasting memory of having been piquantly, though wittily
taunted for some thing censurable in them' (§ 143.3).
     Far more efficacious an educator than Henry, and here I must
disagree with those who admire him as mentor and spokes-
man,[8] is his sister Eleanor. The tutor, says Locke, should
remember that 'his business is not so much to teach him all that
is knowable, as to raise in him a love and esteem for Knowledge;
and to put him in the right way of knowing and improving
himself, when he has a mind to it' (§ 195). Henry does well to lead
Catherine easily from the picturesque, a piece of rocky fragment,
the withered oak and oaks in general, to forests, the inclosure of
them, waste lands, crown lands and government (111), and he
responds warmly to Catherine's announcement that she has
learnt to love a hyacinth. By accident or argument, he asks. 'Your
sister taught me', replies Catherine, 'I cannot tell how'. Where
Mrs Allen's 'pains, year after year' have not succeeded, Eleanor's
loving instruction has. Henry sees that an important start has

been made: 'Who can tell, the sentiment once raised, but you may in time come to love a rose?'. He adds, more seriously, 'The mere habit of learning to love is the thing; and a teachableness of disposition in a young lady is a great blessing. – Has my sister a pleasant mode of instruction?' (174). The arguments that learning should be pleasant, that habits of learning and eagerness to learn should be encouraged, are central to the radical educational theory of Locke.

Rational conversation with a loving tutor is vital; so too is the judicious use of books. But Catherine falls prey to Mrs Radcliffe's sensationalism, her addiction more complicated than once thought. Jane Austen criticises not just *Udolpho*, but what it has meant to Catherine. Bad company has influenced her into reading it; her curiosity is factitiously activated by queries about the black veil; she is encouraged to prefer imagination to the real and the probable and therefore cannot act empirically; she is frightened; and she is corrupted by her only available substitute for the Grand Tour.

'There is no part wherein the understanding needs a more careful and wary conduct than in the use of books', writes Locke, lest 'in [children's] tender years, ideas that have no natural cohesion come not to be united in their heads' (*Education*, p. 57). By false analogy Catherine connects Mrs Radcliffe's Italian scenes to General Tilney and Northanger Abbey, whereas, as Locke says, we must not 'suffer our Understandings to be misguided by a wrong supposition of Analogy where there is none' (*Conduct*, § 38). When Catherine meditates by turns 'on broken promises and broken arches, phaetons and false hangings, Tilneys and trapdoors' (87), when she thinks that General Tilney has 'the air and attitude of a Montoni' (187), she practises an 'instantaneous Legerdemain' by which 'one Idea is substituted for the other' (*Conduct*, § 39).

When she joins Italian fictions to English realities, Catherine makes faulty complex ideas out of simple ones. In Locke's opinion 'there is not any one thing that deserves more to be looked after' in young people because the mind no longer knows what agrees to 'the reality of Things, and what not' (II. xxxiii. 9, xxx. 3). Fancy divorced from nature gives rise to Catherine's elaborate surmises about Mrs Tilney in a passage brimming with conditional words and phrases, 'likely', 'probability', 'conclusion which necessarily followed', 'idea', 'supposition', 'not unlikely', 'remembered', 'plausibility of this conjecture', 'memory', 'might well have', 'perhaps', 'surmises', 'supported by such appearances as made their dismissal impossible' (187–8).'

Typically then, Catherine's busy young mind quickly, too quickly, puts together ideas that do not belong. She herself will come to castigate her theorizing in Lockean terms when she regrets 'the extravagance of her late fancies', her 'folly', the 'liberty which her imagination had dared to take with the character of his father ... the absurdity of her curiosity and her fears' (199), rather as Locke had spoken of taking a 'Liberty' in forming complex ideas (II. xxx. 3). He concludes that we 'run our selves into the most extravagant Errors and Miscarriages' when we 'set up phancy for our supreme and sole Guide, and ... believe any Proposition to be true, any Action to be right, only because we believe it to be so' (IV. xix. 11). So Catherine learns, when she ceases to combine Mrs Radcliffe's Italy with Regency England.

Locke attacks those who fail to 'preserve [the child's] tender Mind' from 'fearful Apprehensions' (§ 138), but Mrs Radcliffe inspires terror deliberately. Henry is equally culpable when he encourages her fears, as even Catherine realises when she says, 'it was in a great measure his own doing' (173). Her perception is remarkable because of her love-struck deference to Henry. She says stoutly, 'I do not think I should be easily frightened', and argues logically that the Abbey has not been left long deserted, nor does the family return to it unawares, 'without giving any notice, as generally happens'. She recognizes that 'this is just like a book', and is 'sure your housekeeper is not really Dorothy'. Miss Tilney, she is sure, would never put her into such a chamber as he had described: 'She was not at all afraid' (158–60). She resists the Radcliffean ideas pressed upon her by an irresponsible and teasing tutor.[9] Jane Austen's parody of the Gothic novel is obvious, but her implications are Lockean. Nor was this the first time that Catherine exercised her independent understanding, as we shall see.

Finally, *Udolpho* is Catherine's Grand Tour, as she explains at Beechen Cliff:

'I never look at it,' said Catherine, as they walked along the side of the river, 'without thinking of the South of France.'

'You have been abroad then?' said Henry, a little surprized.

'Oh! no, I only mean what I have read about. It always puts me in mind of the country that Emily and her father travelled through, in the "Mysteries of Udolpho".' (106)

Locke believed that although the Tour crowned a pupil's wisdom (§ 212), it proved the superiority of English morality and manners. Sir Charles Grandison may dally with a lovely Italian, but the return to English religion, ways, and wife is irresistible. By the time that Jane Austen or even Pope wrote, the Tour seemed not education's crown, but its perversion. Europe corrupted, tutors misled. When Catherine's tutor Henry encourages her hypothesis that people are fiends, she travels in the only way she can through Italy, Switzerland, the South of France, the Alps, and the Pyrenees, shakes off their corruptions when she proves her hypothesis wrong, and returns safely to the central part of England. Unlike most young men, she survives the corruptions of the Grand Tour. When she rejects Mrs Radcliffe and the deceiving tutorship of Henry, when she recognises that 'among the English ... in their hearts and habits, there was a general though unequal mixture of good and bad', when she admits that there might even be some slight imperfection in Henry and Eleanor and some actual specks in the character of their father, a man whom she believes, 'upon serious consideration, to be not perfectly amiable' (200), she has reached Locke's educational goal, which was to acquaint the pupil 'with the true State of the World, and dispose him to think no Man better or worse, wiser or foolisher, than really he is' (§ 94).[10] Catherine escapes the snares of education by shaping her mind herself.

'The dark room of the understanding'

The climactic test of Catherine's understanding is her bold attempt to prove that General Tilney has murdered his wife in the 'cell', the 'prison' of her gloomy bedroom (188–9). Flinging open the door, she sees however 'a large, well-proportioned apartment ... a bright Bath stove, mahogany wardrobes and neatly painted chairs, on which the warm beams of a western sun gaily poured through two sash windows!' (193). It is as though Jane Austen makes an event out of Locke's traditional metaphor for enlightenment. Sensations, he argues, are the Windows by which light is let into this *dark Room*. For, methinks, the *Understanding* is not much unlike a Closet wholly shut from light, with only some little openings left, to let in external visible Resemblances, or *Ideas* of things without ...   (II.xi.17)

'Like the bright Sun-shine', this kind of knowledge leaves 'no room for Hesitation, Doubt, or Examination, but the Mind is presently filled with the clear Light of it' (IV.ii. 1). The dark room of Catherine's mind lights up in the same way when 'astonishment and doubt' give way to a 'ray of common sense' (193),[11] when what Locke called 'this clear Light, some Sparks of bright Knowledge' (IV.xvii. 15), fill her mind with certainty and truth.

This important scene of the mind's illumination is prefigured by others. When, for instance, Catherine's 'fancy' at the Abbey leads her to hope for Gothic windows with 'the smallest divisions, and the heaviest stone-work, for painted glass, dirt and cobwebs', she must admit that 'every pane was so large, so clear, so light!' (162). The mysterious dark chest opens to reveal a white cotton counterpane, and the 'bright morning' after darkness allows her to see that she holds a mere inventory of linen (164, 170–2). Thus this last recognition scene builds upon several in which Catherine's mind proceeds from dark to light, from error to truth, prompted by the evidence of her own eyes.

The scene that follows consolidates what she has learnt. Henry advises her, somewhat unnecessarily, to consult her own understanding, 'your own observation of what is passing around you' (197). Locke too urges the reader to 'stand still, open the eyes, look about, and take a view of the consequence', to look at 'Things as really they are' (II.xxi. 67, xi. 15). Catherine has created mixed modes, 'assemblages of *Ideas* put together at the pleasure of the Mind, pursuing its own ends of Discourse, and suited to its own Notions' (III.ix. 7). As Henry asks, 'What have you been judging from?' (197). Judgment discriminates true from false, says Locke, by perceiving '*the connexion and agreement, or disagreement and repugnancy of any of our Ideas*' (IV.i.2). This bright and comfortable room resists the idea of Mrs Tilney murdered.

Henry also tells her to consult her 'own sense of the probable'. Probability is the conformity of any thing with our own observation, says Locke, and though not the 'broad day-light' of experiential knowledge, provides at least a twilight wherein to check our over-confidence (IV. xv. 4, xiv. 2). It works by deduction, logic, and the use of intermediate ideas (IV. xvii. 2). Catherine consults probability when she sees that if mistaken about the room, she has been 'grossly mistaken in every thing else! – in Miss Tilney's meaning, in her own calculation!' (193).

Henry rebukes her for a 'surmise of such horror', and prompts her to remember other evidence. Memory is for Locke 'necessary in the next degree to Perception. It is of so great moment, that where it is wanting, all the rest of our Faculties are in a great measure useless: And we ... could not proceed beyond present Objects, were it not for the assistance of our Memories' (II. x. 8). What Tilney asks Catherine to recollect seems at first astounding:

Remember the country and the age in which we live. Remember that we are English, that we are Christians ... Does our education prepare us for such atrocities? Do our laws connive at them? Could they be perpetrated without being known, in a country like this, where social and literary intercourse is on such a footing; where every man is surrounded by a neighbourhood of voluntary spies, and where roads and newspapers lay every thing open? (197–8)

But Locke himself, in the full knowledge that cultures were customary and relative, also chose Christian England (III. ix. 22). Whatever dubious habits may obtain elsewhere, implies Henry, likewise, the religion, education, and laws of Regency England are surely to be trusted.

Murder, like the supposed murder of Mrs Tilney, is for Locke the supreme proof of godlessness, of which we should perhaps hear more he thinks, 'did not the fear of the Magistrate's Sword' (like Henry's appeal to civil law), or their 'Neighbour's Censure' (like Henry's neighbourhood of voluntary spies), tie up people's tongues, which 'were the Apprehensions of Punishment, or Shame taken away, would as openly proclaim their *Atheism*, as their Lives do' (I. iv. 8). For Henry Tilney as for Locke, divine law, civil law, and the law of public opinion curb the godlessness which ends in murder. General Tilney cannot possibly have murdered his wife, or so at least argue the twilight demonstrations of probability derived by memory from the daylight knowledge of experience.

Catherine is 'completely awakened' (199) by sense experience, probability and the memory of demonstrable proof. She is helped by Henry's known veracity, and the possibility of other witnesses. Because she has always perfectly relied on the truth of Henry's words (80), and because of 'the wonted Veracity of the Speaker in other cases, or his supposed Veracity in this', as Locke puts it (IV. xv. 1), she can trust his assertion that Mrs Tilney died of a bilious fever. Henry appeals to Locke's 'concurrent Testimony of unsuspected Witnesses' (IV. xvi. 8) when he says that Frederick Tilney 'saw her repeatedly; and from our own observation can bear witness to her having received every possible attention' (196–7).

Equipped then by observation, probability, judgment, memory, and testimony, Catherine sets out to consider what she truly knows. Her action is by Locke's lights brave and unusual, for he often rails against those hardened by a sense of shame 'upon the thought of having done something, which ... will lessen the valued Esteem, which others have for us' (II. xx. 17). Though in tears of shame, humbled, and believing that Henry must despise her for ever, Catherine looks clearly at her own 'voluntary, self-created delusion', at her 'imagination resolved on alarm, and every thing forced to one purpose' (199–200). '*Quod volumus, facilè credemus*', said Locke (IV. xx. 12).

She traces her error back to romances, allowing like Henry, like Locke, that their morality may be local and relative. 'Of the Alps and Pyrenees, with their pine forests and their vices, they might give a faithful delineation; and Italy, Switzerland, and the South of France, might be as fruitful in horrors as they were there represented' (200). She will cautiously accept Mrs Radcliffe's testimony in the absence of direct experience. 'Catherine dared not doubt beyond her own country, and even of that, if hard pressed, would have yielded the northern and western extremities'. But for the central part of England she is decisive, using observation and judgment from probability. 'There was surely some security for the existence even of a wife not beloved, in the laws of the land, and the manners of the age'. She deals in verifiable fact when she asserts that 'murder was not tolerated, servants were not slaves, and neither poison nor sleeping potions to be procured, like rhubarb, from every druggist', a sequence that echoes Locke's '*Rhubarb* will purge, *Hemlock* kill, and *Opium* make a Man sleep' (IV.iii.25). And so she ends in 'conviction', a word twice repeated, that although in the Alps and Pyrenees there were perhaps no mixed characters, 'in England it was not so; among the English, she believed, in their hearts and habits, there was a general though unequal mixture of good and bad' (200). Jane Austen defies Samuel Johnson's disapproval of mixed characters in *Rambler* no.4 when she prefers 'Things as really they are' to pictures of perfection, which made her sick and wicked (*Letters*, pp.486–7). She is of Locke's party rather than Johnson's, when she makes the recognition that no-one is perfectly good or evil the climax of her heroine's education.

Catherine is an ignorant child, who learns to reason aright. The obstacles have been as Locke describes them:

I may be modest, and therefore not oppose another Man's Persuasion: I may be ignorant, and not able to produce a better: I may be in an Errour, and another may shew me I am so. This may dispose me, perhaps, for the reception of Truth, but helps me not to it; That must come from Proofs, and Arguments, and Light arising from the Nature of Things themselves, and not from my Shamefacedness, Ignorance or Errour.

(IV.xvii.22)

Initially she echoes John Thorpe's assertions, and gives way to his assurance. She also defers to Henry's superior knowledge on the picturesque taste (65, 48, 111). But when she learns to act for herself, use her own powers of understanding, form a hypothesis, test it, and find out true from false,[12] she fully deserves the happiness – a word which turns up on about every other page of *Northanger Abbey* – which Locke declares to be the reward of rationality (IV.xxi.1). 'Her mind made up on these several points, and her resolution formed, of always judging and acting in future with the greatest good sense, she had nothing to do but forgive herself and be happier than ever' (201).

Catherine Morland's general integrity

Catherine exercises her understanding carefully and accurately in the episode of the dark room. Jane Austen shows how she acquires that power by means of her ignorance, ability to recognise misleading language, and constancy.

Her mind 'about as ignorant and uninformed as the female

mind at seventeen usually is', Catherine when she arrives at Bath is 'all eager delight; – her eyes were here, there, every where, as they approached its fine and striking environs' (18–19). Being a child, she relishes the 'variety of amusements, a variety of things to be seen and done all day long' (78–9); children, says Locke, 'are surrounded with a world of new things, which, by a constant solicitation of their senses, draw the mind constantly to them, forward to take notice of new, and apt to be delighted with the variety of changing Objects' (II.i.8). Her mind lies as open to experience as Locke's sheet of white paper (II.i.2). Ignorance, a synonym for innocence and integrity, advances knowledge and preserves her from corruption. As Locke sees (*Conduct*, §§ 34–5), the Socratic recognition of ignorance is the beginning of wisdom:

The first and wisest of them all profess'd
To know this only, that he nothing knew.
(*Paradise Regained*, IV. 293–4)

So too Catherine's ignorance, humility, and eager readiness to learn are propitious.

When Henry Tilney says teasingly that Catherine is warped by an innate principle of general 'integrity' (219), he means by it Johnson's 'honesty; uncorrupt mind; purity of manners; uncorruptedness'. Catherine is a teller of truth and a seeker after truth. She cannot lie, she is 'unequal to an absolute falsehood' (174). We may not be born with innate ideas, as Locke argues in the first section of his treatise, but we possess an innate willingness to learn, and a preference for truth. As Henry sees, Catherine has not been 'warped' by her education, or as Locke said, 'bias'd' (*Conduct*, § 35). If indeed we are born innocent, education can provoke a second fall. In Henry's use of 'integrity' may linger something of the obsolete meaning (OED, 1678), 'unimpaired moral state; freedom from moral corruption; innocence, sinlessness'.

The ignorance of inexperience is pardonable, for 'he who wants Leisure, Books, and Languages, and the Opportunity of Conversing with variety of Men' cannot be 'in a Condition to collect ... Testimonies and Observations', says Locke (IV.xx.2). When Catherine cries, 'I never was so deceived in any one's character in my life before', Henry adds comfortingly, 'among all the great variety you have known and studied' (206). Ignorance vanishes with the practice of the understanding: '*Use Legs and have Legs*', says Locke in the *Conduct* (§ 38). What we are to use our understandings for is 'to distinguish betwixt Truth and Falshood, Right and Wrong; and to act accordingly' (§ 189), that is, 'Conduct' (I. i. 6). Catherine becomes in Bath an Everywoman of the rational and ethical life. Jane Austen's three or four families in a country village may be microcosms to the larger world.[13]

Catherine's 'general integrity' may make her strong, but the *tabula rasa* of her mind lays her open to ambush[14] by various abuses of the understanding from Locke's Book III, exemplified in the Thorpes, Henry Tilney, and his father. But Catherine works her way through falsehood to truth by way of juxtaposition, and the absurdity of contradiction.

Isabella Thorpe typifies female education, and John Thorpe stands for public schools. Inaccuracy, hypocrisy, and the usages of custom and fashion reveal her folly, whereas jargon, lies, and lapses of numeracy or memory lay open his. Isabella's language depends on second-hand pickings from other people. It is hyperbolic, deceptive, inconsistent, imprecise. Isabella embodies custom and fashion, and even as she asks Catherine to help her regain James's affections, her mind alights on hats and spring fashions (216). When she applies the fashionable words 'amazing' and 'horrid' to everything indiscriminately, the etymologically minded Henry objects to 'amazingly' being used as an intensifier instead of its original meaning of 'stupify'. He flaunts his knowledge again, this time of *horridus*, 'standing on end', when he says that he read that horrid book *Udolpho* in two days, 'my hair standing on end the whole time' (106). Isabella's usages infect Catherine, but she objects when experience demands it. She will not allow that *Sir Charles Grandison* is 'an amazing horrid book'. Her mother knew it well. It is not like *Udolpho* at all, she says firmly, 'but yet I think it is very entertaining' (41–2).

What Eleanor calls 'propriety of diction' (108), the correspondence of words to things, is an obsessive necessity to Locke, for without distinction in names there can be no distinction in ideas, and without distinction of ideas all is confusion (II. xxix. 12). In civil use, however, usage regulates propriety, even if usage is often 'matter of dispute' (III. ix. 8). Eleanor justly complains that Henry 'is for ever finding fault with me, for some incorrectness of language, and now he is taking the same liberty with you'. Unless they want to be 'overpowered with Johnson and Blair all the rest of the way', they had better leave him to meditate over their faults in the utmost propriety of diction, 'while we praise Udolpho in whatever terms we like best' (107–8). Jane Austen herself used 'nice' in civil use (*Letters*, 9 January 1796).

If Jane Austen objects to pedantry in conversation, she seems to agree on the importance of speaking 'intelligibly' (III.ii.8), for when Catherine says to Henry 'I cannot speak well enough to be unintelligible', Henry replies, 'bravo! an excellent satire on modern language' (133). Value words must especially remain 'steady signs of Things', in Locke's phrase, (II.xxxix.10), but Isabella complains of her 'particular friend' Miss Andrews that 'there is something amazingly insipid about her' (40–1). Catherine lets that pass, but will query her accusation that she herself has failed in friendship: 'Was it the part of a friend thus to expose her feelings to the notice of others? Isabella appeared to her ungenerous and selfish, regardless of every thing but her own gratification. These painful ideas crossed her mind' (98). Though flattered into intimacy with Isabella, Catherine questions her use of value words, and learns about hypocrisy and lies. The child must learn to 'pull off the Mask' says Locke, and not be taken in by the insinuation of 'a fair Carriage, or an obliging Application' (§94). Richardson had copied that passage into *Pamela* (IV.272).

Catherine judges Isabella's letter by juxtaposition. 'Such a strain of narrow artifice could not impose even upon Catherine. Its inconsistencies, contradictions, and falsehood, struck her from the very first'. She bursts out that Isabella must think her an idiot (218), 'one without the powers of reason', as Johnson says. But Catherine can set assertion against known experience, identify discordancies and so judge. She is critical for instance of her friend's hyperboles. When Isabella says of James Morland, 'I thought I never saw any body so handsome before', the narrator comments, 'here Catherine secretly acknowledged the power of love; for, though exceedingly fond of her brother, and partial to all his endowments, she had never in her life thought him handsome' (118). Catherine also sees through lies of fashion, even when she looks ridiculous in Johnson's other definition of idiot, 'fool'. Isabella 'could only protest, over and over again, that no two hours and a half had ever gone off so swiftly before, as Catherine was called on to confirm; Catherine could not tell a falsehood even to please Isabella' (67). Such a stance is typical of her. Though Isabella tells her how easy it would be to tell Miss Tilney she has a prior engagement, Catherine replies, 'No, it would not be easy. I could not do it. There has been no prior engagement'. And in response to Thorpe's lie on her behalf, she rushes to the Tilneys to explain, 'if I had thought it right to put it off, I could have spoken to Miss Tilney myself ... If I could not be persuaded into doing what I thought wrong, I never will be tricked into it' (98–101).

Lies of fashion are more perplexing than such obvious duplicities as Isabella's. After General Tilney's lie of convention that his daughter is not at home,

[Catherine] checked the resentful sensation; she remembered her own ignorance. She knew not how such an offence as her's might be classed by the laws of worldly politeness, to what a degree of unforgivingness it might with propriety lead, nor to what rigours of rudeness in return it might justly make her amenable. (92)

Tricked by the General's protest that Henry must not put himself to any trouble over a meal, Catherine carefully ponders her deception:

... that he was very particular in his eating, she had, by her own un-assisted observation, already discovered; but why he should say one thing so positively, and mean another all the while, was most unaccountable! How were people, at that rate, to be understood? Who but Henry could have been aware of what his father was at? (211)

Such lies, as Locke writes, do indeed create 'perplexity, puddering, and confusion' (IV. iii. 30).

General Tilney's hyperboles amount like Isabella's to hypocrisy. The gallant clichés of his 'can you, in short, be prevailed on to quit this scene of public triumph and oblige your friend Eleanor with your company in Gloucestershire?' (139) conceal a wish to catch at her imaginary fortune. Lockean vocabulary reveals that the General accepts information at second hand: 'Upon such intelligence the General had proceeded; for never had it occurred to him to doubt its authority ... sufficient vouchers for his truth ... absolute facts ... almost instantly determined' (245). The General's affected hospitality conceals greed. He deserves his deception by Thorpe.

Henry mimics his father very nicely when he first dances with Catherine. After chatting 'on such matters as naturally arose from the objects around them', he suddenly switches mode. 'Forming his features into a set smile, and affectedly softening his voice, he added, with a simpering air, "Have you been long in Bath, madam?"'. Not only his 'madam', but his hyperbolic 'have you yet honoured the Upper Rooms?', prove from whom he has learnt the language. The formulae of fashion run through, he concludes, 'now I must give one smirk, and then we may be rational again' (25–6). Catherine resists any notion that she herself is a fashionable female. She will not describe her sprigged muslin and Henry in her journal, nor does she keep one. She can act the part of a fashionable female no more than she can speak it.

What enlightens Catherine is her amusement. Though hardly at first understanding his 'archness and pleasantry', she soon finds herself trying not to laugh (25–6). In Locke, juxtaposition shows up falsehood by means of absurdity (IV.xvii.4). Inconsistency provokes laughter, and laughter provokes judgment. In Jane Austen too, absurdity infallibly shows the truth. 'Could not the adventure of the chest have taught her wisdom? A corner of it ... seemed to rise up in judgment against her. Nothing could now be clearer than the absurdity of her recent fancies' (173).

Jane Austen alerts the reader's own sense of absurdity by numerous rhetorical mismatchings, oxymoron, paradox, tautology, bathos, incongruity, inappropriateness, falsehood, and irony.[15] She prompts our judgment, for instance, by the oxymorons of Mrs Allen's 'busy idleness', or Isabella's 'smiles of most exquisite misery, and the laughing eye of utter despondency' (67); she characterises Isabella by her paradox, 'to shew the independence of Miss Thorpe, and her resolution of humbling the sex, they set off immediately as fast as they could walk, in pursuit of the two young men' (43). Equally nonsensical is tautology. 'A faithful promise! – That puzzles me ... the fidelity of promising!', says Henry (196). Complete incongruity creates more nonsense, like 'the long, long, endless two years and a half' that Isabella must wait to marry James (136) – Fielding had laughed at the folly of using 'Eternal' to mean 'a Duration of five Minutes' (*Tom Jones*, XII.xi). Gothic parody can result in bathos, while repeated hyperbole strips away meaning. Isabella's description of 'Miss Andrews, a sweet girl, one of the sweetest creatures in the world ... netting herself the sweetest cloak you can conceive' (40),[16] creates a nonsense, a vacuum where a word once was.

Relation assists precision. Catherine always compares, whether she sets John Thorpe against Henry Tilney as coachmen, or perceives that General Tilney's reproof of his son is 'dispro-portionate to the offence' (155–7). She resists easy comparisons, even Henry's. Much has been made of his comparison of the dance to marriage,[17] but Catherine actually denies it on the grounds of common sense. 'But they are such very different things!' she exclaims. They cannot be compared together, since 'people that marry can never part, but must go and keep house together. People that dance, only stand opposite each other in a long room for half an hour'. Nor will she budge. 'Yes, to be sure, as you state it, all this sounds very well; but still they are so very different. – I cannot look upon them at all in the same light, nor think the same duties belong to them'. She is more precise than Henry, and she holds her own. Her tenaciously favourable opinion of Bath, even if 'other people must judge for themselves', finally makes Henry admit that her 'fresh feelings' might allow her to enjoy it (76–9).

The disproportion discovered by comparison results in irony. That 'dutiful and affectionate son' John Thorpe asks his mother, 'where did you get that quiz of a hat, it makes you look like an old witch?', and in his 'fraternal tenderness' asks his sisters 'each of them how they did, and observed that they both looked very ugly' (49). Such absurdities alert Catherine and the reader, as if discordancies make us laugh. Laughter, as everywhere in Jane Austen, is a vital test of truth.

John Thorpe harasses Catherine by a different set of vices. Obsessed with the speed of his horses, the state of his equipage, and his sporting prowess, he wonderfully exemplifies Locke's despair about public schools: 'How any one's being put into a mixed Herd of unruly Boys, and there learning to wrangle at Trap, or rook at Span-farthing, fits him for civil Conversation, or Business, I do not see' (§ 70). Thorpe's favourite novel is *Tom Jones* (48). The day he forces Catherine into the carriage, he shows in Locke's words a 'Natural *Roughness* which makes a Man uncomplaisant to others, so that he has no deference for their inclinations, tempers or conditions'. It is 'the sure badge of a Clown not to mind what pleases or displeases those he is with', says Locke tartly (§ 143). In addition to his abduction of Catherine, his unlovely attentions at the ball, and his determination to usurp Henry, he imposes upon Catherine the various corruptions of his understanding. These are his jargon and new words, his precipitancy, his failures of memory and numeracy, and his lies.

Locke complains that newly-coined words bring things into question (III. x. 8), and Thorpe's horsy discourse would in any case identify him as a Yahoo, for Jane Austen in a letter of 19 June 1799. His 'tittupy' is the first cited in the OED; his 'ricketty' earlier than the first, applied to things (65). Jargon makes his discourse confusing and unintelligible. Thorpe cannot remember, relate, or compare, nor is he interested in anything beyond his own circumstances. He is one of those who, as Locke says,

> either perceive but dully, or retain the *Ideas* that come into their Minds but ill, who cannot readily excite or compound them, [and] have little matter to think on. Those who cannot distinguish, compare, and abstract, would hardly be able to understand, and make use of Language, or judge, or reason, to any tolerable degree: but only a little, and imperfectly, about things present, and very familiar to their Senses.
>
> (II. xi. 12)

Thorpe argues first that if everybody were to drink their bottle a day it would be a famous good thing, then asserts that there is no drinking at Oxford, at least beyond four pints. He answers Catherine's rational challenge by 'a loud and overpowering reply, of which no part was very distinct, except the frequent exclamations, amounting almost to oaths, which adorned it' (63–4), and 'manifestly fills [his] Discourse with abundance of empty unintelligible noise and jargon', as Locke describes it (III. x. 4). Thorpe, a stupid man himself, often uses the words 'stupid', 'stuff', 'nonsense', and 'dull', a word which inevitably recalls Pope's *Dunciad*. A man who calls everything stupid inhabits anarchy.

Anarchy of words leads to '*Inconstancy* in the use of them ... 'tis plain cheat and abuse, when I make them stand sometimes for one thing, and sometimes for another', says Locke (III. x. 5). Thorpe's lie that the Tilneys have gone is not unimportant.

If knowledge depends upon truth, untruth brings, as Locke says, 'Confusion, Disorder, and Uncertainty into the Affairs of Mankind; and if not destroyed, yet in great measure [renders] useless, those two great Rules, Religion and Justice' (III. x. 12).

Catherine's safeguard is her ability to detect contradiction. What wit combines, judgment separates (II. xi. 2). She, whose family has been 'plain matter-of-fact people, who seldom aimed at wit of any kind; her father, at the utmost, being contented with a pun, and her mother with a proverb', cannot 'reconcile two such very different accounts of the same thing'. She has not been brought up 'to know to how many idle assertions and impudent falsehoods the excess of vanity will lead'. Her family is not in the habit of 'telling lies to increase their importance, or of asserting at one moment what they would contradict the next'. She reflects on the affair 'in much perplexity', and almost requests from Mr Thorpe 'a clearer insight into his real opinion of the subject; but she checked herself, because it appeared to her that he did not excel in giving those clearer insights, in making those things plain which he had before made ambiguous'. She does well, little as she is 'in the habit of judging for herself' (65 – 6). Isabella and John may lie and lie again, and 'nothing so deformed and irreconcilable to the Understanding, as a Lye', says Locke (IV. iii. 20), but Catherine cannot tell falsehoods even to please her friend. In an uncomfortable scene where Henry is all too ready to mistrust her,

instead of considering her own dignity injured by this ready condemnation – instead of proudly resolving, in conscious innocence, to shew her resentment towards him who could harbour a doubt of it, to leave to him all the trouble of seeking an explanation, and to enlighten him on the past only by avoiding his sight, or flirting with somebody else, she took to herself all the shame of misconduct, or at least of its appearance, and was only eager for an opportunity of explaining its cause.

(93)

Thorpe's precipitancy, the very opposite of standing still and looking about , is often attacked in *Human Understanding* as a cause of error (e.g. II. xxi. 67). 'Make haste! make haste!', he cries characteristically, 'put on your hat this moment – there is no time to be lost – we are going to Bristol' (84). When he tries to rush Catherine into the carriage, she uses the evidence of her own eyes: 'in spite of what she had heard of the prodigious accumulation of dirt in the course of that hour, she could not from her own observation help thinking, that they might have gone with very little inconvenience' (84–6).

Since mathematics make people reasonable (*Conduct*, §6), John Thorpe's faulty calculations are a further sign of idiocy. He denies the authority of numbers, and he rejects the testimony of a more numerate and rational friend:

> '*Three*-and twenty!' cried Thorpe; 'five-and-twenty if it is an inch.' Morland remonstrated, pleaded the authority of road-books, innkeepers, and milestones; but his friend disregarded them all; he had a surer test of distance. 'I know it must be five-and-twenty,' said he, 'by the time we have been doing it. It is now half after one; we drove out of the inn-yard at Tetbury as the town-clock struck eleven; and I defy any man in England to make my horse go less than ten miles an hour in harness; that makes it exactly twenty-five.'
>
> 'You have lost an hour,' said Morland; 'it was only ten o'clock when we came from Tetbury.'
>
> 'Ten o'clock! it was eleven, upon my soul! I counted every stroke. This brother of yours would persuade me out of my senses ...'   (45–6)

Catherine can multiply ten by four (48), but Isabella, anticipating Mary Crawford's 'feminine lawlessness' about time and distance in *Mansfield Park* (95–6), refuses like her brother to believe in numbers:

> 'Past three o'clock!' it was inconceivable, incredible, impossible! and she would neither believe her own watch, nor her brother's, nor the servant's; she would believe no assurance of it founded on reason or reality, till Morland produced his watch, and ascertained the fact; to have doubted a moment longer *then*, would have been equally inconceivable, incredible, and impossible; and she could only protest, over and over again, that no two hours and a half had ever gone off so swiftly before ...
> (67)

In 'false calculations' Thorpe doubles Mr Morland's preferment, trebles his private income, bestows a rich aunt and sinks half the children (245–6), whereas Mr Allen, 'a sensible, intelligent man' like his possible predecessor, Ralph Allen of Bath, acts as carefully as Catherine when he declines to give any absolute promise of sunshine, not having 'his own skies and barometer about him' (20, 82).

Nor is Thorpe's memory any better. He does not remember

whether the clock struck ten or eleven, he forgets that *Udolpho* was written by Mrs Radcliffe, he cannot recall Fanny Burney's name, and even on the subject nearest his heart, forgets that the horse was included in the price (49, 47). Mrs Allen's 'vacancy of mind and incapacity for thinking' (60) are equally revealed by a comparison with Catherine:

> 'Do you remember that evening?'
> 'Do I! Oh! perfectly.'
> 'It was very agreeable, was it not? Mr. Tilney drank tea with us, and I always thought him a great addition, he is so very agreeable. I have a notion you danced with him, but am not quite sure. I remember I had my favourite gown on.'
> Catherine could not answer. (238)

Catherine resists then the corrupt words and ideas of the Thorpes, Mrs Allen, General Tilney, and Henry, even when custom, propriety, friendship, love, hospitality, or fraternal affection press upon her. Her sense of the right results in sincerity, artlessness, integrity, and authentic behaviour when feelings in her correspond to deeds. Imbecility in females may enhance their personal charms, but *Northanger Abbey* shows rather how the blank slate of Catherine's character, unmarked by the corruptions of education or social life, is paradoxically inscribed by ghostly guides to conduct. Those who think Henry Catherine's mentor should look again at the scene where, voluble, superior, and overbearing, he laughs off her fears about Isabella and Captain Tilney, or at the occasion on which he disbelieves her good intentions (152, 94). Henry does not always know best. Whenever Catherine relies on her own observation she is commonly in the right, 'open, candid, artless, guileless, with affections strong but simple, forming no pretensions, and knowing no disguise', as Henry recognises himself (206). Typically Jane Austen has been working towards this cluster of words, to which we may add such synonyms as sincere, honest, and truthful.[18]

Catherine can look a foolish female Quixote, but her steadiness of vision is vindicated and rewarded by marriage with Henry Tilney. She is not obstinate (101) but 'steady', a word used by Locke for courage in keeping to one's duty in battle (§ 115).[19] Under pressure from Isabella, she is 'always distressed, but always steady', and when James complains, 'I did not think you had been so obstinate, Catherine'; 'You were not used to be so hard to persuade; you once were the kindest, best-tempered of my sisters', Catherine replies very feelingly, 'I hope I am not less so now ... but indeed I cannot go. If I am wrong, I am doing what I believe to be right.' She is 'distressed, but not subdued' when 'assailed' by the arguments of her friends. 'Let me go, Mr. Thorpe; Isabella, do not hold me' (97–101). That teasing and irresponsible tutor Henry Tilney learns from his pupil how to behave under his military father's fire. His opposition to the General is as 'steady as the sanction of reason and the dictate of conscience could make it'; he stands firm, 'he steadily refused to accompany his father into Herefordshire ... and as steadily declared his intention of offering her his hand' (247–8).

From Catherine he learns to keep promises and contracts; if she promises to dance with John Thorpe she must, if she promises to walk with the Tilneys she will. Broken promises, like Isabella's to James or the General's to herself, acquire more than local resonance when another cluster of words in the novel, obstinate, firm, steady, change, alteration, constant, fidelity, fickleness, gradually accumulates value by repetition. 'Of all things in the world inconstancy is my aversion', cries the deceiving Isabella (130); when her friend deserts James for Captain Tilney, Catherine must exclaim against 'inconstancy and fickleness, and every thing that is bad in the world' (204). Words make up promises, and their betrayal fractures the social contract.

Northanger Abbey displays the powers of human under-standing. It shows how they work, and describes to what ends they are given. Adequately to demonstrate the variations and commentaries on this topic would be to quote the whole novel, but to summarise, characters may be called genius, scholar, or fool, idiot, simpleton, and blockhead. They may be either quick, wise, intelligent, innocent, and well-informed, or stupid, dull, unintelligent, lazy, heedless, half-witted, and shatter-brained. Their mind, soul, brains, head, senses, powers, habits, and consciousness, their choice of words, diction, and language, prove either their excellence, wit, taste, fire, ingenuity, origin-ality, fancy, imagination, penetration, curiosity, and memory, or their imbecility and intellectual poverty. They know, think, feel, look, perceive, contemplate, reflect, wonder, believe, and learn. They speculate, suspect, deceive, fancy, invent, distinguish, compare, calculate, conclude. In short they reason, and thus come up either with ideas, proof, testimony, witness, information, intelligence, discovery, notions, facts, certainty, doubt, recollection, and conviction, or with nonsense, stuff, perplexity, exaggeration, misapprehension, confusion, error, mistake, and opinion. Their ideas may be possible, probable, reasonable, real and necessary, or incredible and inconceivable. They distinguish truth from falsehood by means of reason, inquiries, authority, argument, discourse, assertion, consequences, causes, distinction, difference, circumstances, conclusions, contradiction, inconsistency, and absurdity. Beside these brilliant charges and counter-charges of reason and nonsense, the Napoleonic wars must pale.

I do not mean to make Jane Austen seem severe, though Robert Alan Donovan is right to talk of her fundamental gravity.[20] The miraculous lightness of *Northanger Abbey* derives from its childish heroine, its test of truth by absurdity, and the fact that Jane Austen plays with all these philosophical concepts rather than presenting them direct. Locke himself had animated his arguments by epigrammatic expressions and homely analogies. Jane Austen's joke is to apply similar ideas to the minutiae of daily life in a mock heroic style inflationary and deflationary at the same time. She sports with ideas on every page. John Thorpe for instance says that he has 'fifty minds' to buy a horse; his sister, a girl with 'such a superior understanding!', as James says dotingly, boasts that 'the sleeves were entirely my own thought' (76, 50, 70). Mrs Allen demands that James 'weigh the merits of a new muff and tippet', and the 'well-read' Catherine, after running over the titles of the 'storehouse of knowledge' in the General's library, remembers 'dozens who had persevered in every possible vice, going on from crime to crime, murdering whomsoever they chose, without any feeling of humanity or remorse; till a violent death or a religious retirement closed their black career' (51, 182–3, 190). Catherine whispers with Isabella 'whenever a thought occurred, and supplying the place of many ideas by a squeeze of the hand or a smile of affection', but soon proves herself reasonable, 'guided only by what was simple and probable' (52–3). When Henry urges Catherine 'to guess for ourselves' about Captain Tilney's intentions on the grounds that 'second-hand conjecture is pitiful. The premises are before you' (151–2), he is loftily reasonable and wonderfully wrong. Henry pushes reason to absurdity when he calls Captain Tilney 'a deceased man – defunct in understanding', and he himself, who really wants Catherine to think him 'a very extraordinary genius', quite strikes Mrs Allen, a woman of no genius herself, with his 'genius' in understanding muslins (206, 20, 27–8).[21] Most revealing of all are such phrases as 'the first experimental conviction' or the conversation between Isabella and Catherine, 'given as a specimen of their very warm attachment, and of the delicacy, discretion, originality of thought, and literary taste which marked the reasonableness of that attachment' (220, 39). 'Experimental' and 'specimen' strikingly show that for Jane Austen, as for Locke, philosophy is not abstract, but the experimental study of humanity.

Mrs Morland may think her daughter a 'sad little shatterbrained creature' (234), but Catherine has done well.[22] So has Jane Austen, who makes philosophy accessible in her fiction. Herself a woman and deprived of formal education, she argues that if a young girl can deploy her understanding, so can anyone. The philosopher is supplanted by the upstart novelist, the maker of something new (IV. xx. 11), but she does him some service by making his ideas 'a Play and Recreation' (§ 148) in *Northanger Abbey*.

'A right popular philosopher'

In *Northanger Abbey* Jane Austen transforms philosophy into fiction, but what she attacks in that fiction is history. Her defence of the novel, like other famous defences of the imagination, claims superiority to them both.

Catherine, whose delight is 'invention', complains that 'history, real solemn history' tells 'nothing that does not either vex or weary me. The quarrels of popes and kings, with wars or pestilences, in every page; the men all so good for nothing, and hardly any women at all – it is very tiresome' (108). Locke had argued similarly that 'all the Entertainment and talk of History is of nothing almost but Fighting and Killing' (§ 116), but Catherine is radical to point out that history generally omits women. Jane Austen's novels supply that unwritten history of women.

History is so very dull, says Catherine, and Eleanor admits that historians are 'not happy in their flights of fancy. They display imagination without raising interest'. But she herself is fond of it, well content to take the false with the true when the facts are verifiable from 'former histories and records'. She likes the 'little embellishments', and reads with pleasure speeches that are well written, though not genuine (109). So too Locke admits that 'in Discourses, where we seek rather Pleasure and Delight, than Information and Improvement ... Ornaments ... can scarce pass for Faults' (III. x. 34).

Since Locke distrusts imagination, Jane Austen's famous defence of the novel takes its place, rather, alongside older apologies for imaginative art. Aristotle's, for instance, who declared that 'Poetry is a more philosophical and a more excellent thing than History: for Poetry is chiefly conversant about general truth, History about particular' (*Poetics*, VI). His definition of poetry as 'invention', Catherine's delight, is elaborated also by Sir Francis Bacon, who argues in a comparison of history (memory), poetry (imagination) and philosophy (reason) that poetry's freedom to demonstrate providential justice makes it superior to history, which is bound to excess (like wars) and bound to time. Jane Austen writes bitterly in her own narrative voice that although 'the abilities of the nine-hundredth abridger of the History of England' are eulogized by a thousand pens, historical writing soon looks out-of-date. The *Spectators*, for instance, contain 'improbable circumstances, unnatural characters, and topics of conversation, which no longer concern any one living; and their language, too, frequently so coarse as to give no very favourable idea of the age that could endure it' (37–8). Bacon concludes bracingly that invention bests both philosophy and history. 'For the expressing of affections, passions, corruptions, and customs, we are beholden to Poets more than to the Philosophers' works, and for wit and eloquence not much less than to Orators' harangues' (92). Jane Austen writes with similar bravado that a novel 'is only some work in which the greatest powers of the mind are displayed, in which the most thorough knowledge of human nature, the happiest delineation of its varieties, the liveliest effusions of wit and humour are conveyed to the world in the best chosen language' (38).

Sir Philip Sidney's *Apology for Poetry* (1595) especially

contains many of the ideas expressed by statement or practice in *Northanger Abbey*. Although several editions of Sidney's defence were available in the eighteenth century, including one printed by Richardson, there is no proof that Jane Austen read it unless one makes much of Maria Bertram's remark (Maria's!) in *Mansfield Park*, 'I cannot but think that good horsemanship has a great deal to do with the mind' (69), which is the assumption with which Sidney begins. But the two writers do look very alike.

Both declare that poetry (or fiction) is in poor repute. Both blame betrayal by its practitioners, readers and critics. Both assert the superiority of poetry/fiction to history, and point out unkindly that history depends on the embellishments of invention. Both argue like Bacon that history's being tied to actual events means that it rarely offers good examples, whereas poetry's portrayal of excellence and poetic justice promotes virtuous teaching more effectively than philosophy. Both stress the pleasures of the imagination, and both agree that the best models are English authors. Sidney's challenging tone of comic vehemence especially echoes in Jane Austen, but where Sidney and Aristotle and Bacon are taken seriously, she commonly is not.[23]

Jane Austen's rounding on the world is as vigorous as it is unexpected:

Yes, novels; – for I will not adopt that ungenerous and impolitic custom so common with novel writers, of degrading by their contemptuous censure the very performances, to the number of which they are themselves adding – joining with their greatest enemies in bestowing the harshest epithets on such works, and scarcely ever permitting them to be read by their own heroine, who, if she accidentally take up a novel, is sure to turn over its insipid pages with disgust. Alas! if the heroine of one novel be not patronized by the heroine of another, from whom she can expect protection and regard? I cannot approve of it. Let us leave it to the Reviewers to abuse such effusions of fancy at their leisure, and over every new novel to talk in threadbare strains of the trash with which the press now groans. Let us not desert one another, we are an injured body. Although our productions have afforded more extensive and unaffected pleasure than those of any literary corporation in the world, no species of composition has been so much decried. From pride, ignorance, or fashion, our foes are almost as many as our readers.

(37)

Sidney is likewise stung by the thought that 'poor Poetry ... is fallen to be the laughing-stock of children' (2). He blames authors, base men with servile wits who 'by their own disgracefulness disgrace the most graceful Poesy' (52–3, 42). Poetry is equally betrayed by the 'ill-favouring breath' of those 'wrong-speakers' (41), who like Jane Austen's reviewers, only criticise, being

> that kind of people who seek a praise by dispraising others, that they do prodigally spend a great many wandering words in quips and scoffs, carping and taunting at each thing, which, by stirring the spleen, may stay the brain from a thorough beholding the worthiness of the subject.

Sidney's solution like Jane Austen's is mockery (30). He slily accuses historians of stealing poesy's 'invention' for the long orations 'put in the mouths of great kings and captains, which it is certain that they never pronounced' (4); Catherine argues too that 'the speeches that are put into the heroes' mouths, their thoughts and designs – the chief of all this must be invention' (108). Sidney claims that the poet can range 'freely within the zodiac of his own wit' whereas historians are bound to the '*was*' (7, 18). The young Jane Austen's own *History of England* was notably imaginative and opinionated, with 'very few Dates', and she would attack the Bertram sisters for knowing all the Kings of England in chronological order (*MP*, 18).

Poetry, says Sidney, sets virtue out in her best colours (19); Jane Austen rewards her virtuous heroine with the justice that only poetry affords. 'My own joy on the occasion is very sincere. I know no one more entitled, by unpretending merit, or better prepared by habitual suffering, to receive and enjoy felicity', she says (251). The historian, says Sidney, 'being captived to the truth of a foolish world, is many times a terror from well doing, and an encouragement to unbridled wickedness' (20) – the quarrels of kings and popes, wars and pestilences, for instance. 'Let other pens dwell on vice and misery', Jane Austen would say, turning her attention back to virtue, in *Mansfield Park* (461).

Poets deliver the ideas in 'excellency', says Sidney. They do not speak in 'table talk fashion ... words as they chanceably fall from the mouth, but peizing each syllable of each word by just proportion according to the dignity of the subject' (10–11); a novel, says Jane Austen, is where you may see 'the liveliest effusions ... conveyed to the world in the best chosen language'.[24] Sidney concludes that poets deliver a golden world and historians only a brazen one (7), an idea asserted and proved by Jane Austen's *Northanger Abbey*.

Poetry is superior to philosophy as well as to history, says Sidney, because it couples the general with the particular in a 'speaking picture' (14–15). A novel, in short. When Jane Austen bodied forth a whole epistemological system in *Northanger Abbey*, she was indeed, as Sidney says of the poet, 'a right popular philosopher' (17). The poet to Sidney is the monarch of all human sciences. 'With a tale forsooth he cometh unto you, with a tale which holdeth children from play, and old men from the chimney corner' (21–2). By poetry men learn philosophy the sweetest and homeliest way, as in *Northanger Abbey*, one of a species of composition which has afforded 'more extensive and unaffected pleasure than those of any literary corporation in the world' and which has 'only genius, wit, and taste to recommend [it]' (37). Poets, says Sidney, teach by delight. His summary, 'this purifying of wit, this enriching of memory, enabling of judgement, and enlarging of conceit, which commonly we call learning' (11), might well describe what Jane Austen does in *Northanger Abbey*. She teaches, as Sidney describes it, by 'plain setting down, how [learning] extendeth itself out of the limits of a man's little world to the government of families, and maintaining of public societies' (12) – the little world at Bath. Sidney's final defence of English as the vehicle for great art (41), and his praise for the 'excellent minds' of the English literary tradition, correspond to Jane Austen's life-long preference for literary models in English.

Jane Austen's ranking of imaginative creation above philosophy and history is edged with defiance, like Sidney's. She flaunts the sheer *invention* of her novel, delivering in the course of it what is in effect the essay on writing that she said she omitted from *Pride and Prejudice*. John Thorpe's favourite novel may have been useful to her, for her deconstructive discussions of her craft closely parallel Fielding's prefatory chapters and parodies of romantic and heroic modes.[25] It has often been remarked that Austen's narrative voice, like Fielding's, suggests an august presence addressing the accomplice reader. Henry Austen, ever protective of his sister's memory, says that compared to *Sir Charles Grandison* 'she did not rank any work of

Fielding quite so high. Without the slightest affectation she recoiled from every thing gross. Neither nature, nor wit, nor humour, could make her amends for so very low a scale of morals' ('Biographical notice', p. 7). And yet she knew in a letter of 9 January 1796 the colour of the clothes in which Jones was wounded, and Mrs Norris's parsimonious benevolence to William is the same as Nightingale's one guinea for Mrs Miller (XIII. viii). The conclusion of *Northanger Abbey* queerly resembles Nightingale's decision to marry Nancy Miller despite his father's wish for a richer match (XIV. vii–viii), and the vignette of a young woman saying, ' ''I am no novel reader – I seldom look into novels – Do not imagine that *I* often read novels – It is really very well for a novel.'' Such is the common cant – ''And what are you reading, Miss – ?'' ''Oh, it is only a novel!'' replies the young lady; while she lays down her book with affected indifference, or momentary shame' (37–8), recalls Sophia Western, in reverse:

The Moment she saw Mrs. *Western*, she shut the Book with so much Eagerness, that the good Lady could not forbear asking her, What Book that was which she seemed so much afraid of shewing. 'Upon my Word, Madam,' answered *Sophia*, 'it is a Book which I am neither ashamed of or afraid to own I have read. It is the Production of a young Lady of Fashion, whose good Understanding, I think, doth Honour to her Sex, and whose good Heart is an Honour to Human Nature'. (VI. v)

Jane Austen's unconstrained conduct of her story generally resembles Fielding's cheerful assertion that he is not 'accountable to any Court of Critical Jurisdiction whatever' (II. i). Her introduction of Catherine shares its mock heroic tone with Sophia's, and the ways in which she draws attention to herself as manipulator are very much in Fielding's style: 'In addition to what has already been said of Catherine Morland's personal and mental endowments, when about to be launched into all the dangers and difficulties of a six weeks' residence in Bath, it may be stated, for the reader's more certain information, that ...' (18). Her remarks on the novelist's control of time, 'Monday, Tuesday, Wednesday, Thursday, Friday and Saturday have now passed in review before the reader ... and the pangs of Sunday only now remain to be described, and close the week'

(97), gestures towards Fielding's promise not to 'imitate the painful and voluminous Historian' but 'hasten on to Matters of Consequence, and leave ... Periods of Time totally unobserved' (II. i). Jane Austen again asserts her freedom to select when she writes, 'this brief account of the family is intended to supersede the necessity of a long and minute detail from Mrs. Thorpe herself, of her past adventures and suffering, which otherwise might be expected to occupy the three or four following chapters; in which the worthlessness of lord and attornies might be set forth [like Fielding's Mrs Fitzpatrick's], and conversations, which had passed twenty years before, be minutely repeated' (34). Or she will jog the reader's memory quite in Fielding's manner: 'I have only to add ... that this was the very gentleman whose negligent servant left behind him that collection of washing-bills ... by which my heroine was involved in one of her more alarming adventures', she writes (251); 'the Reader will be pleased to remember a little Muff', says Fielding (X. v). She reveals with a favourite flattery of Fielding's how she organises information: 'I leave it to my reader's sagacity to determine how much of all this it was possible for Henry to communicate at this time to Catherine, how much of it he could have learnt from his father, in what points his own conjectures might assist him, and what portion must yet remain to be told in a letter from James. I have united for their ease what they must divide for mine' (247); 'Mrs. Waters, as the Reader may well suppose, had at her last Visit discovered to him the Secret of his Birth', says Fielding, cutting corners with equal dexterity (XVIII. x). Jane Austen assumes that readers will 'see in the tell-tale compression of the pages before them, that we are all hastening together to perfect felicity' (250); Fielding alerts his readers to the expectation of an ending by such headings as 'Wherein the History begins to draw towards a Conclusion', and 'The History draws nearer to a Conclusion'.[26] They expose their craft to invite our admiration.

The upstart novelist challenges the philosopher and the historian, standing (as Sidney said of the poet) between the precepts of the one and the examples of the other, and 'if he go beyond them both, no other human skill can match him' (13). But when Jane Austen argues that the novelist possesses the poet's own 'genius, wit, and taste', like Fielding boasting about the poetic genius, invention and judgment of his 'Heroic,

Historical, Prosaic Poem' (IX. i, IV. i), she stakes the bold claim that fiction usurps poetry as well.

Jane Austen speaks up for fiction in as teasing and provocative a voice as Sidney's or Fielding's. Her deliberate parade of her invention, her freedom in taking the reader from Athens to Thebes in an instant, her liberation from the tyranny of particulars, her ability to choose the best subject and express it in the best language – all these are the powers she displays. Though *Northanger Abbey* was finished first, it is not thereby insubstantial. Its Lockean epistemology as much as its realism forms the groundwork of her whole career. In this novel, Jane Austen, like Catherine Morland, shows us her mind.

2

The return to Richardson

Northanger Abbey, says Jane Austen in her 'Advertisement' of 1816, was the novel first 'finished'. Drafted in 1798–9, it was completed and offered to a publisher as 'Susan' in 1803. Jane Austen probably only retouched it in the years before it was published posthumously with *Persuasion* in 1817. But about 1795 she had written an epistolary form of *Sense and Sensibility* called 'Elinor and Marianne', and in 1796–7 composed 'First Impressions', the original of *Pride and Prejudice*. *Sense and Sensibility*, it is thought, was revised in 1809–11 before publication in 1811, *Pride and Prejudice* was radically revised about 1812 before publication in 1813, and *Mansfield Park* was written in 1811–13 before publication in 1814 (see A. Walton Litz's 'Chronology of composition'). It is decidedly odd therefore that although *Northanger Abbey* shows little trace of Richardson except for references to his *Rambler* and to Miss Andrews, the three other novels depend upon him so pervasively. Critics are often bewildered by Jane Austen's fondness for Richardson, Lord David Cecil in the introduction to *Jane Austen's 'Sir Charles Grandison'*, for instance, and even Richardsonians must wonder why Jane Austen, who sharpened her wits upon him in the juvenilia (see Appendix 2) and rejected his epistolary method when she revised 'Elinor and Marianne' and 'First Impressions', might turn back to him in her maturity. If, as Duncan-Jones suggests in 'Jane Austen and *Clarissa*', she referred mockingly to *Clarissa* in a letter of 18 September 1796 when she imagines that in London she might 'inevitably fall a Sacrifice to the arts of some fat Woman who will make me drunk with Small Beer' – the stout brothel-keeper Mrs Sinclair made Clarissa 'inebriated' with drugged 'table-beer' to facilitate the rape (VI. 72) – she would treat that novel with more respect in *Sense and Sensibility*?

I suggest that it was Anna Laetitia Barbauld's 1804 edition of Richardson's correspondence that drew her back to his novels. Claude Rawson argues from her remarks on 'nice' and 'sentimental' that she knew it,[1] while the verbal correspondences between a gentleman's report on 'one of the summer tours which he used to take for his pleasure' and the visit to Pemberley suggests at least an acquaintance with the edition:

> At every inn he put up at, it was his way to inquire after curiosities in its neighbourhood, either ancient or modern; and particularly he asked who was the owner of a fine house, as it seemed to him, beautifully situated, which he had passed by ... within a mile or two of the inn.
>
> (lxix)

Similarly Elizabeth 'after having seen all the principal wonders of the country' on a summer tour with the Gardiners, finds out from her aunt where Pemberley was 'situated. It was not in their direct road, nor more than a mile or two out of it' (240). Jane Austen seems in fact to have drawn on scenes praised by Mrs Barbauld, as well as heeding her warnings. Here too she could have found a defence of fiction in some respects similar to her own, shrewd theoretical observations on style and point of view, and praise for English authors and for unlettered female genius that casts quite another light on her letter to the Regent's Librarian, Mr Clarke. Something must have returned Jane Austen to Richardson and to writing during seven lean years, and perhaps it was Richardson's correspondence.

Mrs Barbauld's edition appeared in the middle of a period about which we know little. In 1801 Jane Austen had been torn by arbitrary parental decree from the family home at Steventon to exile in Bath and Southampton. In 1801 or 1802 she may have lost the only man she ever loved, and certainly changed her mind about marrying another.[2] These 'personal griefs', the deaths of Mrs Lefroy and of her father, the 'literary disappointment' of having 'Susan' purchased but not published, and the 'want of a settled home',[3] are said to account for the absence of letters from 30 November 1800 to 3 January 1801, and for the apparent eclipse of her creative powers during 1801–9. *Northanger Abbey*, however, is a large exception.

I believe that in that time she worked up 'Susan' into *Northanger Abbey*, and revised at least one of her three most Richardsonian novels. Only minor revision to *Sense and Sensibility* need then be done at Chawton in 1809–11. That novel might be more autobiographical than we dared think, even supplying to some extent the place of the missing letters. Given her habit of scribbling from an early age, it is unlikely that she wrote nothing in her exile. Her nephews only infer 'probably correctly' from the absence of any allusion in the Southampton letters to her being engaged upon any novel 'that her pen was idle during these years', but Henry Austen says (p. 4) that some of the novels were the result of gradual performances of her previous life, and why should those years not be 1802–8? It is hard to believe that she substantially revised or wrote three major novels within four years – and her nephews admit that if such a 'large proportion of her most important literary work' were carried out in the period 1809–11, it would indeed have been 'crowded'.[4]

'Elinor and Marianne', the first epistolary version of *Sense and Sensibility*, was written and read to the family before 1796. In November 1797 Jane Austen began a drastic revision, giving the work, as James Austen-Leigh wrote, 'its present form'. Southam argues in *Jane Austen's Literary Manuscripts* (pp. 54–5) that

the change affected structure rather than content; comparing *Sense and Sensibilfty* with the earlier version, Cassandra wrote that it was 'something of the same story & characters'. Twelve years later came the revision of 1809–10 at Chawton, presumably the last before Jane Austen corrected the proofs in 1811 prior to publication in November of that year.

But James Austen-Leigh only says that 'the first year of her residence at Chawton *seems* [my italics] to have been devoted to revising and preparing for the press *Sense and Sensibility* and *Pride and Prejudice*' (p. 101). The second drastic rewriting may well have occurred earlier, at a time closer to events recreated, perhaps, in *Sense and Sensibility*. Only minor correction need then be done at Chawton, at a time when she was already fully occupied with *Pride and Prejudice* and *Mansfield Park*.

The mention of the two-penny post in *Sense and Sensibility* (161) – it was only introduced in 1801 – suggests later revision. So does the mention of Scott, not a popular poet until the *Lay* of 1805 and *Marmion* in 1808, as Mary Lascelles points out (pp. 15–17). Margaret Kirkham has discovered the names Ferrers [sic] and Palmer (*Sense and Sensibility*), Grant and Crawford (*Mansfield Park*), John Knightley, Campbell, Coles, and Perry (*Emma*), and Dalrymple and Carteret (*Persuasion*), in the new arrivals list of the *Bath Journal* during the winter of 1801–2 (p. 140). If Jane Austen did indeed note these names during her stay in Bath, she might have been working on the novels at that time.

One further piece of evidence suggests revision in the early years of the decade. In 1801 the fourteenth edition of *Pamela* revealed for the first time that Mr B. inhabits Brandon Hall. His name is therefore presumably Mr Brandon, as Peter Sabor guesses (note 132). If the 1804 edition of Richardson's *Correspondence* had sent her back to recent editions of his novels such as she might find in circulating libraries, this significant revision would jump to her eye. She may have commandeered Mr B.'s new name for Colonel Brandon, along with his rakish past, sometime after Mrs Barbauld had persuaded her back to Richardson.

The Letters seem also to confirm that this novel, like all her novels, was created gradually over a number of years, as Henry Austen said (p. 4), rather than in the three separate stages 1795, 1797, and 1809–11. When life does feed literature, it arguably does so without delay. Details resembling those in *Sense and Sensibility* turn up in Jane Austen's letters for the years *before* it is usually assumed that the major revision of *Sense and Sensibility* took place. Letters and revision may therefore have been contemporaneous.

Cowper, Marianne Dashwood's favourite, was about to be bought by the Austens on 25 November 1798, and her father was reading it by 18 December. Her uncle is still in his flannels (like Colonel Brandon's flannel waistcoat), but is getting better again on 19 June 1799, and on 20 November 1800 Jane Austen plans for Steventon an orchard of 'larch, Mountain-ash & acacia', rather as Cleveland in *Sense and Sensibility* is 'under the guardianship of the fir, the mountain-ash, and the acacia' (302). On 30 November of the same year Miss Wapshire is 'now seven or eight & twenty ... This promises better, than the bloom of seventeen'. These same two ages are compared in an important conversation in *Sense and Sensibility*.

After the move from Steventon the flow of relevant detail continues. We hear of putrid fevers like Marianne's on 21 May

1801 when Marianne Mapleton is said to have died to the severe suffering of her affectionate family – Marianne Dashwood imagines how she might be mourned by *her* family (346). Death by putrid fever appears close to a mention of Cowper on 7 January and 8 February 1807. On 15 October 1808 Jane asks Cassandra about the bereaved Fanny Austen, 'Does she feel you to be a comfort to her, or is she too much overpowered for anything but solitude?'. Marianne Dashwood also rejects consolation for solitude after Willoughby leaves her, and again, more dangerously, when she catches cold in her solitary wanderings at Cleveland. And on 10 January 1809 Jane Austen speaks of Mrs Middleton, like Sir John Middleton in her book.

The Austens left Southampton in April 1809 and in July were happily at Chawton. No letters survive from the first year and three-quarters at Chawton, as Lascelles says (p. 29). In later letters I detect nothing relevant to *Sense and Sensibility*, and yet this is the period in which she is supposed to have completed the major revision. On 25 April 1811 she is correcting proofs. It does seem that she could have worked on it during the lost years at Bath and Southampton.

Autobiography may also help date the composition of *Sense and Sensibility*. When Jane Austen began *Pride and Prejudice* in the period October 1796 to August 1797, she made her heroine twenty-one like herself. But in other books it is twenty-seven that matters, her age in 1802–3. Charlotte Lucas and Anne Elliot both despair of marrying at twenty-seven. Elinor Dashwood uses the same curiously exact number for her hypothetical discussion about marriage with an older man:

Perhaps ... thirty-five and seventeen had best not have any thing to do with matrimony together. But if there should by any chance happen to be a woman who is single at seven and twenty, I should not think Colonel Brandon's being thirty-five any objection to his marrying *her*.

Marianne's dogmatic response twists arguments to be found in a similar debate in *Sir Charles Grandison* (II. 58), 'A woman of seven and twenty ... can never hope to feel or inspire affection again, and if her home be uncomfortable, or her fortune small, I can suppose that she might bring herself to submit to the offices of a nurse, for the sake of the provision and security of a wife' (37–8).

Within her own family, Jane Austen knew of Philadelphia Hancock's marriage in Bengal to a man highly conscious of being twenty years the elder. Philadelphia gave him a waistcoat; Marianne mocks Colonel Brandon's waistcoat and East Indian past.[5] Seventeen and thirty-five might not do, but twenty-seven and thirty-five would, according to Elinor Dashwood. It is at least possible that this conversation and substantial parts of this book were written after 1797 when Cassandra's lover died, or after 1801, when Jane may have lost a lover as well as a home. In *Sense and Sensibility* the heroine grieves to leave home and a lover departs abruptly, never to return. Did Jane and Cassandra weep together like Marianne and Elinor? Did Jane almost scream with agony? Cassandra fits the role of the older sister Elinor, as Lascelles says (p. 13), while that of the passionate Marianne would fall to Jane.

Neither the Dashwood nor the Austen sisters succumbed under affliction. Richardson's Mrs Eggleton must have seemed on this point to give startlingly prophetic advice to Cassandra, whose fiancé had died in the East Indies of yellow fever in February 1797:

All her friends approved. She found him deserving of her affection, and agreed to reward his merit. He was to make one voyage to the Indies, on prospects too great to be neglected, and on his return they were to be married. His voyage was prosperous to the extent of all his wishes. He landed in his native country; flew to his beloved mistress. She received his visit with grateful joy. It was his *last* visit. He was taken ill of a violent fever; died in a few days, delirious, but blessing her.

(*Grandison*, III. 398)

But Charlotte Lady G. argues that few women have their first loves. A man may prove perfidious or engaged to another [like Willoughby and Edward], or he may die [like the men that Cassandra and Jane loved]. What then? 'Must a woman sit down, cry herself blind, and become useless to the principal end of her being, as to this life, and to all family connexions ...?' (III. 405). The answer for Charlotte as for the Austen sisters is 'no'. Cassandra occupied herself with Edward Austen's motherless children, and Jane often had a niece with her as Emma Woodhouse planned. But in the fictional world where *she* played God, Jane Austen restored Elinor's first love, and gave

Marianne a husband of the same age, perhaps, as her own lost lover.

Jane Austen may have recollected emotion in tranquillity at Chawton, but *Sense and Sensibility* does not read tranquilly at all. Perhaps at Bath and Southampton she gradually worked over the experiences of that sad twenty-seventh year, released them into fiction, and freed her mind for the more detached and accomplished *Pride and Prejudice* and *Mansfield Park*.

Even away from home, then, Jane Austen's imagination may not have been idle. Nor could she have missed such an important publication as the correspondence of her favourite writer. Mrs Barbauld's edition showed a Richardson who encouraged women to write, drew inspiration from women's conversations, and wrote not just of the human heart but of the female heart (clxxii).[6] The revelation of Richardson's self-conscious habits of composition, judiciously analysed by Mrs Barbauld, might have lured Jane Austen to write again.

Mrs Barbauld's encouraging defence of fiction sometimes resembles Jane Austen's in *Northanger Abbey* – even if that novel were finished in 1803 it could have been added at any later time. Mrs Barbauld wonders much as Jane Austen would, 'why the poet should have so high a place allotted him in the temple of Fame, and the romance-writer so low a one, as, in the general estimation, he is confined to, for his dignity as a writer has by no means been measured by the pleasure he affords to his readers'. In truth, she argues, 'there is hardly any department of literature in which we shall meet with more fine writing than in the best production of this kind' (ix); Jane Austen writes, 'our productions have afforded more extensive and unaffected pleasure than those of any other literary corporation' in the world. 'There is no walk in which taste and genius have more distinguished themselves', adds Mrs Barbauld (x); 'only genius, wit, and taste to recommend them', writes Jane Austen. 'If the doors of the great were never opened to a genius whom every Englishman ought to have been proud of ... upon them let the disgrace rest, and not upon Richardson', says Mrs Barbauld stoutly (clxxiv); 'From pride, ignorance, or fashion, our foes are almost as many as our readers', says Jane Austen (37).

Did Mrs Barbauld's enthusiasm for Richardson alert Jane Austen's more serious reconsideration of him? Mr B.'s visit to his daughter Miss Goodwin, Clarissa's death-bed, and Anna Howe's interview with Lovelace are all closely replayed in *Sense and Sensibility*, and even Jane Austen's tenacious memory must have needed prompting nearer the time of composition or revision in Bath and Southampton. Although many of her own books had been sold in 1801, Richardson would never be hard for her to find. The 1808 catalogue of 'upwards of Twenty-five Thousand Volumes' in Marshall's Circulating Library in Upper-Milsom Street, Bath, includes for instance *Pamela*, *Clarissa*, and *Sir Charles Grandison*.

Mrs Barbauld praises other episodes that Jane Austen developed for *Pride and Prejudice* and *Sense and Sensibility*. From *Pamela* she singles out 'the pride and passion of Lady Davers', a character who contributes largely to Elizabeth Bennet's confrontation with Lady Catherine de Bourgh. Mr B., called 'proud, stern, selfish, forbidding' by Mrs Barbauld (lxii–lxiii), is like Mr Darcy, proud and forbidding at first sight, a man to be accused of 'selfish' disdain (10, 193). But Jane Austen prevents the flaws that Mrs Barbauld saw in Richardson. If Mr B.'s 'ideas of the authority of a husband are so high, that it is not easy to conceive of Pamela's being rewarded by marrying him', Darcy will be 'properly humbled' by Elizabeth (369). In real life, says Mrs Barbauld, we should consider Pamela as 'an interested girl', possibly indelicate in her passions, and open to the charge of marrying Mr B. for 'the gilt coach, and dappled Flanders' mares'. Pamela's excessive humility and gratitude on her exaltation shows 'a regard to rank and riches beyond the just measure of an independent mind', she adds (lxiii–lxvi). Jane Austen only lets Elizabeth admit that to be mistress of Pemberley might be something, when all hope of Darcy seems gone (245). And it is not Elizabeth but Mrs Bennet who admires Darcy's rank and riches: 'Oh! my sweetest Lizzy! how rich and how great you will be! What pin-money, what jewels, what carriages you will have!' (378).

From *Clarissa*, Mrs Barbauld picks out the scene where the betrayed Clarissa holds up the marriage licence 'in a speechless agony' (III. letter xxxii), the penknife scene, the prison scene and the death-bed scene, most of which Jane Austen used for *Sense and Sensibility*. The first recurs when the betrayed Marianne, showing Willoughby's letter to Elinor, 'almost screamed with agony – as her last appeal to Willoughby had ended in a 'silent agony' (182, 178) – in a scene which recalls Clarissa's last desperate appeal to Lovelace just before the rape (III. letter xxviii). Jane Austen used the prison scene for Eliza Williams and the death-bed for the 'dying' Marianne, but not Richardson's suicidal penknife scene, as we shall see.

Mrs Barbauld thinks Lovelace unrealistic, for 'where is the libertine who would attempt in England the seduction of young women, guarded by birth and respectable situations in life, and friends jealous of their honour, and an education which would set them far out of reach of any disgraceful overtures?' The libertine Willoughby does not in fact seduce Marianne, nor may Wickham seduce Georgiana Darcy, guarded by her brother.

Mrs Barbauld, fearing that 'the gaiety and spirit of Lovelace, in the hands of Garrick, would have been too strong for the morality of the piece', quotes Johnson as her authority:

[Rowe's] Lothario, with gaiety which cannot be hated, and bravery which cannot be despised, retains too much of the spectator's kindness. It was in the power of Richardson alone, to teach us at once esteem and detestation; to make virtuous resentment overpower all the benevolence which wit, and elegance, and courage, naturally excite; and to lose at last the hero in the villain.   (cvii–cviii)

The problem, as Mrs Barbauld saw, was that to attract such a heroine the villain-hero must have 'wit and spirit, and courage, and generosity, and manly genteel address, and also transient gleams of feeling, and transient stings of remorse' (lxxxix). She wished therefore for a final scene to turn the reader with horror from the features of the gay and agreeable seducer, 'when changed into the agonizing countenance of the despairing self-accuser' (xc–xci). Jane Austen, who invites the same danger, wrote that self-accusing scene for Willoughby.

Mrs Barbauld's summary of Grandison could stand beside any summary of Darcy:

a man of birth and fortune, endowed with every personal advantage, and master of every fashionable accomplishment. He is placed in a variety of situations, calculated to draw forth the virtues and energies of his character, as a son, a brother, a guardian, a friend, and a lover; and his conduct is every where exemplary ... He is generous without profusion ... complaisant without weakness, firm in his purposes, rapid in the execution of them; jealous of his honour, yet always open to a generous reconciliation, feeling ... the passions of human nature, yet always possessing a perfect command over them.   (cxiv–cxv)

But if Sir Charles suppresses those passions to the vanishing point, Darcy will express himself in his proposal 'as sensibly and as warmly as a man violently in love can be supposed to do' (366).

Marianne is like Clementina, as described by Mrs Barbauld, 'a young creature involved in a passion ... so strong as to overturn her reason; and afterwards, on the recovery of her reason, after a severe struggle, voluntarily sacrificing that very passion at the shrine of religious principle' (cxix–cxx). But like Jane Austen in *Sense and Sensibility*, Mrs Barbauld queries Richardson's confidence that a first love may readily be conquered:

though, in real life, a passion, however strong, will generally give way to time, at least so far as to permit the disappointed party to fill her proper station in social life, and fulfil the relative duties of it with calm complacence, if not with delight, we cannot easily figure to ourselves that Clementina, with such a high-toned mind, and a passion so exalted, a passion that had shaken the very seat of reason in her soul, could, or with so shattered an intellect ought, to turn her thoughts to a second lover.   (cxii–cxiii)

The same has often been said of Marianne. And yet Jane Austen's bravado in presenting Marianne's happily second-placed love suggests that she thought she could get away with it so long as it looked like 'real life':

Marianne Dashwood was born to an extraordinary fate. She was born to discover the falsehood of her own opinions, and to counteract, by her conduct, her most favourite maxims. She was born to overcome an affection formed so late in life as at seventeen, and with no sentiment superior to strong esteem and lively friendship, voluntarily give her hand to another! ...

But so it was. Instead of falling a sacrifice to an irresistible passion ... she found herself at nineteen, submitting to new attachments, entering on new duties, placed in a new home, a wife, the mistress of a family, and the patroness of a village.   (378–9)

If Mrs Barbauld's critical observations are noteworthy, her technical analysis is remarkable. She praises the unity of *Clarissa* and *Grandison* (lxxxiii, cxvi) compared to Fielding's detached episodes, 'thrown in like make-weights, to increase the bulk of the volume' (cxxvi) – Jane Austen would write mockingly of her own 'light, and bright, and sparkling' *Pride and Prejudice* that it 'wants to be stretched out here and there with a long chapter of sense, if it could be had; if not, of solemn specious nonsense, about something unconnected with the story; an essay on writing, a critique on Walter Scott, or the history of Buonaparté' (*Letters*, 4 February 1813). Characters who digress, like Mrs Allen, Miss Bates, or Mrs Elton, are in fact commonly comic butts. Mrs Barbauld observed that Richardson did not possess that 'terseness or dignity, which is necessary to give brilliancy to moral maxims and observations', his writings being 'blemished' with 'new coined words, and sentences involved and ill-constructed' (cxxxv–cxxxvi). Jane Austen would reserve *her* new-coined words for John Thorpe, and her involved and ill-constructed sentences for Mrs Palmer, Lydia Bennet, Mary Crawford and Mrs Elton. Generally too in her own work she would hope to 'bring the reader with increased delight to the playfulness and epigrammatism of the general style' (*Letters*, 4 February 1813).

Most interesting to any practising writer is Mrs Barbauld's account of point of view. In the narrative and commonest mode, she says, an author like Cervantes or Fielding reveals what he knows at his own pace and indulges in digressions to display his knowledge (an essay on writing, for example, a critique on Sir Walter Scott, or the history of Buonaparté). But since liveliness depends on dialogue, 'all good writers therefore have thrown as much as possible of the dramatic into their narrative', like Madame D'Arblay (xxiii). Jane Austen needed no reminder to read Fanny Burney, but even as she drew on Fielding's omniscient methods in *Northanger Abbey*, she chose dialogue for her dominant narrative form, as Graham Hough sees in 'Narrative and dialogue in Jane Austen'.

Mrs Barbauld calls the first person memoir the least perfect, because it cannot make relating the past probable (xxiv–xxv). Jane Austen makes improbable relations into comic subjects:

This brief account of the family is intended to supersede the necessity of a long and minute detail from Mrs. Thorpe herself, of her past adventures and sufferings, which might otherwise be expected to occupy the three or four following chapters; in which the worthlessness of lords and attornies might be set forth, and conversations, which had passed twenty years before, be minutely repeated.   (*NA*, 34)

Although in the epistolary mode characters write letters dramatically to the moment, it is improbable 'for want of a narrator', says Mrs Barbauld (xxvi–xxvii). In the juvenilia Jane Austen had already attacked exactly the problems she lists, the confidant, the man who must praise himself, the glaring gaps in narration, the digressive longueurs, and the helplessness of the author to intervene (see Appendix 2). But did this lucid account of narrative kinds persuade her to break off her own unfinished epistolary novel *Lady Susan* by means of a decisive authorial intervention? Two sheets are watermarked 1805 as Gilson points out (p. 375), and Lascelles believes that the conclusion was added 'at some time nearer to the date of the fair copy, when Jane Austen had lost patience with the device of the novel-in-letters' (pp. 13–14). Grasping the narrative reins as she would for the rest of her life, Jane Austen writes, 'This Correspondence, by a meeting between some of the Parties & a separation between the others, could not, to the great detriment of the Post office Revenue, be continued any longer'. At some point before 1809 she also decided to rework the epistolary 'Elinor and Marianne' and 'First Impressions' into works controlled by a mixture of narrative and dramatic voices. Though Jane Austen when young was merciless upon incompetent telling of tales, Mrs Barbauld might have made her think with more sympathy about technique.

Finally, Mrs Barbauld remarks that Richardson's lack of a classical education was no matter:

... however an ignorance of the learned languages might, some centuries ago, have precluded the unlearned Englishman from those treasures of literature which open the faculties and enlarge the understanding, our own tongue now contains productions of every kind sufficient to kindle the flame of genius in a congenial mind.

'Reading', she explains, 'provided a man seeks rather after good books than new books, still continues to be the cheapest of all amusements; and the boy who has barely learned to read at a village school-dame's, is in possession of a key which will unlock the treasures of Shakespeare and of Milton, of Addison, and of Locke' (xxxiii–xxxiv). Jane Austen, a voracious reader of good books as well as new books, could know that her reading made

her 'with Books well-bred', as Pope said of Martha Blount.
Richardson, said Mrs Barbauld, was 'one instance, among innumerable others, of natural talents making their way to
eminence, under the pressure of narrow circumstances, the dis-
advantage of obscure birth, and the want of a liberal education'
(xxix). Jane Austen may have encountered such encouraging ideas
before in the influential *Conjectures on Original Composition*
(1759) by Richardson's friend Edward Young, a work to which
she seems to refer in a letter. And in her own copy of Dodsley's
Collection of Poems, she must have read Arthur Seward's 'The
Female Right to Literature' and John Duncombe's 'The Feminiad:
or, Female Genius'.[7] Both generously urge female genius to
write.

Richardson was also, says Mrs Barbauld, a 'friend to mental
improvement in women', but the prejudice against 'any appearance of extraordinary cultivation in women, was, at that period,
very strong' (cxliii–cxliv). Deploring the humiliating 'necessity
of affecting ignorance', like Jane Austen bitterly remarking on
the charms of imbecility in females (*NA*, 111), she advises that
before a woman steps out of the common walks of life, her
acquirements should be solid, and her love for literature decided
and irresistible. Late in her life Jane Austen told her niece that
'if I would take her advice I should cease writing till I was sixteen;
that she herself often wished she had read more, and written less
in the corresponding years of her own life', as the *Memoir* reports
(p. 47). Once, says Mrs Barbauld, 'a reading female was a sort of
phenomenon' (ccv); to Miss Bingley's sneer that Elizabeth is a
'great reader' with 'no pleasure in any thing else', Elizabeth may
reply defensively, 'I am *not* a great reader, and I have pleasure in
many things', but Darcy, sketching the truly accomplished
woman, states that 'she must yet add something more substantial, in the improvement of her mind by extensive reading'
(37–9).

Jane Austen's letter to the Regent's Librarian (*Letters*, 11
December 1815), generally regarded as 'the author's perception
of her own limitations',[8] looks very different set against such
praise for unlearned genius. The Librarian had asked her to write
of a model clergyman very patently himself, and she, who had
probably mastered Locke, replied, 'such a man's conversation
must at times be on subjects of science and philosophy, of which

I know nothing'. She adds demurely that such a man should 'at least be occasionally abundant in quotations and allusions which a woman who, like me, knows only her own mother tongue, and has read very little in that, would be totally without the power of giving'. But in the light of Mrs Barbauld's derisive account of Richardson's pedant Brand, his letters 'larded with Latin quotations ... those Latin phrases which are used, in a manner proverbially, by scholars, as the garniture of their discourse' (xxxiii), her meekness suddenly looks like a wicked attack on the oblivious Mr Clarke. In the full confidence of her untutored powers, she doubles back into a triumphant declaration of unlettered female genius:

A classical education, or at any rate a very extensive acquaintance with English literature, ancient and modern, appears to me quite indispensable for the person who would do any justice to your clergyman, and I think I may boast myself to be, with all possible vanity, the most unlearned and uninformed female who ever dared to be an authoress.

Mrs Barbauld's analysis proves that to succeed, unlearned practitioners of fiction such as Richardson, or women, need only read literature in English. This, I shall argue, is what Jane Austen did.

3

Sense and Sensibility

When Nancy Steele calls out 'Oh, la! here come the Richardsons' (275), Jane Austen deftly allows that *Sense and Sensibility* is connected to Richardson's novels by a multitude of discoverable threads. Both as much-loved objects, and as artifacts already commented on in the Barbauld edition of the *Correspondence*,[1] they provided her with characters, scenes, and themes for this and the two other novels she published first.

Her knowledge of him 'was such as no one is likely again to acquire', said James Austen-Leigh with pardonable pride (p. 89), and like her brother, like her own mother, like Catherine Morland's mother, Jane Austen very often read *Sir Charles Grandison*. 'Every circumstance narrated in [it], all that was ever said or done in the cedar parlour, was familiar to her; and the wedding days of Lady [Grandison] and Lady G. were as well remembered as if they had been living friends'. Habitually she recalled the date of the year upon which episodes in the novel were supposed to have taken place,[2] for 'Richardson's power of creating, and preserving the consistency of his characters, as particularly exemplified in "Sir Charles Grandison", gratified the natural discrimination of her mind', says Henry Austen (p. 7). She helped a niece write a *Grandison*-based play, but seeing that it is not as close as her own novels to the original, it may not be primarily hers. *Grandison* was thus important to Jane Austen, but so were *Clarissa* and *Pamela*.

Jane Austen quarried Richardson directly and substantially. Some similarities are known,[3] but the more one lays his works beside her first three, the more obvious the inspiration. If Richardson said of his Clementina, you can see her thoughts 'by what she omitted, and what she chose' (*Grandison*, II. 247), Jane Austen is creatively critical too. Affectionate but never

48

reverential, she rapidly surveys the possibilities that he offers, adopting, adapting, fusing together, and diverging from the material that she finds.

Dull flat appropriations of Richardson coexist curiously in *Sense and Sensibility* with deeply satisfying episodes which explode and reconstruct what he had done.[4] The similarities and differences between *Sense and Sensibility* and *Pamela*, *Sir Charles Grandison*, *Clarissa* and *Paradise Lost*, *Clarissa*'s own progenitor, illuminate both her working methods and some difficult critical cruxes in her book.

Pamela and *Sir Charles Grandison*

After 'such a Setting-out in matrimony; who would have expected Charlotte to make such a wife, mother, nurse!', exclaims Harriet Byron in *Grandison* (III.460). The lively Marianne is 'matronized' just as surprisingly by a sober marriage. But as if to compensate, Jane Austen provides Colonel Brandon with an oddly rakish past, derived from Richardson.

In a flashback uncharacteristic for Jane Austen, Brandon tells of his hopeless love for his unhappily married cousin Eliza Brandon, whose adulterous affair with another man resulted in a daughter. This tale, which closely resembles an episode in *Pamela* about Mr B.'s illegitimate daughter by Sally Godfrey, links him briefly to the villain-hero whose name he bears. Both guilty women have recommended their 'precious' trusts to others, that is to Mr B. and Brandon. Mr B.'s daughter Miss Goodwin is a young boarding-school lady, who with four others visits a farm-house in Bedfordshire run by a 'good woman'; Brandon has placed Eliza 'under the care of a very respectable woman, residing in Dorsetshire, who had the charge of four or five other girls of about the same time of life'. Miss Goodwin calls Mr B. her uncle, and Brandon calls little Eliza 'a distant relation; but I am well aware that I have in general been suspected of a much nearer connection with her' (208). She is thought to be his natural daughter (66) as Miss Goodwin is indeed Mr B.'s (II. 288, 290–7).

Jane Austen swerves away from Richardson's inert details in complex and interesting ways. Colonel Brandon, though not the child's father, is mildly complicitous because he loved the erring woman. He does not take the child home as the B.'s did, and his absence from her allows for further developments. While Mr B.'s daughter is 'between six and seven' (II. 292), Eliza Williams at the dangerous age of seventeen repeats her mother's fault with a man we already know, Willoughby. The delayed revelations that Brandon is innocent though interested, and Willoughby attractive but villainous, can then make up a plot.

Sir Charles Grandison is a more largely prevalent source for *Sense and Sensibility*, with Fanny Burney, Jane West, Elizabeth Inchbald and Maria Edgeworth as minor contributors.[5] The omnipresence of *Grandison* has been explored by Alvin C. Metcalfe, whose work I summarise in Appendix 1. But here by way of example and addition is what Jane Austen made of three themes common to both novels.

Marriage with a rake, a topic debated by a 'court of love' in *Grandison*, closely affects Marianne's relation with Willoughby. Richardson had written,

The woman who chooses a Rake ... what has she chosen? He married not from honest principles: A Rake despises matrimony: If still a Rake, what hold will she have of him? A Rake in *Passion* is not a Rake in *Love*. Such a one can seldom be in Love: From a laudable passion he cannot. He has no delicacy. His Love deserves a vile name: And if so, it will be strange, if in his eyes a common woman excel not his modest wife.

(I. 429–30)

Elinor agrees. It is 'the worst and most irremediable of all evils, a connection, for life, with an unprincipled man', she says (184), and even Marianne will acknowledge, 'I never could have been happy with him, after knowing, as sooner or later I must have known, all this. – I should have had no confidence, no esteem. Nothing could have done it away to my feelings'. Her mother chimes in, 'Happy with a man of libertine practices! – With one who had so injured the peace of the dearest of our friends, and the best of men! – No – my Marianne has not a heart to be made happy with such a man! – Her conscience, her sensitive conscience, would have felt all that the conscience of her husband ought to have felt'. Elinor, like Richardson before her, sees the reality of marriage to a rake, and asks,

'how little could the utmost of your single management do to stop the ruin which had begun before your marriage? – Beyond *that*, had you endeavoured, however reasonably, to abridge *his* enjoyments, is it not to be feared, that instead of prevailing on feelings so selfish to consent to it, you would have lessened your own influence on his heart, and made him regret the connection which had involved him in such difficulties?'

(350–1)

In this example Jane Austen seems to call on Richardson's authority in order to disentangle Marianne from Willoughby. But she probes his opinions more carefully in his next topic, 'marriages of persons of unequal years' (I. 430). Sir Charles has advised his uncle Lord W., victim of gout and a termagant mistress, to marry Miss Mansfield, a genteel woman of decayed family and small fortune. He explains, 'I am always for excusing men in years, who marry prudently ... Male nurses are unnatural creatures! ... Womens sphere is the house, and their shining-place the sick-chamber' (II. 58). He adds airily,

My Lord W.'s wife will probably, be confined six months, out of twelve, to a gouty man's chamber. She must therefore be one who has outlived half her hopes: She must have been acquainted with affliction, and known disappointment. She must consider her marriage with him, tho' as an act of condescension, yet partly as a preferment. Her tenderness will, by this means, be engaged; yet her dignity supported: And if she is not too much in years to bring my Lord an heir, he then will be the most grateful of men to her. (II. 90)

Marianne uses Richardson's very words and ideas (gout and rheumatism were thought to be the same)[6] vigorously to challenge Sir Charles's complacency:

'A woman óf seven and twenty ... can never hope to feel or inspire affection again, and if her home be uncomfortable, or her fortune small, I can suppose that she might bring herself to submit to the offices of a nurse, for the sake of the provision and sécurity of a wife. In his marrying such a woman therefore there would be nothing unsuitable. It would be a compact of convenience, and the world would be satisfied. In my eyes it would be no marriage at all, but that would be nothing. To me it would seem only a commercial exchange, in which each wished to be benefited at the expense of the other.'

But as Elinor at once points out, her case is different. (Anyway, Lord W. is fifty, and Colonel Brandon is only thirty-five; where Lord W. suffers pain, Colonel Brandon feels just a twinge.) 'I must object to your dooming Colonel Brandon and his wife to the constant confinement of a sick chamber, merely because he chanced to complain yesterday (a very cold damp day) of a slight rheumatic feel in one of his shoulders'. Marianne protests that 'he talked of flannel waistcoats ... and with me a flannel waistcoat is invariably connected with aches, cramps, rheumatisms, and every species of ailment that can afflict the old and the feeble' (38). Jane Austen here defies the dictionaries and quotation books that associate flannel with Welshmen, underclothing, shrouds, old age, and Betsey Barker's cow.

But both marriages proceed, despite the 'inconveniences' of gout and great disparity in years (II. 269). Unlike Miss Mansfield though, Marianne is not 'one who has outlived all her hopes'. 'She was born to overcome an affection formed so late in life as at seventeen', writes Jane Austen sardonically, even if Marianne like her predecessor has indeed been acquainted with affliction and known disappointment. She marries the man whom 'two years before, she had considered too old to be married, – and who still sought the constitutional safeguard of a flannel waistcoat!' (378). Prudent Miss Mansfield marries a wealthy man she has never even met; Marianne marries a rich man whom she knows, a man who loves her. Colonel Brandon, neither so old nor so gouty as Lord W, and with his mistress safely dead, can prove her true Grandison after all.

The third topic important to both books is the superiority of prudent second attachments over romantic first ones. Richardson reviews the whole of *Grandison* in a crucial debate (Volume VII, letter xlii) about Harriet, Clementina, Emily Jervois, and Charlotte Grandison, all of whom except Harriet marry the object of their second-placed affections. So does Sir Charles. This letter and the next may well have been inserted in proof to answer criticism of *Grandison*'s ending similar to that of *Sense and Sensibility*'s.[7]

The exemplary grandmother Mrs Shirley cannot consent to the 'hardship of Lady Clementina's situation'. Having rejected the man of her choice, Clementina is now being urged for 'reasons of family convenience, and even of personal happiness' to marry a nobleman 'highly deserving and agreeable, and everyway suitable to her'. To the question 'Can the woman be happy in a second choice, whose first was Sir Charles Grandison?', Mrs Shirley replies, 'Young people set out with false notions of happiness; gay, fairy-land imaginations; and when these schemes prove unattainable, sit down in disappointment and dejection'. She herself was once cured of the 'romantic notions' she held from sixteen to 'quite twenty'; Marianne is sixteen and a half when she meets Willoughby (49), nineteen when she marries Brandon. Mrs Shirley, who had 'very high ideas of first impressions; of eternal constancy; of Love raised to a pitch of idolatry', thought when Mr Shirley was proposed to her, 'what was a good sort of man to an Oorondates?'. Her friend Mrs Eggleton had however urged her to accept, arguing that 'Esteem, heightened by Gratitude, and enforced by Duty ... will soon ripen into Love: The only sort of Love that suits this imperfect state: a *tender*, a *faithful* affection'. Years of happiness with Mr Shirley proved Mrs Eggleton right, and Marianne too, 'with no sentiment superior to strong esteem and lively friendship, voluntarily ... give[s] her hand to another!' (378). With Brandon, a good man but no Oorondates, she lives happily ever after.

'First sight impressions', concludes Mrs Shirley confidently, and '*beginning* inclinations ... are absolutely trifles to overcome and suppress, to a person of prudence and virtue'. Lively Lady G., another 'proof' of happy marriage with a sober husband, reinforces the argument in the following letter. Harriet was '*romantic*', she says, not to realise 'how few of us are there, who have their first Loves? And indeed how few first Loves are fit to be encouraged?'. Time qualifies every disappointment. Even the romancer Harriet would have married. So will Clementina. 'Leave her sea-room, leave her land-room, and let her have time to consider; and she will be a Bride'. She points to herself as an 'encouragement for girls who venture into the married state, without that prodigious quantity of violent passion, which some hare-brained creatures think an essential of Love'. Marianne also does not fall 'a sacrifice to an irresistible passion', but marries Brandon willingly, 'at last' (378).

Brandon's and Elinor's debate on the same topic in chapter xi differs mainly in its timing; Richardson puts his towards the end where nothing hangs on it, but Austen places hers early on, while Brandon still sounds out his chances of success. To his assumption that Marianne does not approve of second attachments, Elinor agrees that 'her opinions are all romantic', the word used critically of Harriet. She adds that 'a few years however will settle her opinions on the reasonable basis of common sense and observation', like Mrs Shirley's 'plain common sense'. To Brandon's protest that her youthful prejudices are 'amiable', Elinor replies firmly that 'there are inconveniences attending such feelings as Marianne's'. Colonel Brandon lists various possibilities for second attachment very much as Lady G. had spoken of perfidiousness, other engagements, or death. 'Is it equally criminal in every body? Are those who have been disappointed in their first choice, whether from the inconstancy of its object, or the perverseness of circumstances, to be equally indifferent during the rest of their lives?'. Elinor only knows that Marianne never yet admitted 'any instance of a second attachment's being pardonable'. Brandon, who believes that this cannot hold, regrets that 'the romantic refinements of a young mind' (like Mrs Shirley's 'poetical refinements') may be succeeded by opinions too common and too dangerous (55–7). He seems then to criticise Richardson's assurance that first loves are easily overcome. But Marianne, we are finally told, 'was born to discover the falsehood of her own opinions, and to counteract, by her conduct, her most favourite maxims' (378). Her first affection overcome, she submits to new attachments, and finds the real happiness predicted for Clementina. Marianne descends, that is, from Richardson's two exemplars of second-placed love, the lively Charlotte and the 'fair enthusiast' Clementina.

Jane Austen's mind was also charged with *Grandison* when she turned the sisters Lucy and Nancy Selby into Lucy and Nancy Steele, to whom she gave the skittishness and foolish pink ribbons of Sir Charles's aunt (III. 22, 272); Aunt Eleanor hints at a romantic past, and Miss Steele is full of mysterious becks and winks about the doctor whom, according to family tradition (James Austen-Leigh's *Memoir*, p. 158), she never managed to marry. (Jane Austen presumably also noted Harriet's aunt Marianne.) To the habits of one Jane Austen adds the name of another, and so creates a character.

What are we to make of all these parallels? Metcalfe follows R. Brimley Johnson and Q. D. Leavis in thinking them a very bad thing. Johnson, writes Metcalfe, believes that 'all three [novels of the first group] are built around parody and imitation … the latter group are less book-built, more humane – in one view – more original and independent'. In the second group of novels, however, Metcalfe thinks that Jane Austen 'may indeed have come to regard such methods [adaptations of other novels] as immature' (p. 167). Leavis decides in 'A critical theory' (I, 66),

The wit similarly has a pedigree, so have the characters and much of the plots, and even the details of the intrigue. Much more in the novels is dependent on reference to, reaction against, and borrowings from, other novels, than is commonly realized ... they can be accounted for in even greater detail than other literary compositions, for Jane Austen was not a fertile writer.

She is right in everything except her disapproval. Annotated editions of novels as well as of poetry show just how much major writers draw upon the work of predecessors. They cannot impregnate the air, but must have something more substantial for their minds to work upon. What matters is what the author makes of it, and how she makes it hers.

Jane Austen's differences reveal her creativity. As Metcalfe sees, Grandison's broken utterance before leaving for Italy simply expresses anxiety, but Willoughby's conceals his treachery. It must have startled readers of Richardson when Willoughby proved not to be the Sir Charles he promised to be. Richardson knows heroes from villains, but Jane Austen generates plots in that gap between appearance and truth. She does not so much construct a 'composite', in Metcalfe's word, as make a character lead divided lives. Willoughby, who seems a Sir Charles, is actually a rake, and Colonel Brandon, who seems a stuffy Lord G., is actually a socially responsible Grandison. Jane Austen argues in *Sense and Sensibility* as in all her novels that no man's character may be guessed at by exteriors. Readers must work as hard as heroines to identify the real Sir Charles Grandisons of her tales. Out of commentary on Richardson she builds her books.

Clarissa

The *Clarissa* connection in *Sense and Sensibility* provides especially striking examples of Jane Austen's experimental uses of Richardson. Southam argued from possible links between Richardson's pedant Brand and Jane Austen's Mr Collins that she was 'well-read in *Clarissa*', and Duncan-Jones saw other links yet. But it has usually been assumed, as Bradbrook says, that 'Richardson's greatest novel, the tragic *Clarissa*, did not, generally speaking, supply Jane Austen with characters or situations suitable for her kind of satirical comedy'. A.D. McKillop, while seeing that she could have learned something from *Clarissa*, regards Willoughby as 'a much reduced and softened Lovelace, a Lovelace cut down to size', and Wright remarks in his book that he is a 'less interesting, because less complete, version of Richardson's Lovelace' (p.94). Duckworth perceives that something of Clarissa's conflict between religious obedience and passionate love recurs in Marianne Dashwood (p.20), while Mudrick observes brightly that 'at least one of Jane Austen's women might have done almost as well as Clarissa captivating Lovelace and giving him fits: Marianne Dashwood'.[8]

Jane Austen surely knew the masterpiece of her favourite author as well as she knew the rest. A bill is said to exist for the *Clarissa* which a niece remembered seeing in the sitting-room at Steventon,[9] and she certainly knew about the fat woman and her small beer. To judge from *Sense and Sensibility*, *Clarissa* was as familiar as *Grandison* and *Pamela*. Her two Elizas take much of their stories from Clarissa, while Marianne begins as Anna Howe, flirts dangerously with the role of Clarissa, and returns at the end to Anna Howe's. Colonel Brandon runs through a whole sequence of characters for his characterisation. Starting as a Hickman, he develops into a rakish Mr B. or Belford, continues as an avenging Morden, seems to be a potential Lord W., and ends as he began, a Charles Hickman-Grandison. I shall elaborate briefly on Jane Austen's modes of adoption and divergence, exploring in detail the controversial last interview which proves Willoughby a Lovelace indeed.

Brandon begins as a sober Hickman to a lively Anna Howe. The gravity, reserve, and serious but mild manners for which Elinor, briefly adopting Clarissa's part, defends him, are the very ones for which Marianne attacks him, just as Anna Howe dismisses Hickman as 'mighty sober, mighty grave, and all that'. Brandon's flannel waistcoat reveals a singularity in dress that typifies Hickman, 'a set and formal mortal' who is so particular that he would certainly 'fall into a King-William-Cravat, or some such antique chin-cushion' (II.letter i). Brandon takes on additional characteristics from *Grandison*'s Lord G., naturally enough, because Lord G. and Charlotte Grandison compare themselves to Hickman and Anna Howe in an extraordinary passage which shows how much Richardson was concerned in his new book to 'prove' that such a marriage would work (I. 229). For instance, Brandon 'has seen a great deal of the world; has been abroad; has read, and has a thinking mind. I have found him capable of giving me much information on various subjects, and he has always answered my inquiries with the readiness of good-breeding and good-nature'. Lord G. also shines. He is 'a traveller ... a connoisseur in Antiquities, and in those parts of *nice* Knowledge, as I, a woman, call it, with which the Royal Society here, and the learned and polite of other nations, entertain themselves'. Lord G. appears to advantage 'under the awful eye of Miss Grandison. Upon my word, Lucy, she makes very free with him'; Marianne is similarly contemptuous of Brandon's knowledge of the climate and mosquitoes of the East Indies. Willoughby jeers at Brandon for being 'very respectable', with 'more money than he can spend, more time than he knows how to employ, and two new coats every year' (50–1); Hickman had simply been 'honest', and 'of family, with a clear and good estate'. 'I cannot say I love the man', says Anna. 'nor, ever shall, I believe' (II. letter i), but both she and Marianne will love the man they now despise. Jane Austen's differing is that where Anna merely attacks Hickman, Marianne criticises Brandon to praise Willoughby, and Willoughby criticises Brandon to woo Marianne.

Jane Austen adopted the stories of Eliza Brandon and her daughter Eliza Williams – the surname probably came from a runaway daughter in *Grandison* – with very little change from *Clarissa*. They are the worse for it. Even the confusing repetition of the name Eliza reveals how cursorily she thought the episode through. After the prevention of Brandon's elopement with the first Eliza, his father's ward and his own cousin, Eliza had been made to marry his brother. When Brandon returned from military service she was divorced. 'Can we wonder that with such a husband to provoke inconstancy, and without a friend to advise or restrain her ... she should fall?'. His search for her was 'as fruitless as it was melancholy. I could not trace her beyond her first seducer, and there was every reason to fear that she had removed from him only to sink deeper in a life of sin'. (Clarissa, seduced away by Lovelace, was placed in a brothel.) At last he discovered her. 'Regard for a former servant of my own, who had since fallen into misfortune, carried me to visit him in a spunging-house, where he was confined for debt; and there, in the same house, under a similar confinement, was my unfortunate sister'. (Clarissa, arrested for debt, was taken to the prison of the officer's house, where she was visited by Lovelace's rakish friend, Belford.)

Brandon had been appalled. 'So altered − so faded − worn down by acute suffering of every kind! hardly could I believe the melancholy and sickly figure before me, to be the remains of the lovely, blooming, healthful girl on whom I had once doated' (206−7). So too Clarissa was 'greatly altered' by her ordeals (VI. letter lxvii), her 'melancholy' condition and her illness nigh unto death apparent to everyone. At twelve promising to be 'one of the finest women in England', she had died a 'Flower of Nature ... in the blossom of her youth and beauty', 'cut off in the bloom of youth' (VII. letters liii, lx, lxxi). Brandon says, 'That [Eliza] was, to all appearance, in the last stage of a consumption was − yes, in such a situation it was my greatest comfort', since 'Life could do nothing for her, beyond giving time for a better preparation for death; and that was given'. Nor did Clarissa choose to live, but like Eliza rejoiced in 'the happiness of a timely preparation'; 'The preparation is the difficulty − I bless God, I have had time for that' (VII. letters liv, lx). All Brandon could do was to see Eliza 'placed in comfortable lodgings, and under proper attendants'; Clarissa was placed in two handsome apartments with a nurse and the voluntary attendance of Mr Goddard the apothecary, Mrs Lovick, and the Smiths, the name of Willoughby's powerful relative. Brandon visited Eliza 'every day during the rest of her short life; I was with her in her last moments' (206−7). Where Belford visited Clarissa only as a woman seduced by his friend, Brandon's love for Eliza lends him a rake's glamour without his liability. Elinor, at least, finds that Sir John Middleton's hints of 'past injuries and disappointments' have earned her 'respect and compassion' for Brandon (50).

Colonel Brandon elsewhere resembles Clarissa's cousin Colonel Morden, who admired his cousin as a child but came too late from seven years' absence abroad to save her. Morden, who again like Brandon to Eliza II was trustee as well as kin, challenged

Lovelace to a duel and vengefully killed him. In Jane Austen's more pacific version Brandon and Willoughby meet 'by appointment, he to defend, I to punish his conduct. We returned unwounded' (211). Willoughby suffers the realistic limbo of marriage with Miss Grey instead of Lovelace's expiatory death. Colonel Morden attended Clarissa's death-bed as Colonel Brandon keeps watch over Marianne when he thinks she is dying. Clarissa could only pitifully imagine she was in her mother's arms (VII. letter liii), but Marianne, her mother present, gets well.

Colonel Brandon in fact plays Morden to three 'Clarissas', Eliza I, Eliza II, and Marianne. The Eliza scenes fail for closely copying their original; the Marianne scenes, which scrutinise and rework *Clarissa*, convince and move. Marianne may seem more like Clementina della Porretta when she falls in love through reading books with the hero, or when she goes mad like her out of love-melancholy,[10] but since Clementina often recalls Clarissa we might as well go back to that source. Behind all three may lie the lovely archetypal madwoman Ophelia, for if Clarissa quotes from *Hamlet*, both Clementina and Marianne read it with their lovers.

Marianne is especially like Clarissa. Though Jane Austen does not permit her heroine to be actually ruined by Willoughby, the way that the two Elizas are surrogates for Marianne, together with her public commitment to him, her forwardness, her secret correspondence, and her agony of distress when she is rejected, make her look very much as if she has been.[11] Marianne is seduced, so to speak, by proxy, through her likeness to Eliza I and her own involvement with Willoughby, the seducer of Eliza II. Brandon, who speaks of the first Eliza as 'a lady who in temper and mind greatly resembled your sister, who thought and judged like her' (57), and again as 'a lady ... resembling in some measure, your sister Marianne' (he explains that there is 'a very strong resemblance between them, as well in mind as in person'), is attracted to Marianne for qualities that he found first in Eliza, 'the same warmth of heart, the same eagerness of fancy and spirits' (205). If Marianne is like the Clarissa-like Eliza, she too must be vulnerable, 'fall', and 'die'.

Marianne's 'deathbed' in the sick-room matches very closely to the first Eliza's as Brandon himself points out, and also to Clarissa's, the woman whom Eliza copies (VII. letter liii). Elinor

watches Colonel Brandon take Marianne's 'pale hand', dis-
covering 'in his melancholy eye and varying complexion as
he looked at her sister, the probable recurrence of many past
scenes of misery to his mind, brought back by that resemblance
between Marianne and Eliza already acknowledged, and now
strengthened by the hollow eye, the sickly skin, the posture
of reclining weakness, and the warm acknowledgement of
peculiar obligation' (340). In Marianne appear all the effects
of seduction and decline, as defined by her likeness to Eliza,
and through her to Clarissa.

Marianne's illness seems as deathly serious as Clarissa's;
Colonel Brandon cannot resist 'the admission of every melancholy idea, and he could not expel from his mind the persuasion
that he should see Marianne no more'. 'Feverish wildness'
alternates with slumber as it did in Clarissa, and she calls
on her mother as Clarissa calls on her absent mother when she
is dying (VII. letter xli). Marianne's ideas, 'still, at intervals,
fixed incoherently on her mother', make Elinor anticipate 'her
suffering mother arriving too late to see this darling child,
or to see her rational'. (Clarissa's mother did arrive too late
to see her.) Marianne's apothecary Mr Harris promises her 'the
relief which a fresh mode of treatment must procure', but like
Clarissa's apothecary Mr Goddard he is too sanguine. Marianne
remains in a heavy stupor resembling Clarissa's absence of
consciousness, and Mrs Jennings, at least, fears the worst.
'Her conviction of [Marianne's] danger would not allow her
to offer the comfort of hope. Her heart was really grieved. The
rapid decay, the early death of a girl so young, so lovely as
Marianne, must have struck a less interested person with concern' (309–13).

At this point Jane Austen conflates Clarissa's madness after
the rape with her swift decline towards death when she writes
of Marianne's hallucinations, her broken sentences, her yearning
after her mother. The large difference is that where Clarissa
presses on inexorably to her Father's house in heaven, Marianne
survives. Both books then ask, was that drive suicidal? Once
restored to 'life, health, friends, and to her doating mother' (315),
Marianne seems to think so:

I saw that my own feelings had prepared my sufferings, and that my want
of fortitude under them had almost led me to the grave. My illness,

I well knew, had been entirely brought on by myself, by such negligence of my own health, as I had felt even at the time to be wrong. Had I died, – it would have been self-destruction. (345)

In spite of Lovelace's belief that the pious Clarissa would not 'shorten her own life, either by violence or neglect', in spite of Clarissa's own insistence that 'altho' I wish not for life, yet I would not, like a poor coward, desert my post when I *can* maintain it, and when it is my *duty* to maintain it' (VI. letters lxviii, lxvi), she does in fact die. Jane Austen may pragmatically have acquiesced with Lovelace's question, 'is death the *natural* consequence of a Rape? ... if not the *natural* consequence, and a lady will destroy herself, whether by a lingering death, as of grief; or by the dagger, as Lucretia did; is there more than one fault the *man's*? Is not the other *hers*?' (VII. letter xci), for she lets her heroine live.

Clarissa and Marianne did though set out to kill themselves like Lucretia, and for the same reason, that though innocent they 'fell'.[12] Clarissa blesses God that she is not 'a guilty creature!' (VI. letter lvi), and Marianne, overwhelmed by her feelings as thoroughly as Clarissa was overcome by an opiate, is just as innocent. Colonel Brandon says as much when he imagines how Marianne, abandoned by Willoughby, will

turn with gratitude towards her own condition, when she compares it with that of my poor Eliza, when she considers the wretched and hopeless situation of this poor girl, and pictures her to herself, with an affection for him as strong, still as strong as her own, and with a mind tormented by self-reproach, which must attend her through life. Surely this comparison must have its use with her. She will feel her own sufferings to be nothing. They proceed from no misconduct, and can bring no disgrace. On the contrary, every friend must be made still more her friend by them. Concern for her unhappiness, and respect for her fortitude under it, must strengthen every attachment. (210)

Eliza II's child testified visibly to her liaison with Willoughby, just as Lovelace hoped that Clarissa was pregnant after the rape (VI. letter lxxviii). Marianne is not raped, not pregnant, and yet she falls ill under similar circumstances as the pregnant Harriet, now Lady Grandison. Both are caught in a rainstorm far from shelter, and both are thought to be dying as a result of the fever they consequently catch (III. 419–20). Here again Marianne seems linked to a woman whose sexual life has already begun. In spite of all this evidence of 'fall' however, a matter which will recur in the section on *Paradise Lost*, Marianne is neither Lucretia nor Clarissa. She lives on, marries her champion, and becomes the 'wife, mother, mistress, friend' that Clarissa could never be.

The dying Clarissa kisses the portrait of Anna Howe, '*sweet and ever-amiable friend–companion–sister–lover!*', and reproaches herself, '*What a deep error is mine! – What evils have I been the occasion of!*' (VII. letters iv, xli). Richardson describes the grieving confidant, the inconsolable mother, the remembering relatives; Marianne only imagines the pain her death would have caused:

Had I died, – in what peculiar misery should I have left you, my nurse, my friend, my sister! – You, who had seen all the fretful selfishness of my latter days; who had known all the murmurings of my heart! – How should I have lived in *your* remembrance! – My mother too! How could you have consoled her! – I cannot express my own abhorrence of myself.
(346)

Jane Austen criticises *Clarissa* in her rewriting, for Marianne's drive to destruction is more reprehensible than her predecessor's.

From these dangerous associations with Belford, Morden, and Clarissa, Jane Austen turns Brandon and Marianne back to their original roles of Hickman and Anna Howe. Richardson's list in the Postscript to *Clarissa* of the principal characteristics of a good man, '*Goodness of heart, and Gentleness of manners, great Assiduity*, and *inviolable* and *modest* love', applies neatly to Brandon, faithfully and humbly in love with Marianne, 'of gentle address, and I believe possessing an amiable heart' (51). As Richardson explains,

Ladies … in chusing companions for life … should rather prefer the honest heart of a Hickman, which would be all their own, than to risque the chance of sharing … the volatile mischievous one of a Lovelace: In short, that they should chuse, if they wished for durable happiness, for rectitude of mind, and not for speciousness of person or address: Nor make a jest of a good man in favour of a bad one, who would make a jest of them and of their whole Sex.   (Postscript, p.365)

Marianne like Anna Howe jests at her good man, but gives her heart to Colonel Brandon as thoroughly as she once gave it to Willoughby. She exchanges the doom of Clarissa for the happier one of her friend.

Edward Ferrars changes too from a stuffy, sober Hickman to the Sir Charles Grandison Elinor always thought he was, rushing to her once released like Sir Charles bolting homeward to Harriet. If Brandon is glamorized by a touch of Belford, Edward is pushed towards rake rather than saint by a brief association with the Baron from the *Rape of the Lock*.[13] His act of cutting the scissors sheath to pieces is not Freudian, but erotic through its provenance in Pope's poem. The scene surely alludes to the moment when 'the glitt'ring *Forfex*' descends on Belinda's lock (III. 147) to signify that for Elinor as for Belinda, life as a sexual creature now begins. (The idea also extends to Lucy, whose lock in Edward's ring Elinor thinks must have been procured 'by some theft or contrivance' rather than by free gift (98). Jane Austen uses the same signal in *Northanger Abbey* and in *Mansfield Park*.) Although Marianne invited the purloining of the lock, 'which you so obligingly bestowed on me', says Willoughby (183), Elinor will be the first to marry.

Sense and Sensibility could be summoned up by Richardson's aims for *Clarissa*. His first, as he explained in his various addenda, and repeated in the Preface to *Grandison*, was to warn young women 'against preferring a Man of Pleasure to a Man of Probity, upon that dangerous, but too commonly received Notion, *That a reformed Rake makes the best Husband*'. This Marianne accepts. His second, 'to caution Parents against the *undue* Exercise of their natural Authority over their Children, in the great Article of Marriage' (Preface to *Clarissa*), is however inverted when Marianne's mother actually encourages her attraction to a man of pleasure, thus throwing the responsibility for their happiness to the young protagonists.

The last important link between Marianne's story and Clarissa's is that the sin of a prohibited correspondence (I. letter xvii) leads them both astray. Marianne's open nature is betrayed like Clarissa's when she enters into clandestine correspondence. But unlike Clarissa, she is given a second chance – Jane Austen provides the happy ending for her that readers had demanded for *Clarissa*. She lets her Lovelace live, but married and out of reach; she combines Clarissa and Anna in Marianne and marries her to Colonel Brandon, who is sober Hickman, rakish Belford, protective and appreciative Colonel Morden, and benevolent Sir Charles, all in one.

To show how successfully Jane Austen could rewrite *Clarissa*, I shall choose only that extraordinary scene where Willoughby, now married, hears that Marianne is dying. He rushes to explain himself to Elinor, and her vulnerability to him creates a famous critical crux. Litz praises the scene as 'fine' (p. 82), but Wright, for instance, complains that 'Elinor forgives him – but we can hardly forgive Jane Austen' (p. 95). Mudrick, calling Elinor's attitude to Willoughby curious and unexpected, accuses Jane Austen of unprofessional subjectivity, in his book. 'We ... observe Elinor – and presumably the author – almost in love, and quite amorally in love, with him ... through the flagrant inconsistency of her heroine Jane Austen is herself revealed in a posture of yearning for the impossible and lost, the passionate and beautiful hero, the absolute lover' (p. 85). This is nonsensical as a description of Willoughby. In any case, I think that Jane Austen's own experience of loss went into her creation of Marianne, not Elinor, as I explained.

It is then interesting to realise that this controversial episode is a virtual word-by-word reworking of the equally extraordinary scene at the ball where Anna meets Lovelace, the man who drugged her friend and raped her. Anna is forced to hear him out, only to find herself won by the appearance and personality of the rake (VI. letter lxxiv). The two scenes are startlingly alike and revealingly unalike at the same time.

Elinor is alerted at the end of Volume III, chapter vii by 'the bustle in the vestibule' that someone has come; Lovelace, 'the moment he was brought into the great hall, set the whole assemblee into a kind of agitation'. Elinor in chapter viii starts back 'with a look of horror at the sight of him' and obeys 'the first impulse of her heart in turning instantly to quit the room'; Anna Howe 'thought I should have sunk, as soon as I set my eyes upon him', so that her mother asks, 'can you bear the sight of that wretch without too much emotion? – If not, withdraw into the next apartment'. Elinor has her hand already on the lock when its action is suspended by Willoughby's hasty advance; Lovelace opens the door for Anna, only to have her turn and snap her fan in his face. Willoughby asks for 'half an hour – for ten minutes'; Lovelace asks for 'one calm half-hour's conversation' with the family, for 'ten words' with her. 'I entreat you to stay', says Willoughby; 'let me intreat from you one quarter of an hour's audience', says Lovelace. Elinor returns a firm 'No, sir'; 'Not for a *kingdom*', says Anna Howe. Willoughby's business is 'with you, and only you'; Lovelace accosts Anna with 'I must have a few moments conversation with you'. Both women hesitate, both sit down. Elinor concludes 'that prudence required dispatch, and that her acquiescence would best promote it'; Mrs Howe advises her daughter that 'to get rid of him, hear his *ten words*'. Elinor speaks impatiently; Anna remarks, 'I have no patience with such a devil'.

The remainder of Jane Austen's scene telescopes together various other scenes from *Clarissa*. Willoughby's concern about Marianne being out of danger repeats a phrase often used of the dying Clarissa. He thought she had been 'dying of a putrid fever', 'dying – and dying too, believing me the greatest villain upon earth, scorning, hating me in her latest moments'; Anna calls Lovelace 'a practised villain' in her interview with him as Willoughby calls himself 'a fine hardened villain' in his interview with Elinor. (The *Grandison* Preface speaks of Lovelace 'hardening' himself more and more.) With a 'forced vivacity' Willoughby says to Elinor 'let us be cheerful together. – I am in a fine mood for gaiety', conjuring up memories of Lovelace's bizarre buffoonery in the shop when he knows Clarissa to be dying. 'Do you think me most a knave or a fool?', asks Willoughby, a question that might well be asked of Lovelace. He wants to make Elinor 'hate me one degree less than you do *now*'; Anna speaks of Lovelace as being 'so hateful to me', and of 'his hated sight'. Willoughby will offer 'some kind of explanation, some kind of apology, for the past; to open my whole heart to you, and by convincing you, that though I have been always a blockhead, I have not been always a rascal, to obtain something like forgiveness from Ma – from your sister'. Lovelace makes the same demand, 'I beg your interest with your charming friend', and requests Anna's mediation though 'conscious of my demerits ... I *have* been, indeed, the vilest of men'.

But Marianne has already forgiven Willoughby, as Clarissa forgave Lovelace. Willoughby knows that 'diabolical' motives may have been imputed to him; Anna calls Lovelace a devil, a Satanic allusion common in the novel. Willoughby's account of the trifling manner in which he entered upon the affair with Marianne is as selfish as Lovelace's insouciance, making Elinor turn her eyes upon him 'with the most angry contempt'. She says, 'do not let me be pained by hearing any thing more on the subject'; Anna Howe, 'glowing with indignation', breaks across Lovelace's excuses with 'If I must speak on this subject, Let me tell you, that you have broken her heart'.

Willoughby explains that though vanity set him off, he soon found himself (like Lovelace to Clarissa) 'sincerely fond of her'. 'The happiest hours of my life were what I spent with her, when I felt my intentions were strictly honourable'. So too Lovelace's wavering between honourable and dishonourable intentions form the essential tension of Clarissa's story, even to the point where like Willoughby he is prepared to marry the woman he has learnt to love. Willoughby's confession that he seduced Eliza Williams makes Elinor, 'hardening her heart anew', accuse him of 'guilt in that dreadful business'; Anna, remembering the seduction of her friend, reproaches Lovelace with vehemence. Willoughby attempts to blame the victim:

I do not mean to justify myself, but at the same time cannot leave you to suppose that I have nothing to urge – that because she was injured she was irreproachable, and because *I* was a libertine, *she* must be a saint. If the violence of her passions, the weakness of her understanding – I do not mean, however, to defend myself. Her affection for me deserved better treatment, and I often, with great self-reproach, recal the tenderness which, for a very short time, had the power of creating any return.

But if Eliza I, Eliza II, and Marianne are all interchangeable Clarissas as I have suggested, what is said here of Eliza applies to Marianne, as Willoughby's final transition makes clear. 'But I have injured more than herself; and I have injured one, whose affection for me ... was scarcely less warm than her's; and whose mind – Oh! how infinitely superior!' This singular section appears implicitly to comment on Richardson's novel, which, while presenting Clarissa as 'the most excellent woman in the world', like Willoughby's idea of Marianne as the 'secret standard of perfection in woman' (379), constantly questions Clarissa's sensuality and lack of alertness. Marianne's complicity too is matter for debate.

Elinor though blames Willoughby for his 'cruel neglect' of young Eliza. 'You must have known, that while you were enjoying yourself in Devonshire, pursuing fresh schemes, always gay, always happy, she was reduced to the extremest indigence'. Lovelace too is a schemer, an intriguer always eager to 'start a new game' (I. letter xxxi). When Clarissa is indigent and about to die, he flirts in libertine gaiety at the ball. Willoughby says that his relative Mrs Smith would have forgiven him if he had married Eliza; *'Marry and repair, at any time'* is Lovelace's consolation (VII. letter xlix). But when Willoughby first met Marianne, he replayed Clarissa's story from the start:

I had left her only the evening before, so fully, so firmly resolved within myself on doing right! A few hours were to have engaged her to me for ever; and I remember how happy, how gay were my spirits, as I walked from the cottage to Allenham, satisfied with myself, delighted with every body!

Lovelace had also burst out, 'I am taller by half a yard, in my imagination, than I was! – I look *down* upon every-body now. – Last night ... I took off my hat as I walk'd, to see if the lace were not scorch'd, supposing it had brush'd down a star, and, before I put it on again, in mere wantonness, and heart's ease, I was for buffeting the moon'. Lovelace's 'whole soul is joy. When I go to bed, I laugh myself asleep: And I awake either laughing or singing' (III. letter vi). But like Lovelace glorying in his capture, Willoughby has no intent to marry.

Willoughby's broken sentences and painful feelings in the interview scene resemble Lovelace's once Clarissa is dead, but his 'hackneyed metaphor' of a 'dagger to my heart' reflects Lovelace's despairing admission in *his* interview that he has deserved Anna's 'killing words ... and a dagger in my heart besides'. Elinor asks him to relate 'only what in [his] conscience' he thinks necessary for her to hear; Mrs Howe believes that Lovelace 'is touched in conscience for the wrongs he has done you'. Willoughby's remorse, his recognition that Marianne 'was infinitely dearer to me than any other woman in the world, and that I was using her infamously', summarises Lovelace's feelings after Clarissa's death. Willoughby reveals his 'most constant watchfulness' over the house where Marianne was staying in London, 'how often I watched you, how often I was on the point of falling in with you', much as Lovelace in his Satanic way watched the Harlowe house on a 'fourth, fifth, or sixth midnight stroll' (I. letter xxxi). But Willoughby had 'entered many a shop to avoid your sight, as the carriage drove by', whereas Lovelace by his watching and visiting drove the dying Clarissa out of her London refuge, and vented his frustration in savage foolery at the shop (VI. letter cxxiii).

Lovelace meets Anna at a ball; at a ball Willoughby publicly repudiates Marianne. He says that Marianne was 'beautiful as an angel on one side ... Sophia, jealous as the devil on the other hand'. This is a clear echo of Lovelace, torn between the 'angel of a woman' Clarissa, and Sally Martin the 'devil' of a prostitute (VI. letter cxxiii), for later in the chapter Willoughby characterises his wife as impudent, passionate, malicious, and virulent. Like Lovelace before him, he chooses Vice over Virtue. Marianne had called out to him, 'asking me for an explanation, with those bewitching eyes fixed in such speaking solicitude on my face!', and just so in a spectacular baroque dream Lovelace had envisaged Clarissa intervening to save him from Colonel Morden. But the moment that he clasped the 'angel' in his arms she was taken up to heaven by seraphim (VI. letter cxxiv). Willoughby describes his own Faustian agony with equal force:

Marianne's sweet face [was] as white as death. – *That* was the last, last look I ever had of her, – the last manner in which she appeared to me. It was a horrid sight! – Yet, when I thought of her to-day as really dying, it was a kind of comfort to me to imagine that I knew exactly how she would appear to those, who saw her last in this world.

As he rode to what he thought was Marianne's death-bed, Willoughby imagined her 'constantly before me, as I travelled, in the same look and hue'; so Lovelace, riding up and down, awaited fatal tidings of Clarissa, 'forbidden to attend the dear creature, yet longing to see her' (VII. letter xliv). Death seems inevitable for both women. Marianne had 'almost screamed with agony', Willoughby's letter in her hand (182); Lovelace, says Anne Howe, has broken Clarissa's heart.

Willoughby concludes to Elinor, 'have I said all this to no purpose? Am I ... less guilty in your opinion than I was before? – My intentions were not always wrong. Have I explained away any part of my guilt?' So too Lovelace had argued in the interview with Anna, 'you will allow that a very faulty person may see his errors; and when he does, and owns them, and repents, should he not be treated mercifully?'. Elinor seems to agree. 'You have proved yourself, on the whole, less faulty than I had believed you. You have proved your heart less wicked, much less wicked'. Willoughby longs for Marianne's forgiveness, of which he is already assured, pleading 'my misery and my penitence' and the fact that 'she is dearer to me than ever'. Lovelace also asserts that he still loves the forgiving Clarissa and is penitent, although Anna thinks that he has not the air of one, and 'vindicated not any part of his conduct' except the arrest of Clarissa. Willoughby's explanation, thinks Elinor likewise, is only 'comparatively' a justification. But as soon as he shows his distress at Marianne's illness, he arouses in Elinor the pity that he asks for:

Her thoughts were silently fixed on the irreparable injury which too early an independence and its consequent habits of idleness, dissipation, and luxury, had made in the mind, the character, the happiness, of a man who, to every advantage of person and talents, united a disposition naturally open and honest, and a feeling, affectionate temper.

In very similar words Clarissa says of Lovelace, 'Poor wretch! I pity him, to see him fluttering about; abusing talents that were given him for excellent purposes' (VI. letter lxxv). Jane Austen expands on the idea, at the end of her scene:

The world had made him extravagant and vain – Extravagance and vanity had made him cold-hearted and selfish. Vanity, while seeking its own guilty triumph at the expense of another, had involved him in a real attachment, which extravagance, or at least its offspring, necessity, had required to be sacrificed. Each faulty propensity in leading him to evil, had led him likewise to punishment. The attachment, from which against honour, against feeling, against every better interest he had outwardly torn himself, now, when no longer allowable, governed every thought ...

Willoughby dreads Marianne's marriage for the same reason as Lovelace fears Clarissa's death. Marianne 'can never be more lost to you than she is now', as Elinor says.

Willoughby's departure leaves Elinor in a contrariety of emotions that critics have often puzzled over. His hopes for pity and 'compassionate good-will' are answered when Elinor says that she 'forgave, pitied, wished him well'. Though impatient, she finds that her 'heart ... had undergone many changes in the course of this extraordinary conversation'. She analyses her response with remarkable honesty in Volume III, chapter ix, considering where her principal sympathies lie:

Willoughby, he, whom only half an hour ago she had abhorred as the most worthless of men, Willoughby, in spite of all his faults, excited a degree of commiseration for the sufferings produced by them, which made her think of him as now separated for ever from her family with a tenderness, a regret, rather in proportion, as she soon acknowledged within herself – to his wishes than to his merits.

Clear-eyed she acknowledges that 'his influence over her mind was heightened by circumstances which ought not in reason to have weight; by that person of uncommon attraction, that open, affectionate, and lively manner which it was no merit to possess; and by that still ardent love for Marianne, which it was not even innocent to indulge. But she felt that it was so, long, long before she could feel his influence less'. In an 'agitation of spirits' she wishes Colonel Brandon success, while still feeling 'a pang for Willoughby'. Later, she realises that it was neither in her 'power, nor in her wish, to rouse such feelings in another, by her retailed explanation, as had at first been called forth in herself. Reflection had given calmness to her judgment, and sobered her own opinion of Willoughby's deserts; – she wished, therefore, to declare only the simple truth, and lay open such facts as were really due to his character, without any embellishment of tenderness to lead the fancy astray' (339, 349).

Here Jane Austen pays tribute to Richardson's dramatic art. She let Willoughby like Lovelace tell his own story, which as Richardson well knew invites our sympathy. 'Write to the moment', he said proudly of his epistolary method, 'no *pathetic* without it!' (*Grandison*, III.24). Elinor luckily reports Willoughby's story to her mother at second-hand, for 'had Mrs Dashwood, like her daughter, heard Willoughby's story from himself – had she witnessed his distress, and been under the influence of his countenance and his manner, it is probable that her compassion would have been greater' (349). A Willoughby or a Lovelace, face to face, overwhelms the most sober or most prejudiced observer by emotions that only reflection can dispel. Even Anna Howe, as ferociously loyal and indignant as Elinor, cannot resist Lovelace when she actually sees and hears him.

In a passage that Jane Austen cannot have missed, for it was repeated triumphantly by Lady Bradshaigh when she demanded a fortunate ending to *Clarissa* (*Correspondence*, VI. 90–1), Anna Howe admits in words as admiring as Elinor's,

> ... nobody was regarded but him. So little of the fop, yet so elegant and rich in his dress: His person so specious: his air so intrepid: So much meaning and penetration in his face: So much gaiety, yet so little of the monkey ... all manly ... his courage and wit ...

Richardson often warns, and so does Jane Austen, how women are taken in by the eye. As Anna Howe admits in an allusion to Pope, it must be true that 'the generality of women were *Rakes in their hearts*, or they would not be so much taken with a man who had so notorious a character'. In *Clarissa* as in *Sense and Sensibility*, evil is evil still, though it comes in fine array.

These then are resemblances between the two interview scenes. But how differently Jane Austen plays hers! The fact that Elinor is alone and unprotected deepens her responsibility, vulnerability, and complicity in an intimate correspondence with a married man. Jane Austen's copying in the Eliza stories had been uncharacteristically slavish, but here in this brilliant transformation, her similarities and differences construct the most powerful, the most problematic scene in *Sense and Sensibility*.

Paradise Lost

The fourth book to shape *Sense and Sensibility* is *Paradise Lost*. If Milton proved as invigorating to eighteenth-century poets as Dustin Griffin says, in *Regaining Paradise: Milton and the Eighteenth Century*, why not to novelists as well? Richardson depends extensively on Milton when Lovelace like the father of lies glorying in his stratagems creeps and spies round Clarissa's house, for he is a seducer, a destroyer stupidly good before her goodness. Pitiable for the traces of his former glory, Lovelace forces as ambivalent a response as does Satan. The angelic Clarissa stands alone against this devilish rake, attendant devils, shape-changing whores, and deceiving friends.

The struggle for Willoughby's soul is similarly enacted between the 'angel' Marianne and the 'devil' Miss Grey, at the ball.

(Although the name 'Willoughby' derives from Fanny Burney's
Evelina, Marianne is named as if by association, for a rake famous
for diabolism, Dashwood.) Clarissa falls, her initiation into
sexual experience resulting like Eve's from isolation and a broken
prohibition. She has entered on a prohibited correspondence, and
her 'gloomy father's curse' is heavy upon her.[14] Although
Marianne breaks no parental command, when Mrs Dashwood is
incapable of imposing any, she is wrong to go alone with
Willoughby to Allenham. Unable to resist going to London, she
learns to know evil. Although not seduced, the eager sensuality
of her relationship with Willoughby and her dishevelled, tearful
posture after his betrayal all signify her transition from innocence
to experience.

Clarissa showed how Milton could profitably be reworked as
fiction, but Jane Austen probably drew on Milton direct. The
possibility that she had *Paradise Lost* in mind when she wrote
Sense and Sensibility is suggested by the characterisation, stories,
and settings of Marianne, Willoughby, and Colonel Brandon. If
Marianne is Eve, Willoughby Adam, and Colonel Brandon Adam
after the fall, the grief we feel for Marianne may already have been
demanded for Eve. And if the fortunate fall can comfort us, the
ways of Jane Austen in *Sense and Sensibility* may be justified at
last.

At times Willoughby and Marianne resemble Adam and Eve.
If Milton asserts that 'beauty is excelld by manly grace' (IV.
490–1), Willoughby embodies 'manly beauty and more than
common gracefulness'. His very clothes are 'manly'. He is a
'hero' (43), as Adam is the first hero of them all. Eve 'Her
unadorned golden tresses wore/Dissheveld' (IV. 304–6);
Willoughby can cut off a 'long lock of [Marianne's] hair, for it
was all tumbled down her back' (60). To Marianne, Willoughby
is faultless, satisfying the 'ideas of perfection' that her fancy
had delineated; Eve satisfies her longing for reflection in Adam
(IV. 477), and Marianne too sees that Willoughby is in her image,
for 'their taste was strikingly alike' (47–9). Marianne is to
Willoughby the standard of perfection in women (379), as Eve,
adorned with 'perfet beauty', is the fairest of her daughters
(IV. 634, 324). 'Fair Angelic *Eve*' (V. 74) and Marianne, 'beautiful
as an angel' (327) are much alike, for Marianne is 'so lovely, that
when in the common cant of praise she was called a beautiful girl,

truth was less violently outraged than usually happens'. Her smile was sweet, 'hardly [to] be seen without delight', writes Jane Austen (46); 'So lovely faire', writes Milton,

> That what seemd fair in all the World, seemd now
> Mean, or in her summd up, in her contain'd
> And in her looks, from which that time infus'd
> Sweetness into my heart, unfelt before,
> And into all things from her Aire inspir'd
> The spirit of love and amorous delight.   (VIII. 471–7)

Marianne is as frank, affectionate, open, artless, and confiding as Eve (48, 327). When at their first meeting Marianne falls and sprains her ankle, she falls for Willoughby and she is tempted to her Fall. Eve 'Yeilded with coy submission, modest pride, / And sweet reluctant amorous delay' (IV. 310–11); Willoughby, 'perceiving that her modesty declined what her situation rendered necessary, took her up in his arms without farther delay' (42). Adam and Eve 'Imparadis't in one anothers arms' are the very pattern of open and artless love, 'alone' (IV. 506, 333–40); Willoughby's society becomes Marianne's 'most exquisite enjoyment', in which as narcissistically as Eve she has 'no eyes for any one else'. She and Willoughby dance together half the time, or 'were careful to stand together and scarcely spoke a word to any body else' (48, 53–4). Alone with Willoughby and 'never ... happier', Marianne walks about the garden at Allenham and goes all over the house (67). Adam and Eve also walk about their paradisal garden, and 'thus talking hand in hand alone/ They pass'd on to thir blissful Bower' (IV. 689–90). Milton often uses the word 'happy' in the double sense of 'fortunate' and 'filled with bliss', and so does Jane Austen when she writes that it was 'the season of happiness to Marianne', or makes Willoughby say that 'the happiest hours of my life were what I spent with her, when I felt my intentions were strictly honourable, and my feelings blameless' (54, 321). Adam and Eve's 'happiest life' was likewise 'Simplicitie and spotless innocence' before the Fall (IV. 317–18). Adam leads Eve in her virgin modesty blushing to the nuptial bower (VIII. 510–11); when Willoughby carries Marianne through the garden to the house, 'the only form of building in which happiness is attainable', she crimsons over (72, 43) with the colour that Milton said is love's proper hue (VIII. 619). Alone, imparadist, and in love, Marianne to Willoughby was 'infinitely dearer to me than any other woman in the world' (326), just as Eve was bone of Adam's bone and flesh of his flesh, and of course uniquely dear (VIII. 495).

But something is wrong at Allenham. This is the first of four separate occasions in which Jane Austen reworks Harriet Byron's triumphal possession of her husband's home, but where Grandison Hall is indeed Harriet's rightful nuptial bower, these subtleties derive from Marianne's having no right to be at Allenham at all. She visits it alone with Willoughby, before they are engaged, and before the owner is dead. The words 'impropriety' and 'not ... justified' (68–9) are used when Marianne succumbs to the temptation to look at Allenham. In the second variation, Maria Bertram will boast of Sotherton though her engagement to Rushworth is hateful to her. In the third, Elizabeth Bennet, when all hope of Darcy seems gone, visits Pemberley, and thinks ruefully that it might have been hers. In the fourth, Anne Elliot, tempted to marry Sir William Elliot and repossess her home, admits that it has passed into better hands. Jane Austen's four varyings are rich with complicated anxieties.

Willoughby plays the part of Adam, but here and elsewhere he also plays Satan, a doubling of roles which seems odd unless one remembers Richardson's 'Men and Women are Devils to one another. They need no other tempter' (*Grandison*, I. 439). Willoughby's scheming, his lying, the words used of his departure such as 'evil ... good ... misery ... guilt ... blameable ... think ill of ... secret ... suspect ... suspicion ... alteration ... secrecy ... concealing ... concealment ... deceitful ... alteration', his 'sense of guilt that almost took from me the power of dissembling' (322, 78–81, 324) like Satan's standing 'Stupidly good, of enmitie disarm'd,/ Of guile' at the sight of Eve (IX. 465–6), all mark him as a tempter. Satan lives wretched: 'Me miserable! which way shall I flie/Infinite wrauth, and infinite despaire?/Which way I flie is Hell; my self am Hell' (IV. 73–5). So does Willoughby. 'I was miserable', he says, telling of his remorseful flight. 'What an evening of agony it was ... I ran away from you all as soon as I could ... am I less guilty in your opinion than I was before?' (324–9).

Marianne's habitual and wilful isolation leads like Eve's to 'solitary rambles' at Cleveland that nearly cause her death (303).

Often she is described as 'wandering', a word used for moral as well as physical straying. Her 'fall' follows a secret understanding with the tempter, her secret sexual and epistolary 'correspondence' that Richardson had called a sin in *Clarissa*. Marianne is 'wrong' to correspond with Willoughby, and when she is tempted to follow him to London (186, 154, 187), she learns like Eve to know evil. After Satan's tempting dream Eve's cheek had glowed (V. 10), and Marianne too had coloured when Mrs Jennings mentioned Allenham, turned away in great confusion, and blushed with a blush no longer innocent (67–9). Again at the ball she blushes with pain and distress, and her face, which was 'glowing with sudden delight' at the sight of Willoughby (176) now 'crimsoned over' at his indifference; after the Fall, the distemper in Eve's cheek also 'flushing glowd' (IX. 887).

Eve's passions lead her into wilful wandering, temptation, and carnal experience. As Raphael had warned Adam,

> In loving thou dost well, in passion not,
> Wherein true Love consists not; love refines
> The thoughts, and heart enlarges, hath his seat
> In Reason, and is judicious ...
> Not sunk in carnal pleasure ...   (VIII. 588–93)

Marianne's eager passions likewise cause a fall prefigured at the start of the book when Jane Austen rejects the Grandisonian device of rescue from a seducer's coach in favour of a literal fall caused by a 'false step' on a steep hill (41). Marianne later points out 'the important hill' to her sister. 'There, exactly there ... on that projecting mound, – there I fell; – and there I first saw Willoughby' (344). Barton, which she speaks of, is 'a pleasant fertile spot, well wooded, and rich in pasture', just as Paradise is said to be pleasant, fertile, and covered with trees (IV. 214–17). With its high hills rising 'immediately behind, and at no great distance on each side' (28–9), it recalls the 'rural mound' on a steep hill that is Paradise (IV. 134, 172). It is wild (86) as Paradise is 'wilde' (IV. 136); its 'prospect' which 'commanded the whole of the valley, and reached into the country beyond' (29) resembles Adam's view from Paradise, a 'prospect large/Into his neather Empire neighbouring round' (IV. 144–5). In such a setting only one thing can happen, and it does. Marianne will fall 'from what high state of bliss into what woe!' (V. 543), but she will also fall in the sexual sense when the Clarissa sub-plots draw her in to their loveless, Lovelacian lust. Adam's fall with Eve out of 'foul concupiscence' provokes God's 'Thunder' (IX. 1078, 1002) from the sky; 'To know that Marianne was in town was ... a thunderbolt', says Willoughby, using the same word twice (325). Innocent love becomes carnal and enflaming in *Paradise Lost* (IX. 1013–15); so too the 'ardent love' of Willoughby will be 'not even innocent to indulge' (333).

The Miltonic pattern of prohibited correspondence, disobedience, temptation, lying, loyalty to a fallen partner, fall, and punishment, is re-enacted in the Edward Ferrars and Lucy Steele sub-plot, which is linked to the main one by Marianne's bitter identification of Edward as 'a second Willoughby' (261). Drawn in like Richardson's Mr B. (II. 294) when a pupil and a boarder (130), Edward also is involved in a prohibited correspondence. He colours very deeply when he lies about the lock of hair in his ring, he falls with Lucy and stands by her when they are found out, and disobeying his all-powerful parent, he is 'dismissed for ever from his mother's notice' (98, 267–8). The large words 'transgressed' and 'unpardoned' are used of Lucy (377). But Colonel Brandon, playing God as if he were Sir Charles Grandison indeed, offers him a 'living' which grants him new life. But it cannot, as Earth itself could not, provide them with 'a very comfortable income' (283).

Knowledge of good and evil allows 'high Passions, Anger, Hate,/Mistrust, Suspicion, Discord' to overwhelm Adam and Eve's reason (IX. 1123–30); Elinor had urged restraint upon Marianne, 'But the feelings of her sister were instantly expressed ... a voice of the greatest emotion ... wildest anxiety ... misery ... wretchedness ... silent agony ... oppressed ... pangs ... almost choked by grief ... almost screamed with agony ... excess of suffering' (176–82). Willoughby too remembers how 'very, very painful' his feelings were when Marianne came to town (325). Even at their first parting Marianne had suffered a 'violent affliction', while 'his countenance shewed that he strongly partook of the emotion which overpowered Marianne' (75).

The Fall accomplished and the carnal experience past, Adam and Eve blame each other; Marianne at some times believes Willoughby to be 'as unfortunate and as innocent as herself, and at others, lost every consolation in the impossibility of acquitting him' (201). But if, like Satan's malignity (IV.503), this 'evil' has come from without, Elinor can advise her 'whoever may have been so detestably your enemy, let them be cheated of their malignant triumph, my dear sister, by seeing how nobly the consciousness of your own innocence and good intentions supports your spirits. It is a reasonable and laudable pride which resists such malevolence' (189). Although Marianne suspects Willoughby has been turned against her by 'blackest art, like the 'Devilish art' of Satan (IV.801), his cruel letter makes her rail like Eve against the man she once loved (188–90). Willoughby implicitly blames Marianne when he complains of the 'violence of [Eliza's] passions, the weakness of her understanding' (322); 'Thus they in mutual accusation spent/The fruitless hours, but neither self-condemning', writes Milton (IX.1197–9). Only at the final interview does Willoughby blame himself, and only when she has recovered from her near-fatal illness does Marianne's spirit too become 'self-reproving' (346).

In response to God's curse Adam and Eve abandon themselves to sorrow (X.717); when Marianne and her mother left Norland, their first Eden, they 'encouraged each other now in the violence of their affliction. The agony of grief which overpowered them at first, was voluntarily renewed, was sought for, was created again and again. They gave themselves up wholly to their sorrow, seeking increase of wretchedness in every reflection that could afford it, and resolved against ever admitting consolation in future' (7). Again, when Willoughby leaves her, Marianne forbids 'all attempt at consolation [and] wandered about ... indulging the recollection of past enjoyment and crying over the present reverse ... she courted the misery which a contrast between the past and present was certain of giving' (83). Adam rebukes Eve's despairing desire for 'self-destruction' (X.1016), a word Marianne uses when she admits, 'had I died, – it would have been self-destruction' (345). Like Eve, she resolves to live.

Eve abases herself 'submissive in distress' to Adam, who 'As one disarm'd, his anger all he lost,/And thus with peaceful words uprais'd her soon' (X.942–6); Elinor like Adam 'impatient to sooth, though too honest to flatter', gives her sister 'instantly that praise and support which her frankness and her contrition so well deserved' (347). But Marianne like Eve must leave Paradise, and her return to the district where she might have lived with

Willoughby is charged through and through with Miltonic significances:

> The second day brought them into the cherished, or the prohibited, county of Somerset, for as such was it dwelt on by turns in Marianne's imagination ...
>
> Cleveland was ... situated on a sloping lawn. It had no park, but the pleasure-grounds were tolerably extensive; ... the lawn was dotted over with timber, the house itself was under the guardianship of the fir, the mountain-ash, and the acacia, and a thick screen of them altogether, interspersed with tall Lombardy poplars ...
>
> In such moments of precious, of invaluable misery, she rejoiced in tears of agony to be at Cleveland; and as she returned by a different circuit to the house, feeling all the happy privilege of country liberty, of wandering from place to place in free and luxurious solitude, she resolved to spend almost every hour of every day ... in the indulgence of such solitary rambles. (302–3)

But Cleveland is in fact Paradise *after* the Fall, its garden ruined as the archangel Michael had predicted. Blights have spoilt and frosts have nipped the plants; a 'heavy and settled rain' falls. Marianne walks wilfully to parts of the grounds where there was something more of wildness than the rest, where the trees were oldest and the grass was longest and wettest, and 'assisted by the still greater imprudence of sitting in her wet shoes and stockings' (303–6), discovers like Eve her terrible vulnerability to death. Once recovered, Marianne promises 'I shall now live solely for my family. You, my mother, and Margaret must henceforth be all the world to me' (347). Her echo of 'thou to mee/Art all things under Heav'n, all places thou' from the closing lines of *Paradise Lost*, XII. 617–18, promises however that she will find another Adam – indeed the significant adjective 'manly' has already been used of Colonel Brandon (338). Marianne hopes that her 'spirit is humbled, my heart amended, and that I can practise the civilities, the lesser duties of life, with gentleness, and forbearance' (347); Eve, resigned to the loss of Paradise, promises to obey, to depend upon providence, to be worldly wise by being simply meek (XII. 561–9). In return she will gain 'A Paradise within thee, happier farre' (XII. 587). So Elinor, the crisis past, is 'all happiness within' (316), a happiness that will also be Marianne's. Just as Pope saw not destruction but continuity in Milton's lines, just as Cowper looked on marriage as a kind of earthly Paradise and second Eden, so Jane Austen seems to accept Milton's idea that marriage recovers some of the happiness and freshness of the primitive world. Marriage, it seems, corrects the Fall.[15]

When Marianne looks at Barton, at scenes 'of which every field and every tree brought back some peculiar, some painful recollection', she weeps from an emotion, thinks Elinor, 'too natural in itself to raise anything less tender than pity' (342); when Eve and Adam abandon Eden with wandering steps and slow, 'Som natural tears they drop'd, but wip'd them soon' (XII. 645). Marianne regards the familiar places with 'resolute firmness' when she walks slowly and feebly to view the important hill (344). But now Colonel Brandon enters on an echo of *Paradise Lost*'s last line when, as Jane Austen writes, he 'took his solitary way to Delaford' (341), now he comes forth to play Adam to a fallen Eve and escort her into the real sublunary world. To him Marianne will devote her 'whole heart', 'one Flesh, one Heart, one Soule' (VIII. 499) with Colonel Brandon. Her fall has indeed been fortunate.[16] At nineteen she finds herself 'submitting to new attachments, entering on new duties, placed in a new home, a wife, the mistress of a family, and the patroness of a village' (379). As reluctant as Eve to leave Paradise, she does not now renew her lament on leaving Norland, 'when shall I cease to regret you! – when learn to feel a home elsewhere! – Oh! happy house, could you know what I suffer in now viewing you from this spot, from whence perhaps I may view you no more! – And you, ye well-known trees! ... No; you will continue the same ... insensible of any change in those who walk under your shade!' (27). Eve had said essentially the same:

> Must I thus leave thee Paradise? thus leave
> Thee Native Soile, these happie Walks and Shades ...
> Who now shall reare ye to the Sun? ...
> How shall I part, and whither wander down
> Into a lower World, to this obscure
> And wilde, how shall we breath in other Aire ...?
>
> (XI. 269–85)

How breathe in other air indeed, but Marianne accepts God's dispensation for Eve, to study household good, and promote her husband's good works (IX. 233–4).

'O goodness infinite, goodness immense!/That all this good of evil shall produce,/And evil turn to good', says Adam (XII. 469–71). Brandon and Marianne too are happy. 'Thy going is not lonely, with thee goes/Thy husband, him to follow thou art bound;/Where he abides, think there thy native soile' (XI. 290–2). And Marianne does. 'Haile wedded Love', says Milton, for 'By thee adulterous lust was driv'n from men ... by thee/Founded in Reason, Loyal, Just and Pure,/Relations dear, and all the Charities/Of Father, Son and Brother first were known' (IV. 750–7). Willoughby in his first happy days had been 'a son and a brother' to the Dashwood family, but he chose, instead of wedded love with Marianne, the 'bought smile/Of Harlots, loveless, joyless, unindeard' (IV. 765–6) when he married a woman he did not like (71, 329). Wedded love is ideally to Milton a 'Perpetual Fountain of Domestic sweets' (IV. 760), and although Willoughby imagines that 'domestic happiness' is out of the question for him now, he in time finds 'no inconsiderable degree of domestic felicity' in his marriage (379).

And yet for all that Milton can do, for all that Jane Austen can do, we must feel pangs for Marianne as we do for Eve. Both are lowered, as Pope said of Eloisa, from angel into woman. Once innocent and knowing only good, they now know evil too. They turn from children into women, they exchange happiness, artlessness, and affectionate trust for a knowledge of loss and pain, they are 'Despoild of Innocence, of Faith, of Bliss' (IX. 411). When they are flung into the light of common day, we grieve for our first mother, for Marianne, and for ourselves. Our response has been tightly controlled by Jane Austen along Miltonic lines.[17] Southam is right to see in 'General Tilney's hot-houses' that *Sense and Sensibility* is the 'most poignant and most nearly tragic of Jane Austen's works'. But when Mudrick concludes ringingly that Marianne, 'the life and center of the novel, has been betrayed; and not by Willoughby' (p. 93), he should be slugging it out with God, not with Jane Austen.

The reason that Marianne and Willoughby behave like Adam and Eve is not because their creator was imaginatively barren, nor because she sank under powerful predecessors. It is not Jane Austen but the characters who are derivative and bookish. The very alacrity with which Marianne and Willoughby take on the roles of Clarissa and Eve, Lovelace and Adam and Satan, suggest that these stories allow them to act out forbidden things much as *Lovers' Vows* gives the characters dangerous permission in *Mansfield Park*. Jane Austen's concern to warn against second-hand behaviour had already appeared in *Northanger Abbey*, where she set the real and the probable against the products of a heightened imagination. Her signal, again, is absurdity. Marianne's hyperbolic apostrophe to the garden she must leave is one example, and here is another. Remembering 'dear, dear Norland', Marianne imagines the dead leaves that cover its woods and walks:

> 'Oh!' cried Marianne, 'with what transporting sensations have I formerly seen them fall! How have I delighted, as I walked, to see them driven in showers about me by the wind! What feelings have they, the season, the air altogether inspired!' ...
> 'It is not every one,' said Elinor, 'who has your passion for dead leaves.' (87–8)

Shelley would display a similar passion for dead leaves in *Ode to the West Wind*, published seven years after *Sense and Sensibility*, but wind already meant to the Romantics inspiration by natural powers.[18] Marianne's identification with blown leaves and her melancholic relish of autumn, a cliché of eighteenth-century poetry after Milton's *Il Penseroso* as Griffin shows, deserve deflation. Anne Elliot, by contrast, will resist indulgence in the sweets of poetical despondency, and urge Captain Benwick to abandon his. Gothic fiction, Romantic cant, and the Miltonic sublime are all exposed by a proper sense of the real.

Marianne, though, ridiculously persists in seeing Barton as another Eden, unique in glories. 'Look at those hills! Did you ever see their equals? To the left is Barton park, amongst those woods and plantations ... And there, beneath that farthest hill, which rises with such grandeur, is our cottage'. In Paradise there is a comparable upward progess. The rank of trees 'ascend/Shade above shade, a woodie Theatre/Of stateliest view'. Like Marianne's cottage, the 'happy rural seat' of Paradise is on a hill higher than the rest (IV. 247, 142–3). Edward like Elinor pricks these Miltonic pretensions by drawing her literally down to earth: 'It is a beautiful country ... but these bottoms must be dirty in winter ... among the rest of the objects before me, I see a very dirty lane' (88). When Cowper shows Satan floundering over a boggy

Syrtis in *The Task*, 'The Garden', Book 3, he translates Milton's mythical world to the English countryside of muddy roads and disappearing tracks, as Griffin says (p. 223). When Jane Austen likewise 'Englishes' her Miltonic scene, she shows why it will not do at Barton.

One last clue as to what Jane Austen is up to in this novel appears I think in the horse that Willoughby presses on Marianne (59). He calls it Queen Mab, who in *Romeo and Juliet* 'gallops night by night/Through lovers' brains, and then they dream of love'. The fairy midwife's dreams are unpleasantly 'Begot of nothing but vain fantasy' (I. iv). Jane Austen, though elsewhere a stout defender of imagination, seems here to share her distrust of fancy with Shakespeare, Spenser, and Milton, whose Satan attacks Eve through the 'Organs of her Fancie' (IV. 802). When Marianne's '*mind*' is not to be controlled, when Willoughby proves to be everything that her 'fancy had delineated', when her 'imagination' deludes her that a tender and contrite letter will appear from Willoughby and be followed by his eager self, when 'the same eager fancy' which led her into an extreme of indulgence and repining introduces excess into her scheme of self-control (85, 49, 202, 343), *Sense and Sensibility* borrows from *The Faerie Queene* words and values used of Marianne's lack of moderation: fancy, imagination, excess, reason, wandering, and error. Fancy is dangerous here.[19] Elinor, telling of Willoughby's remorse, allows no 'embellishment of tenderness to lead the fancy astray' (349), and Edward, who fancied himself in love with Lucy, must disillusion himself. The fancy that nearly destroys Marianne is nourished above all by her reading. Her ideas and words derive uncritically from books.

In that *Grandison* debate on second-placed affection, Richardson argues that romances lead young women astray. 'When our eye has led our choice', says Mrs Shirley, 'imagination can easily add all good qualities to the plausible appearance' – like Marianne's busy imagination when she is saved by Willoughby (43). She who is almost driven wild by the beautiful lines of Cowper, a poet who actually went mad as Tony Tanner points out, she who idolises her favourite authors and reads them with 'so rapturous a delight' (47), is indeed one who sets out with 'fairy-land imaginations' (III. 396) and succumbs to the 'false-colourings' with which poets and romance-writers set off their passionate accounts. Passions, says Mrs Shirley, should be our servants, not our masters; 'fancy' must not be our guide. Since we may not trust a 'pitiably misguided' imagination, 'let us take our rules ... from plain common sense, and not from poetical refinements' (III. 400). Like Mrs Shirley refusing to sympathise with Clementina, we are not in the end to pity Marianne, a 'fair enthusiast'[20] like Clementina, a victim of Romanticism in every way. We cannot really regret 'the holiness of [her] heart's affections' as Tanner calls it (p. 99), for she handed that heart's holiness to a self-confessed deceiver, a mercenary fortune-hunter, an unscrupulous seducer who abandoned his mistress and his child. If we care about Marianne we will not want her to marry Willoughby, for all his handsome air and skill in reading Cowper. It is the right ending after all when Marianne, living her life at first-hand, admits the goodness of the daily world, and ceases to long for the heightened one of poetry and romance. Like Clementina, like Charlotte, like Anna Howe, she submits to a confederacy of friends and the knowledge that she will marry a good man. Her dependence on delusion is past; the paradise within is happier far.

Critical discontent about *Sense and Sensibility* is common. Litz argues in his book that we must regard it as 'a youthful work patched up at a later date, in which the crude antitheses of the original structure were never successfully overcome' (p. 73), while Q. D. Leavis complains that it is 'so narrowly symmetrical in its construction, its stylization so artificial and its object so obtrusively evident', that Marianne must be simply 'the peg on which to hang a literary joke' (p. 85). Jane Austen may well, as Litz suggests, have started with the simple oppositions she found in West or Edgeworth, but we can assume that each revision worked in rich elements from *Pamela, Grandison, Clarissa,* and *Paradise Lost*. We in turn can read her book through them. *Sense and Sensibility* is coherent as the story of Clarissa with a swerve at the end to Anna Howe, it is coherent as the story of Charlotte Grandison and Clementina, above all it is coherent when read as the story of Eve in a paradise made actual and unobtainable at Barton. Out of such composites, Jane Austen made compositions.

4

Pride and Prejudice

Odd though it seems, Jane Austen probably worked up *Pride and Prejudice* and *Mansfield Park* at much the same time.[1] Certainly her mind was as full of *Sir Charles Grandison* when she wrote the one as when she wrote the other. I shall show first how the light, bright, and sparkling *Pride and Prejudice* substitutes density and relation for the diffuseness of Richardson. Sometimes critically but often not, she seizes upon his detail, combines, separates and varies it, and makes it hers.

'A new set of company'

Though written in Richardson's old age, *Sir Charles Grandison* displays a surprising abundance of invention. What he discarded Jane Austen pounced on, for almost the entire cast of *Pride and Prejudice* lay to her hand in the third letter of his book.[2] Casting about for a subject, he had introduced Harriet Byron to 'a new set of company' (I. 44), soon to be shouldered out by the Grandisons. These lively sketches Jane Austen profitably developed. I shall show what she made of her plunder in the secondary characters first.

To begin with the Bingleys. Richardson's Mr Singleton, 'in possession of a good estate', a man good humoured, humble, modest, ready to confess an inferiority to every one, with smiles and laughs at the service of every speaker, has 'rare *fun* at the dinner', and elaborates admiringly on the attractions of all the guests, especially Miss Byron (I. 42, 72). Jane Austen's Mr Bingley, a 'single man in possession of a good fortune', shares the same qualities, 'easiness, openness, ductility of ... temper', humility before Darcy's opinion, and readiness to be pleased. 'Bingley had never met with pleasanter people or prettier girls in his life; every body had been most kind and attentive to him, there had been no formality, no stiffness, he had soon felt acquainted with all the room; and as to Miss Bennet, he could not conceive an angel more beautiful' (16). But where Mr Singleton (meaning 'simpleton') has a brief, foolish life, Bingley's attachment to Jane, and his ready compliance with Darcy's opinion of her, precipitate the plot. He is even linked to the great Sir Charles Grandison in a youthful piece of parody. Where Richardson had twice run through all his hero's dancing partners (II. 323, 346), Mrs Bennet's attempts to do the same for Charles Bingley makes her husband cry out, 'if he had had any compassion for *me* ... he would not have danced half so much! For God's sake, say no more of his partners. Oh! that he had strained his ancle in the first dance!' (13).

Miss Bingley and her sister, 'very fine ladies; not deficient in good humour when they were pleased, nor in the power of being agreeable where they chose it; but proud and conceited' (15), look back to Richardson's Miss Cantillon, 'pretty: but visibly proud, affected, and conceited', who 'could hardly let her eyes be civil to me; and yet her really pretty mouth *occasionally* work'd itself into affected smiles, and an affectation of complaisance' (I. 42, 61). These ideas are explored in the cold civility, insolent smiles, civil disdain, and proven duplicity of the Bingley sisters (42, 102, 94, 149).

Charlotte Grandison contributes to the elder Bingley sister Mrs Hurst, who is a social gadfly playing with bracelets and rings (55) much as Charlotte once played with her diamond ring (I. 397). And if Charlotte remarks that if there were an hundred Sir Charleses, 'we would not let *one* of them go into the city for a wife', and says carelessly, 'I am very bad at remembring the names of city-knights' (II. 322–3), the Bingley sisters find it comic that Jane, who attracts their brother, has an uncle 'who lives somewhere near Cheapside'. The sisters indulge 'their mirth for some time at the expense of their dear friend's vulgar relations' and laugh heartily at their own bad pun, 'that is capital'. But Bingley reproves them, 'If they had uncles enough to fill *all* Cheapside ... it would not make them one jot less agreeable' (37).

Charlotte Grandison too is rebuked both here and later, when she jeers at her cousin Everard for marrying a 'widow *Cit*'. '*Cit*!

Lady G. And in a trading kingdom?', answers Harriet (III. 267).[3] In *Pride and Prejudice* the extra comic twist is that where Charlotte is actually upper-class, the Bingley sisters, members of 'a respectable family in the north of England; a circumstance more deeply impressed on their memories than that their brother's fortunes and their own had been acquired by trade' (15), are not. This theme of class snobbery will widen to include not only Darcy but Lady Catherine and Elizabeth, as we shall see.

Mrs Hurst's name comes from a brief anecdote about a 'first foolish impression' in *Grandison* – Jane Austen's original title for *Pride and Prejudice* was 'First Impressions' – in which Miss Hurste falls for a military man in a market town (II. 551); the Bennet girls, out shopping, are dazzled by their first sight of Mr Wickham, who 'wanting only regimentals to make him completely charming' (72), is soon found to have accepted a commission in the corps. The unmarried Charlotte Grandison bestows her name on the unmarried Charlotte Lucas (Miss Lucas appears in *Pamela* and again as one of Clarissa's pseudonyms), and the married Caroline Grandison gives her first name to the married Bingley sister. Caroline Hurst's husband is as much a vacancy as Caroline Grandison's, and his rare stirrings into life are invariably comic.

In *Grandison*, the rescued heroine collapses into a family of two sisters, a brother-in-law, and an eligible, unmarried brother; Jane Bennet's detention in an exactly similar household nurtures exactly similar hopes. Jane looks set to follow the happy fate of Harriet, whose escape from a rake is ludicrously replaced by Mrs Bennet's plot to keep her at Netherfield, even if it kills her. Jane's visit was purely social, and a cold prolongs it. Her stay at Netherfield, where only Bingley wants her, is far more awkward than Harriet's at Grosvenor Square. The plot-line complicates again when Elizabeth follows her sister and increases the tension by close proximity to Darcy. Harriet was ashamed of her foolish masquerade dress, but Elizabeth's mud-stained clothes, sneered at by the Bingley sisters, provoke Darcy's startled admiration.

Second, the Bennets. Mary Bennet is prefigured in the rudeness of Richardson's Walden to the learned Miss Clements. 'We know ... that you are a well-read Lady. But I have nothing to say to observations that are in everybody's mouth' (I. 50). But whenever Mary piques herself on the solidity of her reflections, or offers 'new extracts' and 'new observations of thread-bare morality', she looks ridiculous (20, 60). Richardson may regret that folly in a pretty face has advantages in some people's eyes over wisdom in a plain one (I. 59), but Elizabeth's 'easy and unaffected' piano playing is listened to with much more pleasure than Mary's higher, but pedantic and conceited excellence (25). In response to Lydia's disgrace, Mary can only quote from *Evelina* and offer 'moral extractions' (289).

Mrs Bennet derives from Lady Betty Williams, 'immersed in the love of public diversions! so fond of routs, drums, hurricanes', whose daughter runs away with an ensign not worth a shilling (II. 408, III. 13). As the *Grandison* Index says sternly, 'her Daughter's misconduct owing in a great measure to her careless education of her'. Mrs Bennet encourages her daughters to follow the regiment to Brighton, remembering what she herself had endured five and twenty years before (229).

Similarly Mr Collins derives some of his attributes from Richardson's pedant Walden, who 'quaint and opinionated, despising every one who has not had the benefit of an University Education', provokes Harriet Byron's sharp comment, 'every scholar, I presume, is not, necessarily, a man of sense' (I. 42, 53). Mr Collins is not 'a sensible man, and the deficiency of nature had been but little assisted by education or society' (70). Harriet laughs at Walden's 'conscious worthiness' and his 'parcel of disastrous faces' (I. 57, 82), just as Mr Bennet draws out Mr Collins to be as absurd as he has hoped (68).

Mr Collins is formed by accretion and telescoping. If Mr Bennet asks 'whether these pleasing attentions proceed from the impulse of the moment, or are the result of previous study?' (68), Charlotte Grandison had commented tartly of Uncle Selby that 'he *studies* too much for his pleasantries: He is continually hunting for occasions to be smart' (II. 414). But most irreverent of all, Jane Austen draws on Richardson's hero for her comic suitor, reworking an opinion that Sir Charles might be 'a grave formal young man, his prim mouth set in plaits' (II. 274) into her 'young man' with a 'grave and stately' air and 'very formal' manners (64). The criticism is acute, for Sir Charles is often a Malvolio cross-gartered, like Mr Collins. Finally, as I shall show, aspects of Sir Hargrave Pollexfen helped to make up a character comic and menacing at the same time, drawn from a number of sources but miraculously animated into life. Richardson abandons his pedant, but Jane Austen pulls hers into the theme of snobbery, rank, and wealth through his deference to Lady Catherine and his obsequiousness to Darcy.

The heiress Miss de Bourgh is funny for two reasons. Sir Charles's account of the Italian heiress Olivia is uninformative enough, 'a woman of high qualities, nobly born, generous, amiable in her features, genteel in her person, and mistress of a great fortune in possession' (II. 117), but when Mr Collins says that Miss de Bourgh is an heiress 'of very extensive property ... charming ... there is that in her features which marks the young woman of distinguished birth ... perfectly amiable' (67), hyperbole reveals servility. Olivia tried to poniard the hero and make him marry her, but Miss de Bourgh is utterly extinguished by her mother, and can neither speak nor act.

All these are fairly simple derivations, developments, or inversions, but Wickham's character provides a much more complicated example of combination. When Elizabeth finds that he is a secret seducer like Captain Anderson, a gamester like Everard Grandison, a false friend like Lorimer, and a dangerous villain like Sir Hargrave Pollexfen, her discoveries make up a plot.

Wickham's aspect as a military fortune-hunter derives from Richardson's Captain Anderson, whose address to Charlotte Grandison he describes in II, letter xxix. If Sir Charles takes 'notice, with some severity on our Sex, on the general liking, which he said women have for military men ... Do not a cockade, and a scarlet coat, become a *fine gentleman*, and help to make him so, in your eyes?', Mrs Bennet remembers 'the time when I liked a red coat myself very well – and indeed so I do still at my heart ... and I thought Colonel Forster looked very becoming the other night ... in his regimentals' (29). 'Womens eyes are wanderers', says Sir Charles, 'and too often bring home guests that are very troublesome to them, and whom, once introduced, they cannot get out of the house' (II. 8); the young Bennets, whose 'eyes were immediately wandering up the street in quest of the officers' (72), introduce Wickham as a guest who will never leave.

Captain Anderson appealed to Charlotte Grandison because he was the principal officer in that part of the country, 'caressed, as if he were a general'; Elizabeth falls into the same trap. She thinks the officers of the regiment a very creditable set, but Mr Wickham was 'far beyond them all in person, countenance, air, and walk' (76). Charlotte thought Anderson 'a sprightly man ... well received by every-body; and particularly a favourite of three young ladies, who could scarcely be civil to each other, on his account: And this, I own, when he made assiduous court to me, in preference to them, and to every other woman, gave him some consequence with me'. When Wickham, 'the happy man towards whom almost every female eye was turned', chooses Elizabeth as the 'happy woman' with whom he engages in conversation, she is flattered into hearing him out (76). Even after Wickham abandons her for Miss King, Elizabeth's 'vanity was satisfied with believing that *she* would have been his only choice, had fortune permitted it' (149). The idea persists right up to Wickham's belief 'that however long, and for whatever cause, his attentions had been withdrawn, her vanity would be gratified and her preference secured at any time by their renewal' (233).

Captain Anderson appeared to Charlotte as 'a man of sense, as well as an agreeable man in his person and air. He had a lively and easy elocution. *He* spoke without doubt, and *I* had therefore the less doubt of his understanding. The man who knows how to say agreeable things to a woman, in an agreeable manner, has her vanity on his side; since, to doubt her veracity, would be to question her own merit'. The young Bennets are similarly 'struck with the stranger's air' when they first meet Wickham. 'His appearance was greatly in his favour; he had all the best part of beauty, a fine countenance, a good figure, and very pleasing address ... a happy readiness of conversation' (72). Even Jane cannot 'question the veracity of a young man of such amiable appearance as Wickham'. The hint that vanity misleads is vital for the plot. The proud perceiver Elizabeth, told that Wickham's story may be false, says confidently, 'I beg your pardon; – one knows exactly what to think' (85–6). Only when she reads Darcy's letter does she say, 'I, who have prided myself on my discernment! – I, who valued myself on my abilities! ... and gratified my vanity' (208). Like Charlotte, she must realise that 'as to his real character, had information been in her power, she had never felt a wish of enquiring. His countenance, voice, and manner, had established him at once in the possession of every virtue' (206). She will learn instead to love Darcy, a man who creates disagreeable first impressions. Unlike Wickham and Captain Anderson, he does not perform to strangers (176).

Captain Anderson seeks Charlotte Grandison's fortune, but Jane Austen, who kept her heroine poor for other reasons, creates the rich Miss King to confirm Wickham's fortune-hunting. Charlotte, regretting 'my rash, my foolish promise' just as Elizabeth deplores 'the preference which she believed she had most incautiously shewn' (207), calls her affair an '*entanglement*', for she cannot with justice say love; Elizabeth's 'heart had been but slightly touched', she thinks. But she, unlike her predecessor, sympathises with the young man's need for money. In so doing, comments the author in one of her rare judgments on Elizabeth, she is 'less clear-sighted perhaps in his case than in Charlotte's [Lucas]' (149–50). It is part of her self-discovery when she acknowledges his views to have been 'solely and hatefully mercenary' (207).

Both Anderson and Wickham consider themselves disappointed men, but Jane Austen uses outside witnesses fully to clarify the extent of Wickham's warping. Charlotte Grandison says bitterly, 'I could not help *despising* him, when I found myself so grosly imposed upon'; Elizabeth uses the same large word twice, in 'gross duplicity on one side or the other', and 'so gross a violation of every thing right' when she admits the truth about Wickham (205, 208). But neither woman has really suffered. Elizabeth picks up Harriet's consolation to Lucy that 'when the Love-fever was at its height, did you make any-body uneasy at your passion? Did you run to woods and groves, to record it on the barks of trees? – No!', with her 'I am now convinced … that I have never been much in love … though I should certainly be a much more interesting object to all my acquaintance, were I distractedly in love with him'. Harriet believes a passion for an unworthy man is conquerable without 'pains' (I. 67), and Elizabeth can see and write of Wickham's new attachment 'without material pain' (149–50). Richardson lets his fortune-hunter go; Jane Austen prolongs the usefulness of her right to the end of her book.

Wickham also proves like Everard Grandison to be a gamester, and a rake who ruins young women. Everard loses everything at the gambling table (II. 442); Wickham's gaming debts horrify Jane. Sir Charles clears Everard's debts with cold benevolence, but when Darcy clears Wickham's, he deals secretly with a man he loathes, out of love for Elizabeth (298, II. 512).

Sir Charles insists like Darcy to Wickham that Everard make good a seduction. 'Had she been the poorest honest girl in Britain, and you had seduced her, by promises of marriage, I must have made it a condition of our continual friendship, that you had married her' (II. 513). Everard actually marries a rich City widow. He has shown his 'consciousness of inferiority' by his change of colour, uneasiness, and apprehension (I.231); once Elizabeth reveals she knows all about Wickham, he is apprehensive and anxious, his alarm appearing in his heightened colour (234). By substituting Elizabeth for Darcy in this uncomfortable confrontation, Jane Austen saves Darcy from looking a prig, and grants Elizabeth the sweet chance for revenge.

Wickham also proves to be like Richardson's vicious Lorimer, who sought to harm his boyhood friend Sir Charles. His profligacy once revealed, Lorimer attempts revenge on the good Doctor Bartlett and dies in horror not to be described (volume II, letter xxxvi). Equally melodramatic terms are used of Wickham, 'vicious propensities', 'a life of idleness and dissipation', 'extravagance and general profligacy' (200–5). But Jane Austen employs more subtle modes of blackening Wickham's character when he takes 'revenge' neatly and nastily on his own friend's sister (202). The fact that Darcy's father helped Wickham's as Sir Charles's father helped Lorimer's makes his choice of victim worse. But Wickham, instead of dying horribly, suffers like Willoughby the more realistic punishment of marriage to a silly wife. Thus Jane Austen makes up not just a character but a plot, by her 'combining'. Elizabeth's realisation that Wickham is not Grandison, but an Anderson, an Everard, and a Lorimer, is a large step to self-knowledge.

Finally, Wickham stands revealed as Richardson's villain, Sir Hargrave Pollexfen. Richardson had used an outside informant to give 'such an account of Sir Hargrave, as let me know that he is a very dangerous and enterprising man ... laughing and light as he is in company, he is malicious, illnatured, and designing ... He has ruined, Sir John says, three young creatures' (I. 63). Elizabeth's admission that Darcy, though not disinterested, has told the truth about Wickham, is a major turning point. Wickham is only prevented from ruining three young creatures, Georgiana,

Miss King, and Lydia, by the most strenuous interventions of other people. But where Harriet knew of Sir Hargrave's wickedness even before he proposed to her, Elizabeth's similar understanding is delayed. Taken in at first, she holds to her hostile views right up until the time that Wickham, proved a liar by Georgiana's gentleness, elopes with Lydia. Sir Hargrave disappears from Richardson's novel until his repentance and death, but the delayed revelation that Wickham is villainous resolves Jane Austen's plot.

Sir Hargrave Pollexfen abducts the heroine from a masquerade and threatens her with forced marriage; Wickham abducts the heroine's young sister instead. Lydia derives from several characters in *Grandison*. Like Richardson's 'fine tall *portly* young lady' Miss Barnevelt (I. 72), she is stout, well-grown and assured (45). Defending her right to go to the ball, she says boldly, 'though I *am* the youngest, I'm the tallest' (8). Miss Barnevelt is a 'loud and fearless laugher', bold and free, a woman who prefers 'a brave man, a gallant man' (I. 58, 42, 62); Lydia, who is characterised by mindless laughter, even at the end of the book is 'untamed, unabashed, wild, noisy, and fearless', and of course a soldier-lover (315). Her identifying word '*fun*,' which Johnson stigmatises as 'a low cant word', probably came from Richardson's Mr Singleton:

We had rare *fun*, at dinner ... what with one thing and with another, we *box'd it about*, and had rare *fun* as I told you – So that when I got home, and went to bed, I did nothing but dream of being in the same company, and three or four times wak'd myself with laughing.   (I. 72)

Jane Austen catches the same tone for Lydia, shallow, mindlessly merry, delighted with trivia. 'We had such a good piece of fun the other day at Colonel Forster's ... only think what fun! ... Lord! how I laughed! ... I think I should have died ... We had such fun! ... it was such fun! I was ready to die of laughter. And then we were so merry all the way home! we talked and laughed so loud' (221–2); 'I could live and die with Sir Hargrave', writes Singleton, 'you never knew ... such a bright man as Sir Hargrave'. But where Singleton vanishes like the others after this hopeful start, Jane Austen pursues and explores the character in her gay unthinking Lydia, who once a Phaedria remains a Phaedria still. 'Good gracious! when I went away, I am sure I had no more idea of being married till I came back again! though I thought it would be very good fun if I was' (316).[4]

Lydia's story resembles that of Richardson's Miss Cantillon, pert without fear or wit (I.59), who runs away with a nominal captain. 'Her mother vows, they shall both starve, for her: And they have no other dependence ... Poor wretches! What will become of them? For every-thing is in her mother's power as to fortune. − She looked so sly! *so* silly! *so* slatternly! Unhappy coquettish thing!' (III.13). In Jane Austen's varying, the runaway is unabashed and the mother only too willing to forgive.

Lydia's folly is encouraged by exposure to public places, an important topic in *Grandison*. Sir Charles, arguing that young women like his ward Emily 'should be innocently indulged', has deliberately taken her to places of public entertainment so that she can see the subjects of polite conversation, judge of such entertainments as they deserved, 'and not add expectation (which runs high in young minds, and is seldom answered) to the ideal scenes ... and thus a boundary is set to her imagination' (II.8). Mr Bennet's flippant perversion of Sir Charles's scheme makes Elizabeth despair: 'We shall have no peace at Longbourn if Lydia does not go to Brighton', he says. 'Let her go then ... At any rate, she cannot grow many degrees worse, without authorizing us to lock her up for the rest of her life'. But Brighton, far from being bounded in Lydia's imagination, 'comprised every possibility of earthly happiness'. With 'the creative eye of fancy' she saw officers, the glories of the camp, tents, and herself, 'tenderly flirting with at least six officers at once' (232).

Although Mr Bennet's name may derive from the Bennets in *Pamela* − his friends Mr Shepherd and Mr Martin must wait until *Persuasion* and *Emma* for their own apotheoses (*Pamela*, III.50, 183) − he himself is a comic version of the tyrant father Sir Thomas Grandison, snubbing, chiding, and jeering at his daughters for their matrimonial plots. Richardson's patriarch perversely forces his daughters on to the 'London market' as soon as they show signs of independence. Here, says Charlotte,

the flocks of single women which croud to Ranelagh and Vaux-hall markets, dressed out to be *cheapened*, not *purchased* ... convinced [me] that the maids are as much above either shame or controul, as the wives. But were not *fathers* desirous to get the *drugs* off their hands ... these freedoms would not be permitted. As for *mothers*, many of them are for escorting their daughters to public places, because they themselves like racketing.   (II. 553)

Mr Bennet, a man with five daughters to dispose of, has no right to criticise his daughters' ways of finding husbands. He takes no part in guiding their choice, or exerting himself 'to restrain the wild giddiness of his youngest daughters' (213). This darkly self-indulgent side to his character corresponds to the same qualities in Sir Thomas. But where that cynical father had urged his daughters to 'strike at once, while your face is new' and not prostitute themselves 'at every polite place' (I. 340–1), Elizabeth must beseech her father not to let Lydia go to Brighton, for at sixteen she will 'be the most determined flirt that ever made herself and her family ridiculous ... without any attraction beyond youth and a tolerable person ... wholly unable to ward off any portion of that universal contempt which her rage for admiration will excite ... Vain, ignorant, idle, and absolutely uncontrouled!' (231). Sir Thomas casts out his daughters, and promptly dies; Mr Bennet must bear every consequence of Lydia's leaving home.

'Let her go, then', says Mr Bennet (232); 'Let them take their *fill of love*', says Sir Thomas, 'and if they run their heads into an hedge, let them stick there by the horns' (I. 331). Even when the worst has happened Mr Bennet cries unfeelingly, 'this is a parade ... which does one good; it gives such an elegance to misfortune!'; 'What tragedy-movements are here! What measured steps!' says Sir Thomas (I. 335). He reduces Charlotte Grandison to tears, and Mr Bennet forbids Kitty to stir out ever again 'till you can prove, that you have spent ten minutes of every day in a rational manner' (299–300). 'Snubbing, chiding, and studying to find fault' (I. 321), Sir Thomas abdicates responsibility for his daughters much as Mr Bennet does for girls he considers silly and ignorant (5). Sir Thomas exercises his 'satirical vein' upon his daughters (I. 334), and Mr Bennet directs his pleasantry even at his favourite daughter. 'Her father had most cruelly mortified her', thinks Elizabeth (364); 'If you were not my father', says Charlotte, 'I would say you are very cruel' (I. 341). Sir Thomas may repent at the point of death (I. 356), but how much more affecting when Mr Bennet, trapped in his satiric carapace, sees for an instant just what he has done. 'Let me once in my life feel how much I have been to blame. I am not afraid of being over-powered by the impression. It will pass away soon enough' (299).

Lydia's elopement with Wickham closely parallels Harriet's abduction. Both accounts show the relatives reproaching them-selves, blaming others, and tracing the fugitives through the number of the coach. Both also dramatise the fear that marriage may be required to repair a loss of virginity, the extent of the woman's culpability, the desire to think better of the villain, the threat of a duel, the tidings by letter that the pair have been discovered, the broken, exclamatory utterances that the dread-ful affair provokes, the retrospective filling-out of detail, and the gratitude that results. Jane Austen draws then on Richardson, but departs significantly from his treatment of the episode.

Lydia's willing elopement, the very opposite of Harriet's unwilling abduction, occurs in chapter iv of Volume III, shatter-ing the smooth progress of Elizabeth and Darcy's reconciliation in the encouraging atmosphere of Pemberley. So much more is simply in train here than in *Grandison*, before the hero and heroine have even met. Jane Austen as well as Richardson an-nounces the event in a letter, 'written in evident agitation'. Jane Bennet is typically afraid of alarming her sister, just as Mr Reeves warns Mr Selby not to be too much surprised before he begins (I. 116). The words 'dreadful' and 'tidings' ring through Jane Austen's narrative as they do through Richardson's; the 'dreadful news ... cannot be concealed from any one' in the world of *Pride and Prejudice* any more than 'the dreadful tidings' can be kept within Mr Selby's breast in *Grandison* (I. 119). Harriet's Aunt Selby, about whom we know little and care less, 'has been in violent hysterics' (I. 116), but when the hypochondriac Mrs Bennet is 'sadly grieved' and 'really ill', that is quite something. Richardson writes of 'consternation ... wife ... fainted away'; when Jane Austen writes of 'a family so deranged ... a mother incapable of exertion, and requiring constant attendance', we would prefer that mother to be capable. And where Harriet's Selby cousins 'go distracted' (I. 120), Kitty and Mary are 'tolerably calm, and no change was visible in either, except that the loss of her favourite sister ... had given something more of fretfulness than usual, to the accents of Kitty' (289).

The pursuit takes similar stages in both books. Place names sprinkle the letters from the pursuing uncles, Mr Gardiner in

Pride and Prejudice (Volume II, chapter V) and Mr Reeves in *Grandison*, and both men hit upon the idea of finding out the fugitives from their transport. In *Grandison* they enquire at every turnpike and trace the chairmen's number and previous fare (I. 129, 118); Mr Bennet plans to go to Epsom where they changed horses, to see the postilions, and discover the number of the hackney coach which took them from Clapham (293).

Harriet's Uncle Selby is quick to blame. 'Why parted we with such a jewel out of our sight? You *would* not be denied: You *would* have her to that cursed town' (I. 120). But in *Pride and Prejudice* it is wonderfully Mrs Bennet herself, the prime mover of Lydia's participation in Brighton, the cause of her fall in every way, who complains of 'some great neglect or other' of the hosts in words that echo Uncle Selby's, 'why did the Forsters ever let her go out of their sight?'. Lydia is no jewel, and the extent of her culpability distresses Elizabeth and Jane. Harriet in her masquerade dress had blamed herself for her 'wretched levity', 'Giddy creature that I was, vain and foolish!' (I. 150), but Lydia is truly 'given up to nothing but amusement and vanity … idle and frivolous'. The large alteration is that where Harriet blames herself, it is only Elizabeth who sees what Lydia has become, Elizabeth who cares and knows that her sister's 'sense of decency and virtue' is in doubt. For this she reproaches herself as Lydia never will. How much more moving too than Mr Reeves's complaint, 'my mind is the greatest sufferer' (I. 129), is Mr Bennet's uncharacteristic 'Who should suffer but myself? It has been my own doing, and I ought to feel it' (299).

In both episodes, the seduction is feared to have already taken place. Harriet rejects the remedy of marriage which Lydia very much wants. 'What may she have suffered by this time?' grieve Harriet's relatives (I. 119); 'my mother and father believe the worst', writes Jane (275). Richardson's phrase the 'dreadful subject', echoed in Jane Austen's 'the dreadful sequel' (290), produces 'dreadful uncertainties' about Harriet's fate (I. 193, 128); though Mr Gardiner thinks it 'right to be prepared for the worst, there is no occasion to look on it as certain' (288). Harriet's relatives hope to keep the matter quiet (I. 168) as do Lydia's (311), but whereas 'the last violence' was not offered the resisting Harriet (I. 134), no such confidence can be placed in the all too willing Lydia.

At first Harriet's friends think her abducted by another rake, but cannot credit it. 'Had we not the proof I mention'd, Greville, bad as he is, could not be such a villain' (I. 120). It is an expression of Jane's character, rather, that she 'does not think so ill of Wickham, as to believe him capable of the attempt' (284). Where Harriet need not marry, Lydia must. Harriet's reputation might be forcibly ravished from her, but Lydia is all too prompt to surrender hers. 'When the day dawns', gloats Sir Hargrave, 'she will be glad to own her marriage' (I. 156); 'And they are really to be married! ... and for *this* we are to be thankful ... we are forced to rejoice! Oh, Lydia!', says Elizabeth (304).

Duels follow elopements in *Grandison*. Sir Charles lays Sir Hargrave low with a 'jerk, and a kind of twist' in a way that leaves him free to expatiate on the horrors of duelling: 'How many fatherless, brotherless, sonless families have mourned all their lives ... irreparable injury to the innocent family and dependents of the murdered?', he says (I. 140, 206). These solemnities turn to farce in the mouth of Mrs Bennet. 'Now here's Mr Bennet gone away, and I know he will fight Wickham ... and then he will be killed and what is to become of us all? The Collinses will turn us out, before he is cold in his grave; and if you are not kind to us, brother, I do not know what we shall do' (287). Sir Charles grieves for his saintly mother, the sight of whose wounded husband threw her into fatal fits (I. 262); Mrs Bennet, when Mr Bennet returns unharmed, 'did not express so much satisfaction as her children expected, considering what her anxiety for his life had been before'. Who, she asks, 'is to fight Wickham, and make him marry her, if he comes away?' (298).

Both lost women are eventually found. A letter brings happy tidings of Harriet (I. 129), just as Mr Gardiner sends 'tidings' of Lydia such as he hopes will give satisfaction (302). But the hands that Lydia is in are scarcely as honorable as Sir Charles's. And where Harriet had been conventionally rescued by the hero, Lydia will be saved in a very different kind of way. Jane Austen replaces Sir Charles's modest containment of applause (I. 142) by Darcy's secret benevolence, postponing its revelation until Lydia, the one person who will never realise what she owes to Darcy, blurts it out, and so brings on the match.

Jane Austen rewrites Richardson in a striking variety of ways to develop the Bingleys, the Bennets and their circles. What she

most admired in Richardson was his consistency of characterisation, wrote Henry Austen (p. 7). But where Richardson tackled
a vast number of characters whose reactions are difficult to
distinguish, Jane Austen reduces the range, involves everyone,
and keeps the characters up. Mrs Selby's response to Harriet's
abduction is like her daughters', but Mrs Bennet's incapacity
resembles neither Kitty's fretfulness nor Mary's reflections. It is
all her own. Here as elsewhere, Jane Austen surpassed her master.

'Intricate characters are the most amusing'

For her major as for her minor characters, Jane Austen splits
Richardson's creatures into their disparate elements, then makes
one character into several, or combines several into one. Their
idiosyncratic responses can then become a plot. The marriages
of Jane, Charlotte Lucas, and Elizabeth particularly reveal this
trick. The Grandison sisters reappear in Jane and Elizabeth
Bennet, Caroline's 'sweetness and complacency' (I. 210) showing
in Jane's sweetness and disinterestedness (134). When Harriet's
'equality in her temper' which makes it hard for her to 'find room
in her heart for a particular Love' is added on (I. 10), Darcy can
defend his separation of her from Bingley: 'Her look and manners
were open, cheerful and engaging as ever, but without any
symptom of peculiar regard ... the serenity of your sister's
countenance and air was such, as might have given the most
acute observer, a conviction that, however amiable her temper,
her heart was not likely to be easily touched' (197). Even
Elizabeth admits that 'Jane's feelings, though fervent, were little
displayed, and ... there was a constant complacency in her air and
manner, not often united with great sensibility' (208).

Darcy repeats a slur cast on Harriet, 'I suppose she has been
told that her smiles become her: for she is always smiling' (I. 69),
when he acknowledges that Miss Bennet is 'pretty, but she
smiled too much' (16). Jane's uncomplaining fidelity to Bingley,
like Harriet's to Sir Charles, makes her 'paler ... but more sedate'
(335), just as Harriet is 'not quite so lively, and somewhat paler'
when Sir Charles is away (II. 30). But Jane's happiness with
Bingley repeats that of Caroline Grandison and her husband, 'an
happy pair! They want not sense; they have both fine understandings! But O! my Lucy, they are not the striking, the dazzling

qualities in men and women that make happy. Good sense, and solid judgment, a natural complacency of temper, a desire of obliging, and an easiness to be obliged', which result in 'the silent, the serene happiness' (II. 98). Serenity, complacency, and good sense are words to apply to Jane, but Mr Bennet sees other consequences when he warns against Jane and Bingley's 'pliancy of temper', 'each of you so complying, that nothing will ever be resolved on; so easy, that every servant will cheat you; and so generous, that you will always exceed your income' (15, 348).

Charlotte Grandison's marriage to a man who seems at first ridiculous is mirrored by her namesake Charlotte Lucas. Harriet knows that her friend 'hates not Lord G. There is no man whom she prefers to him. And in this respect, may perhaps, be on a par with eight women out of twelve, who marry, and yet make not bad wives' (II. 347); Charlotte Lucas is 'convinced that my chance of happiness with [Mr Collins] is as fair, as most people can boast on entering the marriage state' (125). As Charlotte Grandison unanswerably asks,

What can a woman do, who is addressed by a man of talents inferior to her own? Must she throw away her talents? Must she hide her light under a bushel, purely to do credit to the man? She cannot pick and choose, as men can. She has only her negative; and, if she is desirous to oblige her friends, not always *that*. Yet it is said, Women must not encourage Fops and Fools. They must encourage Men of Sense only. And it is *well* said. But what will they do, if their lot be cast only among Foplings? If the Men of Sense do not offer themselves? (I. 230)

The game is all to Mr Collins, as he well knows. But while Sir Charles had remarked that 'daughters of a decayed family of some note in the world, do not easily get husbands. Men of great fortunes look higher ... and men of genteel businesses are afraid of young women better born than portioned' (II. 268), Elizabeth will not hide her light under a bushel for such an absurdity as Mr Collins, even when he explains that 'it is by no means certain that another offer of marriage may ever be made you. Your portion is unhappily so small that it will in all likelihood undo the effects of your loveliness and amiable qualifications' (108). Miss Lucas, for whom a man of sense never offers, marries in Mr Collins a man neither sensible nor agreeable. His society is irksome and his attachment to her imaginary. 'But still he would be her husband. – Without thinking highly either of men or of matrimony, marriage had always been her object; it was the only honourable provision for well-educated women of small fortune, and however uncertain of giving happiness, must be their pleasantest preservative from want'. She thus escapes what Richardson called 'insolent ridicule' of old maids (I. 232), and her barbarous brothers need not fear that Charlotte will die an old maid (122–3).

Charlotte Grandison learns to love and respect her husband, their happiness confirmed by the birth of a daughter. Jane Austen offers no such hope for Charlotte Lucas. Instead of love, she supplies *Grandison*'s solution, comfort. Miss Grandison in echo of Biddy Tipkin in Steele's *Tender Husband* had said, 'I have a *joy*: You a *comfort*: But comfort is a poor word: and I can't bear it' (II. 264). 'Joy' belongs largely to Mrs Bennet and Lydia, but Jane Austen sets up powerful contrasts between 'comfort' and 'happiness'. Elizabeth reacts violently to Charlotte's steady remark that she only wants a comfortable home. 'She could not have supposed it possible, that ... she could have sacrificed every better feeling to worldly advantage' (125). She bursts out to Jane, 'you shall not, for the sake of one individual, change the meaning of principle and integrity, nor endeavour to persuade yourself or me, that selfishness is prudence, and insensibility of danger, security for happiness' (135–6). But she is forced to back down when she realises that Charlotte will be 'tolerably' happy (125), a qualifier that Richardson had used in the recommendation of prudential marriages: 'Convenience, when that's the motive, whatever foolish girls will think, will hold out its comforts, while a gratified Love quickly evaporates', writes Charlotte Grandison (II. 333, 442). Elizabeth must admit that comfort, a word repeated at least six times in the episode, must do for Charlotte, so long as there are not enough Darcys to go round.

Comfort will suffice for Charlotte Lucas, but Jane Austen reserves happiness, a word that rings through the last volumes of *Grandison* as it does through the closing pages of *Pride and Prejudice*, for Elizabeth and Jane. She even promises Elizabeth 'years of happiness' (337), when in a swift glance ahead such as no epistolary novelist could indulge in, she steps outside her own time-scheme. Happiness is hard-won and carefully defined. Richardson hopes that love will ripen into friendship (II. 517);

Elizabeth finds her respect for Darcy 'heightened into somewhat of a friendlier nature'. In *Grandison*, Harriet's love for Sir Charles progresses from esteem, to grateful regard, to making his interest her own, and his happiness her study (II. 547); after reading Darcy's letter, Elizabeth 'respected, she esteemed, she was grateful to him, she felt a real interest in his welfare', and wonders how she can bring about happiness for them both (265 – 6). Charlotte Lucas gets as much and as little as she sought, but Elizabeth and Jane gain comfort and happiness, both.

Charlotte cynically advises Jane not to be guarded, because 'in nine cases out of ten, the woman had better show *more* affection than she feels. Bingley ... may never do more than like her, if she does not help him on'; Harriet too had worried that 'we women, when we love, and are doubtful, suffer a great deal in the apprehension, at one time, of disgusting the object of our passion, by too forward a Love; and, at another, of disobliging him by too great a reserve' (I. 423). Elizabeth recoils from the idea of Jane 'acting by design', and protests that Charlotte knows it is 'not sound ... you would never act in this way yourself' (22 – 3). But Charlotte is forward to save her life.

Elizabeth allows herself to become infected with her friend's misanthropy, and adapts Charlotte Grandison's words, 'no more, no more ... Why, this human nature, I believe, is a very vile thing! I think, Lady L. I won't marry at all' (II. 99), when she complains, 'the more I see of the world, the more I am dissatisfied with it: and every day confirms my belief of the inconsistency of all human characters' (135). But she must finally acknowledge the advantages of frankness in courtship. Why should women be blamed, says Harriet, 'for owning modestly a passion for a worthy and suitable object' (II. 1), for instance the man who rescued her? Elizabeth also recognises her obligation to Darcy's 'exertion of goodness', assuring her father repeatedly that he was 'really the object of her choice ... and enumerating with energy all his good qualities' (326, 377). Frankly prompting Darcy's declaration, she accepts him without delay (365).

In these various ways Jane Austen selects, combines, and develops hints from *Grandison*. Her combining for Elizabeth is particularly rich. Charlotte Grandison's lively defiance of convention, her playfulness and archness are what make Elizabeth attractive, but Harriet Byron's frankness, her fault-finding in her suitor, her studying of character, and her humbled repentance of her satiric tongue are what make Elizabeth interesting. Richardson himself revealed that he had designed Harriet Byron as something 'between Clarissa and Miss Howe' (*Selected Letters*, p. 179). But he split the integrity of one from the wit of the other once Charlotte Grandison took over the role of witty foil to virtuous heroine, and became another Anna Howe as she herself remarks (I. 229).

Charlotte Grandison disdains decorum. 'Hang ceremony, said she, sitting down first; let slower souls compliment: And taking some muffin, I'll have breakfasted before these *Pray Madams*, and *Pray my dears*, are seated' (I. 203). She has 'a vein of raillery, that were she *not* polite, would give one too much apprehension for one's ease; But I am sure she is frank, easy, and good-humoured' (I. 179). She practises her wit on her stuffy suitor Lord G., saying, 'I love to jest, to play, to make him look about him' (II. 506). How like this is to Elizabeth, who jumps over stiles and springs over puddles in defiance of female decorum, who 'dearly love[s] a laugh' (32, 57), and who sets out to tease Darcy, as lordly, stiff, and solemn as Lord G. himself. But, explains Charlotte, 'I have a vast deal of roguery, but no ill-nature in my heart', for 'there is luxury in jesting with a solemn man, who wants to assume airs of privilege, and thinks he has a right to be impertinent' (II. 361–2). She pleads that she is not a bad, but 'only a whimsical creature' (II. 506), just as Elizabeth, teasing Darcy, hopes she will never ridicule what is wise and good. Charlotte 'has not much reflexion; she is apt to speak as the humour comes upon her, without considering much about the fit and unfit' (II. 99); Elizabeth admits that 'whims and inconsistencies *do* divert me ... and I laugh at them whenever I can'. But Mr Darcy is not so vulnerable, as Miss Bingley points out. 'Tease calmness and presence of mind! No, no – I feel he may defy us there ... Mr. Darcy may hug himself' (57).

Charlotte Grandison justifies her merry war by asking, 'if it were not one of the truest signs of Love, when men were most fond of women who ... used them worst? These men, my dear, are very sorry creatures and know no medium. They will either, spaniel-like, fawn at your feet, or be ready to leap into your lap' (II. 159). These ideas, together with Charlotte's dislike of 'the officiousness, the assiduities, of this trifling man' (II. 320),

Elizabeth combines, copies and partially inverts. 'The fact is, that you were sick of civility, of deference, of officious attention ... I roused, and interested you, because I was so unlike *them* ... in your heart, you thoroughly despised the persons who so assiduously courted you' (380).

Charlotte fears that she may be thought impertinent for her wit (II. 79); when Elizabeth accuses herself of impertinence, Darcy, as fond as Sir Charles, calls it liveliness of mind instead (380). Charlotte confesses that her reverence for her brother reins in her vivacity (I. 237), while in a nonsensical variation Mr Collins knows that Elizabeth's wit and vivacity must be acceptable to Lady Catherine, 'especially when tempered with the silence and respect that her rank will inevitably excite' (106). The most attracting thing about both heroines, like the pert, saucy Pamela upon whom Elizabeth is often modelled,[5] is a lively and provocative wit which both authors call 'arch'. Charlotte's sweetness and archness 'make one both love and fear her' (I. 179); 'there was a mixture of sweetness and archness in [Elizabeth's] manner which made it hard for her to affront anybody; and Darcy had never been so bewitched by any woman as he was by her' (52). Their resistance does not injure them with the gentlemen (26–7). Courtship is as much play to Charlotte (II. 159) as it is to Elizabeth, but if Charlotte wishes to save her marriage she must suppress her light-heartedness (II. 400); Elizabeth, promised to Darcy, checks herself (371). Charlotte says rudely that Lord G.'s judgment will balance her wit, which, 'with the assistance of your *reproving Love*, will in time teach me *discretion*', but actually discovers in him 'more good sense, more learning, than I had ever till now, that I was willing to enquire after these qualities in him, imagined that he had ' (II. 393, 543). Elizabeth imagines when all seems lost that 'by her ease and liveliness, his mind might have been softened, his manners improved, and from his judgment, information and knowledge of the world, she must have received benefit of greater importance' (312). If Lord G. could sometimes be made to 'laugh *with* Charlotte and sometimes *at* her, she would not make *him* her sport' (II. 330); Darcy, says Mrs Gardiner, wants 'nothing but a little more liveliness, and *that* ... his wife may teach him' (325). Charlotte will teach her husband to jest (II. 399), though Elizabeth, like Harriet Woodvil in Etherege's *Man of Mode*, thinks that

Darcy 'had yet to learn to be laught at, and it was rather too early to begin' (371). Like Sir Charles who loves his sister for her 'pretty playfulness' (II. 99), Darcy finds that Elizabeth's 'lively, playful disposition' first attracts, then holds his attention for ever (12).

Charlotte finds that her pride and petulance must go down by degrees, for 'debasement is the child of pride' (II. 315–17); Elizabeth too is humbled when she knows what Darcy has done (327). But what happens when a lively woman marries? Two scenes in particular, Harriet's defence of Charlotte to Sir Charles in the library and her attempt to talk her out of marrying even as they travel to church (Volume III, letter xix; Volume IV, letter xvi) contribute ideas and vocabulary to Mr Bennet's terrible appeal to his daughter, 'I know that you could be neither happy nor respectable, unless you truly esteemed your husband; unless you looked up to him as a superior. Your lively talents would place you in the greatest danger in an unequal marriage ... My child, let me not have the grief of seeing *you* unable to respect your partner in life' (376). Jane Austen compresses two long scenes and several shorter ones into her brief scene, but the comparative anguish of her version derives from the fact that where Harriet and Sir Charles speak only out of theory, Mr Bennet knows all too much of the practice.

Charlotte Grandison's temperament is no more subdued (II. 6) than Elizabeth's; Georgiana Darcy observes with astonishment bordering on alarm her sportive liveliness with her brother (387–8). Humbled but not crushed, Charlotte makes it a rule to remember nothing that will vex her. 'Is not my memory ... given me for my benefit, and shall I make it my torment?' (II. 263). Elizabeth shows a like happy resilience. 'Every unpleasant circumstance ... ought to be forgotten. You must learn some of my philosophy. Think only of the past as its remembrance gives you pleasure' (368–9). Charlotte can be crude, but we can see what appealed to Jane Austen. Like Elizabeth she 'raillies every one; she can't help it', having 'a kind of constitutional gaiety of heart, and exercised on those she loved best' (II. 398).

Richardson's principal heroine Miss Byron completes Jane Austen's. Harriet tells her age with a teasing reluctance that has no particular significance: 'I am much nearer twenty-one than *nineteen*, I assure you' (I. 38). But when Elizabeth forces Lady Catherine to fight for the information that she is not one and twenty (166), the scene becomes a trial of strength. It does not matter much when Harriet is allowed to have no bad complexion, 'nor are her features, taking them either in whole or part, *much* amiss' (I. 69), but when the lordly male Darcy 'at first scarcely allowed [Elizabeth] to be pretty ... hardly a good feature in her face' (23), it is an insult. The description of Harriet's fair complexion, every feature bearing close examination, lovely face, neck, shoulders, teeth, nose, eyes, Jane Austen in the mood of the juvenilia simply inverts for Elizabeth: 'her face is too thin; her complexion has no brilliancy; and her features are not at all handsome', says Miss Bingley (271).

But the particular excellence that distinguishes Harriet 'from all other *English* women (for it must be acknowledged to be a characteristic of the French women of quality), is, the grace which that people call *Physiognomy*, and we may call *Expression*'. It shows especially in the eyes. This important word recurs when Darcy sees that Elizabeth's face is 'rendered uncommonly intelligent by the beautiful expression of her dark eyes'. 'Had *not* her features and her complexion been so fine as they are', writes Richardson of Harriet, 'that grace alone, that Soul shining out in her lovely aspect ... would have made her as many admirers as beholders' (I. 12); though Darcy 'detected with a critical eye more than one failure of perfect symmetry in her form' (23), he comes to value Elizabeth's expression, a bewitching, even Gallic animation of features that reveals the quality of her sensibility, her mind, her soul. Uncle Selby wishes for Harriet, 'give me the beauty that grows upon us every time we see it: that leaves room for something to be found out to its advantage, as we are more and more acquainted with it' (I. 29); although the Bingley women had been amazed to find Elizabeth reputed a beauty, that, says Darcy, 'was only when I first knew her, for it is many months since I have considered her as one of the handsomest women of my acquaintance' (271).

The frankness of the country girl Harriet Byron contrasts with the false sophistication of town. She is 'tolerably genteel', says Lady Betty (I. 68); Elizabeth is 'tolerable', says Darcy coldly (12). This hint is elaborated into her cross-country dash, its details taken, I think, from the poet Mary Leapor's painfully self-mocking account of herself:[6]

'Why must *she* be scampering about the country, because her sister had a cold? Her hair so untidy, so blowsy!'

'Yes, and her petticoat; I hope you saw her petticoat, six inches deep in mud, I am absolutely certain; and the gown which had been let down to hide it, not doing its office.'   (36)

Just as Pamela's country clothes had attractively revealed '*her own self*' (61), Elizabeth's 'country town indifference to decorum' does her no harm with Darcy. Harriet's 'charming Carmine flush, which denotes sound Health' and the lustre of her fine eyes had no real importance (I.12), but when exercise makes Elizabeth's complexion brilliant and brightens her fine eyes, Darcy is silent with admiration (36, 33).

Country manners release the heroines from mere form. For instance, both prefer reading to the usual accomplishments of females (I.22, 37–9). But their wit is actually aggressive. By defining other people's natures they claim superiority over them. Harriet plays briefly with the novelist's role, and draws 'pictures' (I.34) when she writes letters in other people's characters. She reproduces their tricks of syntax and attitudes to herself, she analyses and contains them. This promising venture was not lost on Jane Austen. Elizabeth is also a novelist within the novel, observing and drawing conclusions. Both she and Harriet are called censorious, and both regret the impulses of their satiric tongues when their squibs are thrown back upon themselves.

Elizabeth is a 'studier of character' who tries her hand at portraits, illustrations, and likenesses (42, 91–4). She may protest that she never ridicules what is wise and good (57), just as Harriet resists the idea that she has 'a satirical vein ... I mean no ill-nature: I love every-body; but not their faults' (I.48). But both heroines do in fact seek faults in a man they find attractive. 'A most *intolerable* superiority! ... If he would but bear malice, would but stiffen his air by resentment, it would be something', says Harriet (II.89); Elizabeth's taunt that 'Mr. Darcy has no defect. He owns it himself without disguise', provokes Darcy's admission of a resentful temper, which she to her cost believes (57–8). It is of no consequence that Harriet will not let Sir Charles despise her, but Elizabeth's challenge to Darcy at the ball, 'you wanted [to] have the pleasure of despising my taste ... now despise me if you dare' (52), ensnares him utterly. Harriet wants to make Sir Charles do something that will make her hate him; 'I will be captious, I think, and study to be affronted, whether he intends to affront me, or not' (II. 15, 13); Elizabeth, as if intending to exasperate herself as much as possible against Mr Darcy, reads and rereads Jane's unhappy letters, and manages to hate him as extravagantly as she could wish (188).

Elizabeth's early 'hatred' of Darcy, confirmed by his separation of Jane and Bingley, corresponds to Johnson's definition, 'to detest; to abhor; to abominate'. She uses such violent expressions as 'deeply rooted dislike, resentment, anger, exasperate', and 'that ground-work of disapprobation, on which succeeding events have built so immoveable a dislike ... his abominable pride, his shameless avowal ... his unpardonable assurance ... the unfeeling manner ... his cruelty' (189–94). But love strangely borders upon hate, as Pamela knew (59). Elizabeth 'certainly did not hate him. No; hatred had vanished long ago, and she had almost as long been ashamed of ever feeling a dislike against him, that could be so called'. In a gradual crescendo of warmth she tries out other words, 'Respect, somewhat of a friendlier nature, respect, esteem, good will, gratitude, a real interest in his welfare', and hopes for the happiness that a renewed proposal would bring (265–6). As Pamela had said before her, 'I know not *how* it came, nor when it begun; but creep, creep it has, like a Thief upon me; and before I knew what was the Matter, it look'd like Love' (214).

'Hate' at last looks pettish. 'Have not you always hated him?', asks her father. 'How earnestly did she then wish that her former opinions had been more reasonable, her expressions more moderate!'. With the same strength of feeling with which she once hated Darcy, Elizabeth says, '"I do, I do like him," she replied with tears in her eyes, "I love him"' (376). For as Charlotte Grandison allows, hatred cannot coincide with play: 'had I either hated or despised him, I would not have been his; and it would have been impossible for me to be so playful with him' (II. 505).

Both Harriet and Elizabeth are biters bit. Where Harriet, suffering a hopeless love for Sir Charles, is 'afraid of my uncle. He will railly his Harriet ... in hopes to divert her ... But my jesting days are over: My situation will not bear it. Yet if it will divert himself, let him railly' (II. 378), Elizabeth, in love with Darcy, feels the force of her father's 'pleasantry ... Never had his wit been directed in a manner so little agreeable to her. "Are you not diverted?" ... "Oh!" cried Elizabeth, "I am excessively diverted"' (363–4). If Uncle Selby accuses Harriet of vanity and pride (I. 34), Elizabeth bursts out, 'I, who have prided myself upon my discernment! – I, who have valued myself upon my abilities! ... and gratified my vanity, in useless or blameable distrust! ... But vanity, not love, has been my folly' (208). Knowing that Darcy is indeed a good man, she grieves heartily over 'every ungracious sensation she had ever encouraged, every saucy speech that she had ever directed towards him' (327); Harriet in similar circumstances writes, 'I cannot ... bear my own littleness', and, 'I intended not to be saucy, vain, insolent'. She adds an extenuation we gladly grant also to Elizabeth, 'if I was so, lay it to a flow of health, and good spirits; to time of life; young, gay, and priding myself in every-one's love' (I. 295, 288).

Both women have aspired to the condition of all-seeing and all-knowing novelist, that is, to the status of God. Presumption, or reliance on one's own judgments, is a theme common enough in the eighteenth century. Robinson Crusoe and Pamela for instance learn that their little busy contrivances are as nothing compared to the designs of Providence. To seek full knowledge was the primal sin, and in practice, even with the advantages of an Adam or a Rasselas, Prince of Abissinia, mortals must be content with less than complete understanding. But where Harriet's 'squibs' (I. 412) have no important result, Elizabeth's quick judgments, her vanity in her abilities, and her rapid, wrong decisions contribute to her plot. When she says proudly 'one knows exactly what to think' (86), she sums up her whole errant, human character. Elizabeth derives first impressions through the dangerous medium of her senses. It is only when she receives quasi-legal information from Darcy's letter or the housekeeper, information that can be checked with Colonel Fitzwilliam or the tenants, that she learns another way to marshall her perceptions, her divine gift of reason.

The last important way that Elizabeth resembles Harriet is in her gratitude – Jane Austen repeated her 'What am I to do with my Gratitude?' in a letter (11 October 1813). Harriet is teased, 'Your gratitude! your gratitude! was the dust you wanted to throw in our eyes, that we might not see that you were governed by a stronger motive ... we were to be popt off with your gratitude' (II. 414–15); Elizabeth, cautiously testing her feelings for Darcy, finds 'a motive within her of good will which could not be overlooked. It was gratitude. – Gratitude' (265). But both Richardson and Jane Austen perceive that the superiority of benevolence is hard to bear, particularly in what he calls '*pecuniary* surprizes'. Harriet writes, 'I don't love them – They are double taxes upon the gratitude of a worthy heart. Is it not enough for a generous mind to labour under a sense of obligation?' (II. 284). When Darcy bribes Wickham into marrying Lydia, 'it was painful, exceedingly painful, to know that they were under obligations to a person who could never receive a return', thinks Elizabeth (326). But Harriet's frankness, 'No prudery! No coquetry! ... you madam, are more than woman' (II. 91–2), like Elizabeth's frankness to Darcy, 'I roused, and interested you, because I was so unlike [the other women]' (380), turn their benefactors into lovers. For the obligation they thought never to repay, their hearts turn out to be sufficient fee.

What of Darcy himself? Much of his story comes, I think, not from *Grandison* but from *Much Ado About Nothing* – Shakespeare was part of Jane Austen's mental furniture too. Darcy, a man 'aweful' in his own house of a Sunday evening when he has nothing to do (50–1), looks at first like gloomy Don John who slanders sweet Hero much as Darcy exposes sweet Jane to the derison of the world. As Beatrice says, he has made Claudio into 'a villain that hath slandered, scorned, dishonoured my kinswoman ... with public accusation, uncover'd slander, un-mitigated rancour' (IV. i. 299–304); Elizabeth believes Darcy to be 'the man, who has been the means of ruining, perhaps for ever, the happiness of a most beloved sister ... exposing one to the censure of the world for caprice and instability, the other to its derision for disappointed hopes, and involving them both in misery in the acutest kind' (190–1). Bingley like Claudio readily believes Darcy, as he will again when all difficulties are cleared.

A quick shift of the focus and Darcy is now Benedick. Darcy's haughty charge that Elizabeth is unhandsome, like Benedick's similar comment about Hero, is an early shot in the merry war with my Lady Disdain, Elizabeth-Beatrice. (McMaster sees other similarities yet, p. 42). The sparring lovers Beatrice and Benedick, Darcy and Elizabeth, lapse into seriousness to save a reputation. At the end Beatrice is teasing again. In reply to Benedick's question, 'For which of my bad parts didst thou fall in love with me?', she replies, 'For which of my good parts did you first suffer love for me?' (V. ii. 51–7); Elizabeth, asking Darcy to account for his having fallen in love with her, wonders 'what could have set you off in the first place'? Her beauty, her manners, her impertinence? (380). As happens so often in Jane Austen, Darcy plays first one role and then another. Elizabeth's perception that he is not Don John but Benedick brings them together at last.

The rest of Darcy's character derives from Richardson's hero. At first Darcy seems an anti-Sir Charles, a parody by inversion reminiscent of the juvenilia. For instance if Sir Charles, an avid dancer, leaves 'the numerous assembly at Enfield while they were in the height of their admiration for him' (II. 348), Darcy refuses to dance at the Meryton ball, and 'every body hoped that he would never come there again' (11). Yet the character of Sir Charles contains all the elements of Darcy:

The good sense of this real fine gentleman is not ... rusted over by sourness, by moroseness: He is above quarreling with the world for trifles: But he is still more above making such compliances with it, as would impeach either his honour or conscience ... [He] is valued by those who know him best, not so much for his birth and fortune ... as for being, in the great and yet comprehensive sense of the word, a *good man* ... he lived to himself, and to his own heart ... he made the judgment or approbation of the world matter but of second consideration.   (I. 182)

Mr Darcy likewise admits that his temper is 'too little yielding – certainly too little for the convenience of the world' (58). In a book where the world's judgments are often proved wrong, Elizabeth will learn to value that unyieldingness. Darcy and Sir Charles do not give everything away, and their forbidding aspect evaporates upon further and truer acquaintance. Harriet complained of Sir Charles's reserve as 'what I do not like' (I. 184); when Darcy blames his own reserve as the cause of the elopement, Jane Austen typically turns characterisation into causation. Sir Charles is obstinate (II. 155), and in a good cause Darcy is very obstinate too. 'I fancy, Lizzy, that obstinacy is the real defect of his character after all', writes Mrs Gardiner (324). Although family pride (I. 384) and passionate temper distinguish both heroes, they descend from their proud elevation to marry women remarkable for mind, not rank. Harriet demands 'assiduities' to prove Sir Charles's affection (II. 383); Elizabeth's heart whispers of Darcy's much more difficult love-test, 'he had done it for her' (326). Harriet guesses, 'such sweetness of manners; such gentleness of voice! – Love has certainly done all this for him' (II. 82); Elizabeth finds Darcy's manner altered and softened by love at Pemberley (255).

Darcy and Sir Charles both save their sisters from eloping with military fortune-hunters. Darcy decorates a room for Georgiana with an 'elegance' and 'lightness' (250) like that exercised on the room, 'elegantly furnished ... with a light green velvet' that Sir Charles offers to Harriet (III. 269). Indeed the situation, setting, rooms and windows of Darcy's house often resemble those of Grandison Hall. Elizabeth says of the garden at Pemberley that she has never seen 'a place for which nature has done more, or where natural beauty had been so little counteracted by an awkward taste'; the garden at Grandison Hall is controlled by 'a great taste' yet 'not an expensive one' (II. 160–1). Sir Charles like Darcy 'will not force and distort nature; but ... help it, as he finds it, without letting art be seen in his works, if he can possibly avoid it'. Darcy's taste is 'neither gaudy nor uselessly fine; with less of splendor, and more real elegance than ... Rosings' (246), terms which derive from Harriet's remark that Sir Charles 'dresses to the fashion, rather richly ... than gaudily ... his equipage is perfectly in taste, tho' not so much in the glare of taste, as if he aimed either to show or inspire emulation' (I. 182–3). In the winding walks and paths of Darcy's garden, lovers meet as unexpectedly as in the winding walks of Clementina's Italian garden (II. 147–50). So far so close, but Jane Austen comments sharply on Richardson's famous minuteness when Mr Collins, superbly unmindful of Johnson's warning not to number the streaks of the tulip, numbers the fields in every direction, tells how many trees there were in the most distant clump, and points out 'every view ... with a minuteness which left beauty entirely behind' (156).[7]

The display of Darcy's portraits in the gallery at Pemberley and his character from the housekeeper copy the portraits and character of Sir Charles Grandison from *his* housekeeper (III. 272, 287), as Moler saw (pp. 104–8). Sir Charles, says Harriet, is 'proved to be the best of brothers, friends, landlords, masters, and the bravest and best of men' (I. 303), just as Elizabeth at Pemberley learns to appreciate Darcy as 'a brother, a landlord, a master'. She will soon discover him to be a hero when he rescues Lydia. 'No question but a man's duties will rise with his opportunities', says Harriet (II. 78); 'how many people's happiness were in his guardianship!' marvels Elizabeth (247–50). Sir Charles bribes the faulty into virtue, but the more realistic Darcy does not attempt to mend hearts along with fortunes. Gone is the idea that philanthropy is to be enjoyed. Where Sir Charles's benefactions were public and publicly applauded, Darcy works painfully and in secret, bribing a man he loathes, and dealing with a woman he must abominate and despise (326). His philanthropy confirms Elizabeth's love as Sir Charles's sparked off Harriet's (I. 389). Elizabeth may smile at his 'easy manner of directing his friend' (371), just as Harriet sees wrily that it is impossible but Sir Charles 'must carry every point he sets his heart upon' (II. 317), but she would surely acknowledge the truth of Harriet's advice to Lucy, to see how cautious we ought to be in passing judgment on the actions of others, especially on those of good men (I. 443). Darcy's fulfilment of the social duties proves him a true Grandison after all.

'In a more gentleman-like manner': three proposals

Jane Austen constructs the three proposal scenes in *Pride and Prejudice* very much as though she were playing her favourite game of spillikins. She gathers up episodes from *Grandison*, scatters them, and picks up sticks to build her own. Sir Hargrave Pollexfen's proposal to Harriet she gives to Collins and then to Darcy, and simply inverts Sir Charles's relationship with Clementina for Darcy's angry response and Lady Catherine's arguments to Elizabeth.

Mr Collins's proposal to Elizabeth in Volume I, chapter xix follows exactly the same sequence as Sir Hargrave's to Harriet, enquiry as to pre-engagement, compliment by common report, voluble laying out of the advantages to the heroine which includes his wealth and her poverty, perseverance in self-deception when the heroine promptly and frankly refuses with thanks and good wishes, demands that she should love him out of gratitude, accusations of wilful suspense turning to accusations of pride, determination, and cruelty in the face of the heroine's withdrawal, hurt pride, and the seeking of approval by relatives. But how differently, how ludicrously, it is replayed!

Sir Hargrave consults Harriet's family before proposing (I. 62), but Mr Collins does so twice, once for Jane and once for Elizabeth. 'I have been assured madam', says Sir Hargrave, declaring himself Harriet's lover (Volume I, letter xvii), 'that your affections are not engaged'; Mrs Bennet does not '*know* of any prepossession'. When Mr Collins finds *all* the Bennet sisters 'as handsome and amiable as they were represented by common report' (71, 70), he enlarges absurdly upon Sir Hargrave's 'running over with the praises he had heard given [Miss Byron] at last Northampton races' (I. 57). Sir Hargrave's proposal, sardonically summarised by Harriet, Jane Austen need only dramatise for Mr Collins:

Had not Sir Hargrave intended me an honour, and had he not a very high opinion of the efficacy of eight thousand pounds a year in an address of this kind, I dare say, he would have supposed a little more prefacing necessary: But, after he had told me, in few words, how much he was attracted by my character before he saw me, he thought fit to refer himself to the declaration he had made at Lady Betty Williams's, both to Mr. Reeves and myself; and then talked of large settlements; boasted of his violent passion; and besought my favour with the utmost earnestness.

Mr Collins is just as abrupt. 'Almost as soon as I entered the house I singled you out as the companion of my future life' (that 'almost' is wonderful). Before he is 'run away with by [his] feelings', he enumerates his reasons for marrying and concludes, 'now nothing remains for me but to assure you in the most animated language of the violence of my affection'. His 'solemn composure' is a fine addition to the brew, as is the detail relating the whole episode to Elizabeth's family circumstances that he is 'to inherit this estate after the death of your honoured father'. Sir Hargrave may lay 'a title to my gratitude from the passion he avowed for me', but Mr Collins argues from strength when he claims that preserving the Bennets from want 'has been my motive, my fair cousin, and I flatter myself it will not sink me in your esteem'.

Where Sir Hargrave boasts of wealth in possession, Mr Collins anticipates wealth as soon as Mr Bennet dies. Where Sir Hargrave points to his rank, Mr Collins claims rank by association with

Lady Catherine. Where Sir Hargrave's fortune, descent and ardent affection will not, he thinks, '*dis*-avail you. Your relations will at least think so, if I may have the honour of your consent for applying to them', the joke in Mr Collins being 'persuaded that when sanctioned by the express authority of both your excellent parents, my proposal will not fail of being acceptable' almost confounds analysis. Typically too Elizabeth's parents respond in character, unlike Harriet's family. Her mother will never see her daughter again if she does not marry Mr Collins, and her father will disown her if she does (112).

Harriet's passing thought, 'I would have played a little female trifling upon him, and affected to take his professions only for polite raillery, which men call *making love* to young women ... but the fervour with which he *renewed* (as he called it) his declaration, admitted not of fooling', becomes Mr Collins's obsession and his comfort:

'I am not now to learn,' replied Mr. Collins, with a formal wave of the hand, 'that it is usual with young ladies to reject the addresses of the man whom they secretly mean to accept, when he first applies for their favour; and that sometimes the refusal is repeated a second or even a third time ...'

'I know it to be the established custom of your sex to reject a man on the first application, and perhaps you have even now said as much to encourage my suit as would be consistent with the true delicacy of the female character.' ...

'As I must therefore conclude that you are not serious in your rejection of me, I shall chuse to attribute it to your wish of increasing my love by suspense, according to the usual practice of elegant females.'

But Elizabeth like Harriet is no trifler. She has 'no pretension whatever to that kind of elegance which consists in tormenting a respectable man ... Do not consider me now as an elegant female intending to plague you, but as a rational creature speaking the truth from her heart'. The phrase becomes the leit-motif of the scene and its conclusion when Elizabeth turns to her father, 'whose behaviour at least could not be mistaken for the affectation and coquetry of an elegant female'. Sir Hargrave's laborious repetitions do not amuse, unlike the courtly and oblivious accumulations of Mr Collins.

Harriet will not 'keep a man in an hour's suspense, when I am in none myself'; Elizabeth will answer 'without farther loss of time'. 'As therefore I could not think of encouraging his addresses, I thought it best to answer him with openness and unreserve', says Harriet:

To seem to question the sincerity of such professions as you make, Sir Hargrave, might appear to you as if I wanted to be assured. But be pleased to know that you are directing your discourse to one of the plainest-hearted women in England; and you may therefore expect from me nothing but the simplest truth. I thank you, Sir, for your good opinion of me; but I cannot encourage your addresses.

'Can I speak plainer?', asks Elizabeth. 'Accept my thanks for the compliment you are paying me. I am very sensible for the honour of your proposals, but it is impossible for me to do otherwise than decline them'. She adds, 'I thank you again and again for the honour you have done me, in your proposals, but to accept them is absolutely impossible'. 'If what I have hitherto said can appear to you in the form of encouragement, I know not how to express my refusal,' she says in exasperation (108–9).

Sir Hargrave complains, 'A man of his fortune to be refused, by a lady who had not (and whom he wish'd not to have) an answerable fortune' (I. 98). His grievance becomes Mr Collins's reproach, that

to fortune I am perfectly indifferent, and shall make no demand of that nature on your father, since I am well aware that it could not be complied with; and that one thousand pounds in the 4 per cents. which will not by yours till after your mother's decease, is all that you may ever be entitled to. On that head, therefore, I shall be uniformly silent; and you may assure yourself that no ungenerous reproach shall ever pass my lips when we are married.

To these unforgivable particularities he adds one more: 'In spite of your manifold attractions, it is by no means certain that another offer of matrimony may ever be made you. Your portion is unhappily so small that it will in all likelihood undo the effects of your loveliness and amiable qualifications'.

Harriet's meek response, 'may your fortune, Sir Hargrave, be a blessing to you', like Elizabeth's wish for Mr Collins to be 'very happy and very rich', only inflame their suitors more. 'You *must* be mine', says Sir Hargrave, 'Every word you speak, adds a rivet to my chains'; 'You are uniformly charming!', cries Mr Collins, with an air of awkward gallantry. Sir Hargrave accuses Harriet of pride, cruelty, and ingratitude; Collins, ready to accuse Elizabeth of cruelty, shows in a voice of displeasure how much he resents her behaviour (114). Harriet withdraws in haste, and Elizabeth 'immediately and in silence withdrew'.

Sir Hargrave, says Harriet shrewdly, 'had paraded so much, before I went down, to my cousins, and so little expected a direct and determined repulse, that a man of his self-consequence might, perhaps, be allowed to be the more easily piqued by it'. Owning that the 'proud repulse had stung him', he turns in vain for consolation from her relatives. But when Mr Collins in his hurt pride (112) turns to Mrs Bennet, she is too eager to make the match, attacks her daughter, and alters his resolve. 'I can never make you happy, nor you me', says Harriet (I. 114); 'You could not make *me* happy, and I am convinced that I am the last woman in the world who would make *you* so', says Elizabeth. These irritating proposals induce brief misanthropy in the heroines. 'Every-thing of this nature now appears silly to me', says Harriet crossly (I. 271); Collins seems to Elizabeth so 'silly' after his proposal to Charlotte that she is thoroughly dissatisfied with the world (135). Her reasons are more complex than Harriet's. Where Harriet merely resents the fop's address, Elizabeth must feel the insult when Collins turns promptly to Charlotte, and Charlotte as promptly accepts.

Harriet's inconsequential rejection of the rake compares with Elizabeth's more difficult refusal of a respectable clergyman who controls the family's prospects. Mr Collins's obedience to his patron even unto matrimony, and his worldly excuse for his passion derive, I think from the 'sensible, sober' young clergyman Mr Williams in *Pamela*.[8] But if he shares Sir Hargrave's vanity and proposal scene, he derives his scholastic gravity and condescension from Richardson's pedantic Walden (volume I, letter xi). Fop and pedant incongruously fuse to make up the awkwardly amorous, the verbosely vain, the immortal Mr Collins.

Mr Darcy's first proposal derives from the same source as Mr Collins's, and fails for the same reasons. Darcy confidently declares his love to the heroine in the manner of Sir Hargrave and Mr Collins. He points out that she is inferior to him, and resents her refusal which is based on her dislike for his manner or personality. Jane Austen builds here on a new selection of detail from *Grandison*, but what especially distinguishes it from the two earlier proposals is the shift from comedy to seriousness. Collins irrupts farcically into Elizabeth's life, but Darcy is already her match in witty wars.

Darcy's expressed passion, volubility, sense of stooping to an inferior, and anger when Elizabeth will not accept him, all derive from Sir Hargrave's proposal at an equally early stage of the story, although when he says 'in vain have I struggled' against the 'degradation' (189), he sounds more like Mr B. complaining, 'in vain ... do I find it to struggle against my Affection' for all his 'Pride of Heart, and Pride of Condition' (216–7), as Duncan-Jones saw in 'Proposals of marriage'. Sir Hargrave speaks in Volume I, letter xvii of his 'ardent affection' and 'violent passion'; Darcy says, 'My feelings will not be repressed. You must allow me to tell you how ardently I admire and love you'. Sir Hargrave's '*volubility*', says Harriet acutely, 'might have made questionable the sincerity of his declarations'; Elizabeth observes coolly that Darcy 'spoke well' but 'was not more eloquent on the subject of tenderness than of pride'. Harriet had explained that Sir Hargrave 'is very voluble in speech; but seems to owe his volubility more to his want of doubt, than to the extraordinary merit of what he says' (I. 45), an insulting confidence that Elizabeth also perceives in Darcy. 'As he said this, she could easily see that he had no doubt of a favourable answer. He *spoke* of apprehension and anxiety, but his countenance expressed real security'. Neither man permits the woman to reply, so intent is he to stress his superiority. Where Sir Hargrave points to his rank and descent, Darcy indicates his 'sense of her inferiority'. 'Could you expect me to rejoice in the inferiority of your connections? To congratulate myself on the hope of relations, whose condition of life is so decidedly beneath my own?', he asks (192). Sir Hargrave despises Harriet, 'What a devil, am I to creep, beg, pray, entreat, and only for a *wife*?' (I. 158), but Darcy's sneer at Elizabeth's relations wounds her to the heart.

Harriet, thanking the fop for his good opinion, 'cannot encourage your addresses'; Elizabeth, saying that she 'never desired [Darcy's] good opinion', rejects him. Harriet will not 'keep a man in an hour's suspense' when she is in none herself, and adds, 'I will not give pain to a man I can like to marry' (I. 110); Elizabeth says, 'I am sorry to have occasioned pain to any one. It has been most unconsciously done, however, and I hope will be of short duration'. At this point Jane Austen seems to copy *Pamela*, but critically. Where Pamela humbly agrees that Mr B. should 'regard the World's Opinion' and allow time, absence and conversation with worthier people to 'effectually enable you to overcome a Regard so unworthy of your Condition' (184), Elizabeth bursts out that the 'feelings which, you tell me, have long prevented the acknowledgment of your regard, can have little difficulty in overcoming it'.

Darcy responds with anger and resentment where Sir Hargrave showed 'anger, and an air of insolence'. He starts like Sir Hargrave, is pale with anger, his colour later heightening as Sir Hargrave's colour came and went (I. 96); he pauses to recover his composure as Sir Hargrave 'stood silent a minute or two ... looking upon me, and upon himself'; he asks, 'I might, perhaps, wish to be informed why ... I am thus rejected', rather as Sir Hargrave demands 'your *objections*, then dear madam? Give me, I beseech you, some one material objection'. Darcy though blames Elizabeth for rejecting him 'with so little *endeavour* at civility', whereas Harriet had admitted that her suitor's professions of regard entitled him 'to civility and acknowlegement'. Sir Hargrave, astonished at the manner of 'your refusal of me in so peremptory, in so unceremonious a manner, slapdash, as I may say, and not one objection to make, or which you will condescend to make!' (I. 113), replies unpleasantly to Harriet's plea that she was 'civil to you', 'Yes, yes, and very determined ... You were very civil. Hitherto *I* have not been uncivil' (I. 152). The charge of incivility affects all of *Pride and Prejudice*, as I shall show.

Elizabeth accuses Darcy of 'so evident a design of offending and insulting me', just as Harriet thought she was 'staying to be insulted'. In return, says Darcy sarcastically, 'My faults, according to this calculation, are heavy indeed!', just as Sir Hargrave thinks he has been upbraided by Harriet (I. 96). The disturbance of Darcy's mind is visible in every feature. '"And this," cried Darcy, as he walked with quick steps across the room, "is your opinion of me! This is the estimation in which you hold me! I thank you for explaining it so fully"' (192). Sir Hargrave too walks about the room, muttering angrily, 'You have no opinion of my morals', and gives himself 'airs that shewed greater inward than even outward emotion' (I.96, 114). But Sir Hargrave's faults are conventional enough. How much more dreadful seems Darcy's separation of Jane and Bingley, or his unkindness to his childhood friend Wickham! Misunderstandings created in this one scene will take the whole story to unravel.

Both suitors call the heroine proud, and Elizabeth's accusation that he has not been 'gentleman-like' sends Darcy storming away like his rakish predecessor (I.96). Elizabeth points to Darcy's 'arrogance, your conceit, and your selfish disdain of the feelings of others'; Sir Hargrave shows anger, insolence, pride and ill-nature. Elizabeth's dislike she says is 'immoveable', for 'it is not merely this affair ... on which my dislike is founded'; though Harriet thinks that 'a dislike of such a nature as [mine] must be a dislike arising from something like a natural aversion', Elizabeth will learn to be ashamed of ever feeling a 'dislike against him, that could be so called' (265). Elizabeth says, 'I had not known you a month before I felt that you were the last man in the world whom I could ever be prevailed on to marry'; 'were Sir Hargrave king of half of the globe, I would not go to the altar with him', says Harriet, 'I would not, of all the men I have ever seen, be the wife of Sir Hargrave' (I.64, 88). Darcy pointedly asks forgiveness for taking Elizabeth's time, and Sir Hargrave with equal sarcasm begs forgiveness (I.95). But with all its similarities to Richardson's scene, Jane Austen's is much richer. Elizabeth will marry the man she vowed she never would, an irony that makes her painful mental tumult after the interview more complex than Harriet's failure to recover herself in an hour (I.97). Elizabeth may recall Darcy's 'pride, his abominable pride ... his cruelty' (193–4), like Harriet accusing Sir Hargrave, but she is wrong.

Darcy like Mr B. (II.6–7) explains himself more successfully in a letter than Sir Hargrave in spoken words. He composes 'two sheets of letter paper, written quite through, in a very close hand. – The envelope itself was likewise full'; 'Two sheets!' Harriet had written of one of her own letters, 'and such a quantity before! Unconscionable!' (I.65). Darcy will not pain Elizabeth by the renewal of addresses 'so disgusting to you' (196); Sir Hargrave had taken offence that his offer '*disgusted*' Miss Byron. K.C. Phillips suggests in his book that Jane Austen usually means by this word the comparatively mild sense of 'distaste' rather than 'nauseatingly unpleasant' (p. 22). But surely she does mean nausea here, for Elizabeth must learn, as in the matter of 'hate', that her vocabulary has been extravagant to the point of childishness.

Where Mr Darcy has a 'look of haughty composure' (195), Sir Hargrave speaks 'haughtily'; where Harriet says, 'You have a very high opinion of yourself. You may have reason for it; since you must know yourself, and your own heart, better than I can pretend to do' (I. 114), Elizabeth had said with equal sharpness, 'I am perfectly convinced ... that Mr. Darcy has no defect; he owns it himself without disguise' (57). Darcy, 'with his eyes fixed on her face, seemed to catch her words with no less resentment than surprise ... The pause was to Elizabeth's feelings dreadful' (190); Sir Hargrave looks at Harriet 'five or six times, as in malice. Ill-natured, spiteful, moody wretch! thought I, trembling at his strange silence ... what an odious creature thou art!' (I. 160). Sir Hargrave's reaction accurately reflects his mind, but Mr Darcy's holds mysteries yet.

Jane Austen's principal revelation is that Darcy is not Sir Hargrave, but Sir Charles. He is also a Grandison in love. Sir Charles loves two women at once, and struggles to repress his affection for Harriet. He is bound in honour to Clementina, as he explains to Harriet in the library, but once rejected by Clementina, returns to Harriet. The difficulties of this peculiar plot are resolved in Jane Austen's reworking of it.

Darcy follows Elizabeth with his eyes (23, 51), an infallible sign of love in Richardson (II. 33). Sir Charles claims that he loved Harriet from the moment he first saw her, 'and you know not the struggle it cost me ... to conceal my Love' (III. 284); 'In vain have I struggled', says Darcy, 'it will not do. My feelings will not be repressed' (189). Early on sensing his 'danger', he had 'wisely resolved to be particularly careful that no sign of admiration should *now* escape him, nothing that could elevate her with the hope of influencing his felicity; sensible that if such an idea had been suggested, his behaviour during the last day must have material weight in confirming or crushing it' (58–60). This idea provides a new turn to the plot. When Darcy in his first proposal represents to Elizabeth 'the strength of that attachment which, in spite of all his endeavours, he had found impossible to conquer', she can respond swiftly with 'the feelings which, you tell me, have long prevented the acknowledgment of your regard, can

have little difficulty in overcoming it after this explanation ...
you chose to tell me that you liked me against your will, against
your reason, and even against your character' (189–90). The
reasons for Elizabeth's outrage are to be found elsewhere, in Sir
Charles's relationship with Clementina.

Clementina's 'Rank next to princely; her Fortune as high as
her Rank ... all so many obstacles that had appeared to me
insuperable' (II. 130), cannot daunt the rich, aristocratic Sir
Charles, but when in an inversion of the scene Darcy speaks of
Elizabeth's 'inferiority', the 'degradation', the 'family obstacles
which judgment had always opposed to inclination' (189), he tells
an actual, brutal truth. These ideas reappear in Lady Catherine's
finest scene, Volume III, chapter xiv, which itself derives from
one 'frightful Interview' between Pamela and Lady Davers, Mr
B.'s sister, and another when Lady Davers is 'beside herself with
Passion and Insolence' (317, 224), as Moler sees (p. 77). The
insolent, disagreeable, and angry Lady Catherine, only able to call
herself 'almost the nearest relation [Darcy] has in the world', has
less right even than Lady Davers to interfere. The union she
planned from the cradle between her daughter and Darcy makes
her even more of a bad fairy than Lady Davers, who, says Mr B.,
has simply 'found out a Match for me, in the Family of a Person
of Quality' (341). 'Do not expect to be noticed by his family or
friends', says Lady Catherine, 'if you wilfully act against the
inclinations of all. You will be censured, slighted, and despised,
by every one connected with him. Your alliance will be a
disgrace; your name will never even be mentioned by any of us'.
Mr B. knows that Lady Davers would never be reconciled: 'the
other Ladies will not visit you; and you will ... be treated as if
unworthy their Notice'. He therefore pities 'my dear Girl too, for
her Part in this Censure; for, here she will have to combat the
Pride and Slights of the neighbouring Gentry'. Pamela sounds
merely spiteful when she replies in all the glory of her married
state, 'I shall have the Pride to place more than half their ill-will,
to their Envy at my Happiness' (225); Elizabeth however chances
all to say, 'These are heavy misfortunes ... But the wife of Mr.
Darcy must have such extraordinary sources of happiness
necessarily attached to her situation, that she could, upon the
whole, have no cause to repine'. She crushes Lady Catherine
utterly.

The arrogant Porrettas insist that the alliance would not be 'a proper one. Their rank, their degree, their alliances, were dwelt upon: I found that their advantages, in all these respects, were heightened; my degree, my consequence, lowered, in order to make the difference greater, and the difficulties insuperable' (II. 218). Jane Austen's reversals of rank and sex make Elizabeth's resistance as a poor young woman all the more remarkable. Lady Catherine dwells on her own family's noble line of 'ancient, though untitled families' and its splendid fortune on both sides. Elizabeth is 'wholly unallied to the family ... Your alliance will be a disgrace'. Sir Charles says that 'they considered the alliance, as highly honourable to me (a private, an obscure man, as now they began to call me) *as* derogatory to their own honour' (II. 130), just as Lady Catherine talks of 'the upstart pretensions of a young woman without family, connections, or fortune'. 'Ours is no upstart Family', wrote Lady Davers, 'but is as ancient as the best in the Kingdom: and, for several Hundreds of Years, it has never been known that the Heirs of it have disgraced themselves by unequal Matches'. Pamela's reply was perhaps too overt for *Pride and Prejudice*, 'how can they be assured, that one hundred Years hence or two, some of those now despised upstart Families, may not revel in their Estates, while their Descendants may be reduced to the other's Dunghils?' (221–2). But Jane Austen appeals to meritocracy nonetheless.

Sir Charles resents the charge that he is 'a man of inferior degree' (II. 169), just as Elizabeth resents being called 'a young woman of inferior birth'. If Sir Charles says that 'I have not deserved ill usage (from my equals and superiors in rank, especially)' (II. 458), Elizabeth makes the same proud claim to equality. 'He is a gentleman; I am a gentleman's daughter; so far we are equal' (356), she says, echoing both the Countess of D. in *Grandison*, 'an antient and good gentleman's family is all I am sollicitous about' (I. 214), and Pamela, that Protestant democrat, 'My Soul is of equal Importance with the Soul of a Princess' (141). 'What the *world* would say, had been no small point' with the Porrettas (II. 176), and Lady Catherine too thinks the alliance will 'make [Darcy] the contempt of the world'. The whole Porretta family will be 'dishonoured' (II. 184): 'Are the shades of Pemberley to be thus polluted?', asks Lady Catherine. Has Elizabeth no regard for the honour and credit of her nephew?

'Do you not consider that a connection with you, must disgrace him in the eyes of everybody?': Mr B. will be the 'Disgrace' of his friends, says Lady Davers to her brother, 'for *you* to throw yourself away thus, is intolerable' (221). 'Is this to be endured!', demands Lady Catherine. Pamela and Mr B. retreat to private domesticity, and Elizabeth and Darcy flee to 'all the comfort and elegance of their family party at Pemberley' (384).

Inversion as well as likeness controls Jane Austen's whole episode. Where the Porrettas complain that Sir Charles rejects their daughter, Lady Catherine rages that Elizabeth will not reject her nephew. Most characteristic difference of all, where Sir Charles's indignation affects his fate no whit, Elizabeth's democratic sturdiness precipitates a second and very welcome proposal from Darcy. 'We have sufficiently tortur'd one another', says Mr B., but now 'we sit together secur'd in each other's good Opinion, recounting the uncommon Gradations, by which we have ascended to the Summit of ... Felicity' (229); Darcy, once 'tortured' by Elizabeth's words, rehearses with her the progress of their prosperous love (367).

These fruitful images of class conflict combine with a scene where the Countess of D. closely questions Harriet, already in love with Sir Charles. A match-maker to manage a Machiavel, she wants Harriet to marry her son (III. 86). Neither Harriet nor Elizabeth can answer directly, affairs being so complicated. But the effectiveness of Elizabeth's frankness to Lady Catherine the match-breaker derives from another exchange with Sir Hargrave.

The Countess of D. had demanded to know if Miss Byron's affections are 'absolutely disengaged'; 'Has he, has my nephew, made you an offer of marriage?' asks Lady Catherine, though her claim that 'I am almost the nearest relation he has in the world, and am entitled to know all his dearest concerns' is much more peremptory than the Countess's solicitousness to have her son 'happily married' (I. 214–5). Harriet, 'not knowing of any engagement' of Sir Charles, had 'no reason to *endeavour* to conquer [her] passion' (II. 158); 'If Mr. Darcy is neither by honour nor inclination confined to his cousin', says Elizabeth, 'why is not he to make another choice? And if I am that choice, why may not I accept him?'. But Darcy is no dutiful nonentity like Lord D. Elizabeth risks everything by defending his liberty to choose, and she gains everything by Lady Catherine's interference. Lady

Catherine's demands are thwarted by echoes of Harriet's resistance to Sir Hargrave:

> ... he asked me, If Sir Charles Grandison had not made an impression on my heart?
>
> What, Lucy, could make me inwardly fret at this question? I could hardly have patience to reply. I now see, my dear, that I have indeed a great deal of pride.
>
> Surely, Sir Hargrave, I am not accountable to you −
>
> You are not, Madam: But I must insist upon an answer to this question ...
>
> Sir Charles Grandison, Sir, is absolutely disinterested. Sir Charles Grandison has made − There I stopt: I could not help it.
>
> No application to my cousin, I assure you, Sir Hargrave, said Mr. Reeves.   (I. 270)

Harriet cares nothing for Sir Hargrave, but Elizabeth speaks from love:

> '*You* may ask questions, which *I* shall not choose to answer.'
>
> 'This is not to be borne. Miss Bennet, I insist upon being satisfied. Has he, has my nephew, made you an offer of marriage? ... I ... am entitled to know all his dearest concerns.'
>
> 'But you are not entitled to know *mine*; nor will such behaviour as this, ever induce me to be explicit.' ...
>
> 'Tell me once for all, are you engaged to him?'
>
> Though Elizabeth would not, for the mere purpose of obliging Lady Catherine, have answered this question; she could not but say, after a moment's deliberation,
>
> 'I am not.'

Sir Charles, who loves two women at once, offers Harriet a 'second-placed love' that makes him a 'widower-bachelor' and 'another woman's *leavings*' (II. 547, III. 32). Darcy calls on the neater solution of *Pamela*, and asks the same woman twice. Even so, some of Harriet's unease comes through in Elizabeth's worry about this 'man who had been once refused! How could I ever be so foolish as to expect a renewal of his love? Is there one among the sex, who would not protest against such a weakness as a second proposal to the same woman? There is no indignity so abhorrent to their feelings!' (341). Sir Charles acknowledges Harriet's right to refuse a rejected man (III. 16), but when Darcy renews his proposal and says with equal delicacy that 'one word from you will silence me on this subject forever' (366), nobody could want Elizabeth to speak it.

Jane Austen's finale takes several stages, the interesting encounter at Pemberley, the puzzling visit without declaration, the explanatory proposal, and the informing of the Bennets, all of which have parallels in *Grandison*. Signs that Darcy will again propose appear at Pemberley (Volume II, chapter i) where he meets Elizabeth unexpectedly as Harriet had once been broken in on by Sir Charles. Sir Charles was 'in the room before I saw him. I started!', says Harriet (III. 289); 'the owner of it himself suddenly came forward ... He absolutely started', writes Jane Austen of her equally accidental meeting. Darcy is 'immoveable from surprise ... Nor did he seem much more at ease ... his accent had none of the usual sedateness; and he repeated his enquiries ... so often, and in so hurried a way, as plainly spoke the distraction of his thoughts ... every idea seemed to fail him'; when in the library Sir Charles had explained his love for Clementina, 'his emotion was visible as he spoke', reports Harriet, 'Why did he hesitate? Why did he tremble?' (II. 134). Elizabeth too must puzzle over Darcy's odd behaviour. Harriet writes, 'Sir! Sir! said I, as if I thought excuses necessary. He saw my confusion ... Sir Charles reconciled us ... to ourselves' (III. 289). Darcy meets Elizabeth's astonishment, confusion, and embarrassment with civility, relieving her from 'the impropriety of her being found there'. But Harriet is married and her confusion pointless. Elizabeth's plight is much more complex and consequential.

The proposals of both men are unaccountably delayed. Greville's warning to Harriet 'NOT TO BE TOO SECURE' (III. 173) is a completely factitious device to heighten the suspense, but when Elizabeth 'would not be secure' she ought not to be (334). Harriet is told not to have Sir Charles, who fails to arrive, if he is indifferent (III. 47); Elizabeth believes Darcy to be 'wavering', and says that if he came no more she would cease to regret him (361). Harriet says that women when courted do not want men to be 'solemn, formal, grave' (III. 92); Elizabeth asks of Darcy's extraordinary visit, 'Why, if he came only to be silent, grave, and indifferent ... did he come at all?' (339).

In the cedar-parlour that Jane Austen knew so well, Sir Charles proposes in 'some little confusion' to Harriet (III. 53); Elizabeth too must feel the 'more than common awkwardness and anxiety' in Darcy's situation. Sir Charles's proposal is long, defensive, and in his own words; Darcy's is brief, indirect, and all the better for it. Elizabeth, her eyes cast down and her tongue not fluent, like Harriet's (III. 76), hears Darcy express himself 'as sensibly and as warmly as a man violently in love can be supposed to do'. Jane Austen boldly forestalls here any such surprise as Charlotte Grandison's, 'Upon my word, Harriet, allowing for every-thing, neither of Sir Charles Grandison's sisters expected that their brother would have made so ardent, so polite, a Lover' (III. 110–11). 'You have given me hope, madam: All your friends encourage that hope', says Sir Charles smugly (III. 98), but it is a fine change that Lady Catherine 'taught [Darcy] to hope' (366–7). Harriet accepts a man called always 'the best of men', Elizabeth accepts a man 'condemned as the worst of men' (138). To prove him 'perfectly amiable' (376) is now her task. A happy letter to Mr and Mrs Gardiner invites their praise and them to Pemberley (382–3), just as Pamela had invited Mrs Jervis (302).

Both couples trace the stages of their love. 'Miss Byron's graces had stolen so imperceptibly upon my heart, as already to have made an impression on it too deep for my tranquillity', says Sir Charles (III. 53–4); Darcy too 'was in the middle before I knew that I *had* begun' (380). Darcy admits that he has been selfish, uncorrected of temper, proud, conceited, spoilt, overbearing and thinking meanly of those beyond the family circle, but blames his aristocratic education much as Mr B. had done. 'Such I was, at eight to eight and twenty; and such I might still have been but for you, dearest, loveliest Elizabeth! What do I not owe you! ... You shewed me how insufficient were all my pretensions to please a woman worthy of being pleased' (369). His confession is far more modest than Sir Charles's complacent request, 'you must perfect, by your sweet conversation ... what Dr. Bartlett has so happily begun; and I shall then be more worthy of you than at present I am' (III. 124).

Before he declared himself, Sir Charles had been kept coldly at a distance out of 'tyrant custom' (III. 345); before *his* engagement is announced Darcy must suffer the 'cold and ceremonious politeness' of Mrs Bennet. 'The sighing heart ... will remind us of imperfection, in the highest of our enjoyments', says pious Harriet (III. 51), but when Elizabeth feels that 'years of happiness could not make Jane or herself amends, for moments of such painful confusion', Jane Austen instantly promises her those years of happiness (335–7).

In *Pride and Prejudice*, Jane Austen confirms Richardson's belief that princes are so 'only as they act' (II. 234). To do so she explores his important word *civil*. Her aristocrat Darcy moves from the cold civility of etiquette to a full and generous life among traders, professional people, and women.[9] The knowledge that Mr Gardiner's every sentence marks 'his intelligence, his taste, or his good manners' is much more pointed in the circumstances than Harriet's early praises of the Reeves's modesty, good sense, and amiable tempers. Though Richardson's Miss Hurste had blushed whenever her husband opened his mouth, her eyes sparkling with gratitude 'upon any one who took the least respectful notice of him' (II. 551), Elizabeth has moved from 'blushing for her mother' (43) to the consolation that 'she had some relations for whom there was no need to blush'. Instead of 'decamping as fast as he could from such distasteful companions', Darcy invites Mr Gardiner to fish 'with the greatest civility'. Elizabeth must wonder at his 'more than civil' behaviour, above all at his 'civility' in wishing her to become acquainted with his sister (255–9).

Georgiana Darcy also welcomes this woman of merit, not birth. Looking and acting like Sir Charles's ward Emily Jervois, she proves as loving and sisterly as she. Emily is tall, 'gentle ... innocently childish beyond her stature and womanly appearance; but not her years' (I. 227, 357); Georgiana is 'tall ... her figure was formed, and her appearance womanly and graceful ... gentle'. Her age, 'little more than sixteen' (261), is dangerous. Like Charlotte Grandison she has already been 'entangled', like Emily she is disabled by diffidence and shyness. She listens with 'astonishment, bordering on alarm, at [Elizabeth's] lively, sportive, manner of talking to her brother', not knowing that 'a woman may take liberties with her husband, which a brother will not always allow in a sister more than ten years younger than himself' (387–8) – the Grandison sisters had observed 'a distance' to their brother 'from awe, from reverence' (II. 18). Like Emily anxious for Harriet to love her (II. 25), Georgiana expresses 'all her earnest desire of being loved by her sister' (383). Emily and Harriet become 'sisters' after Sir Charles proposes (III. 212); in *Pride and Prejudice* 'the attachment of the sisters was exactly what Darcy had hoped to see. They were able to love each other, even as well as they intended' (387). Georgiana's 'civility' (266), like her brother's, means exactly what it seems.

All this suggests yet again that to Jane Austen the characters of *Grandison* were as imaginatively powerful to her as if they had been living friends. To animate her simple characters[10] one or two traits from *Grandison* suffice. The deep, intricate, and amusing characters (42) are so, simply because they are made up of elements from several characters in *Grandison*, elements which the book unfolds. Elizabeth seems to be Charlotte Grandison, my Lady Disdain, but turns into a humbled Harriet, grateful to marry the man who attracted her from the start. Darcy appears to be Sir Hargrave, but is really the Sir Charles that his appearance, his house, and his garden have already proclaimed him to be. By such splitting and recombining, Jane Austen endows her creatures with secret lives.

Direct appropriation from *Grandison*, like those coach numbers, is rare. Sometimes Jane Austen corrects Richardson, as when Elizabeth's proud resistance answers Pamela's expressed unworthiness. Sometimes she parodies by shift of mode, as when Mrs Bennet wails that Mr Bennet 'will be killed, and what is to become of us all?' (287). Sometimes she checks him against her own sense of the real, as when Charlotte Grandison's marriage to a man she does not love becomes Charlotte Lucas's to one not lovable at all. And sometimes she just develops a hint, such as Miss Hurste blushing for her husband. Whatever she does, however we are to describe it, the result is a *complicating* of Richardson. When Harriet's abduction turns into Lydia's elopement, so much more is simply involved. Jane Austen's episode arises inevitably from the past, and brims with prime causes for the future.

Grandison is characterised by story, *Pride and Prejudice* by plot. Nothing may be learnt from Harriet's arrival at Grandison Hall, but when Elizabeth, unable to resist visiting Pemberley, acknowledges her love for Darcy and thinks she can never be its mistress, what, as Henry James asked, 'is character but the determination of incident? What is incident but the illustration of character?' Such scrupulosity of cause and effect is what finally distinguishes Jane Austen from the Richardson of *Sir Charles Grandison*. That book was full of fine but ultimately local insights. Jane Austen's triumph was to make everything connect. She threw his 'precious particles', as James called them,[11] into the kaleidoscope of her mind, and created there the sparkling, shifting scenes that make up her book, *Pride and Prejudice*.

5

Mansfield Park

Jane Austen transposes *Grandison* into a more serious key in *Mansfield Park*. In *Sense and Sensibility* she had sometimes assimilated Richardson's work, sometimes not; in *Pride and Prejudice* she had questioned it, broken it up, redistributed it, and made it her own. Now, when for a third time she turns to *Grandison*, it seems part of her own self. I shall show how her re-creating mind modifies Richardson's marriage plot and its participating characters, and once the connection is established, speculate more freely on four matters vital to both.[1]

'And the Women but barely swim'

Fanny Price like Harriet Byron is 'adopted' into a Northamptonshire family, a compliment to Richardson with which Jane Austen persisted even though it meant dispensing with the useful dramatic device of hedgerows.[2] Each heroine thus acquires two 'sisters', and a 'brother' with whom they rapidly and unilaterally fall in love. Both spend most of their books watching their men become bound to rivals, until the wonderful catastrophes arranged for them by the authors. Clementina della Porretta's sacrifice returns Sir Charles to Harriet, while Mary Crawford's mockery of Edmund Bertram allows him to appreciate Fanny.

Richardson's second heroine supplies further details for Fanny's story, for she too must hear proposals from a man agreeable only to others. The families appeal to grateful duty, persuading their daughters to marry where they cannot love. Sir Thomas Bertram like the Porretta family finally recommends 'no farther attempts to influence or persuade', leaving the event to Henry Crawford's 'assiduities' (356). This word is frequently used of Clementina's unwelcome suitor the Count of Belvedere.

Jane Austen seems here to be conflating Richardson's two main heroines into one, along with hints of Sir Charles's young ward Emily Jervois, who has a slatternly mother like Fanny's, and her love of the hero resulting from gratitude to a guardian, like that of Fanny for Edmund.

Henry Crawford's proposal to Fanny nicely exemplifies Jane Austen's trick of combining. For the third time in her novels she turns to Sir Hargrave's unwelcome proposal, but with Clementina in mind picks out different things. Most obviously she substitutes loving compulsion for Richardson's kidnapping,[3] but Henry's kindness to William and Sir Thomas's paternal appeal are just as binding on Fanny as Sir Hargrave's cloak on Harriet.

Richardson's scene (Volume I, letter xvii) comes almost at the start, whereas Jane Austen, with advantages for complexity of motive and feeling, places hers at the junction of her second and third volumes. In both cases the man is rakish, vain, witty, fine in manner, and a 'laugher' with a history of conquest. Though never before serious on serious subjects, he now proposes to a good woman, praises her extravagantly, boasts of personal and financial merits (Sir Thomas points out Henry's for him), admits past error, and promises reform after the marriage has taken place. Anticipating grateful acceptance, he is bewildered when the heroine, her heart elsewhere, says she cannot like him well enough to marry him. When pushed, she adds that she cannot approve his morals. Accused of being too modest or of loving another, she complains of the indelicacy of persisting in a proposal to an unwilling woman. Though undefended by her guardian, distressed, and called proud and ungrateful, the heroine will not marry where she cannot love.

Briefly to expand on the likenesses. Henry, says Sir Thomas in the painful interview scene (311–25), is 'a young man of sense, of character, of temper, of manners, and of fortune', an echo of Sir Hargrave's claims about himself (I.113). The heroines' contrariness in refusing such merit seems worse when Harriet says simply that Sir Hargrave does not 'hit my fancy', and Fanny that she 'cannot like' Henry. Sir Hargrave's angry comparison of Harriet's response to Tom Brown's impudent verse, '*I do not like thee Dr.* Fell',[4] and Sir Thomas's rebuke that Fanny's answer is very strange, force both women to speak the criticism they had tactfully avoided. Harriet has not 'that opinion of your morals ... That I must have of those of the man ... to whose guidance [I must] intrust my *future*'; Fanny, who cannot explain that she has reason to think ill of his principles, says that she 'cannot approve his character' (349).

The amazed Sir Thomas Bertram, who probably acquires the name of his estate from Sir Thomas Mansfield, a minor character in *Grandison*,[5] counter-attacks with the 'general reflexions on the sex' of Richardson's tyrannical father, Sir Thomas Grandison (I. 348). Implying that Fanny is 'self-willed, obstinate, selfish, and ungrateful', as Sir Hargrave accuses Harriet of *'Pride, Cruelty, Ingratitude'*, Sir Thomas says in reproach, 'I had thought you peculiarly free from wilfulness of temper, self-conceit, and every tendency to that independence of spirit, which prevails so much in modern days, even in young women, and which in young women is offensive and disgusting beyond all common offence'. Sir Thomas Grandison railed with like vehemence against the public 'gaiety and extravagance' of the modern women when his own daughters showed independence in the marriage choice (I. 331, 340–1). Jane Austen also carefully acknowledged Richardson's *Rambler*, no. 97, on the same subjects in chapter iii of *Northanger Abbey*.

Harriet and Fanny refuse for good reasons. Sir Hargrave, complains Harriet, lays 'a title to my gratitude from the passion he avowed for me', just as Fanny later asks sharply, 'was I to be – to be in love with him the moment he said he was with me? How was I to have an attachment at his service, as soon as it was asked for?'. As Harriet declares, it 'is a very poor plea ... as you yourself would think ... were one of our sex, whom you could not like, to claim a return of love from you upon it'. Fanny too argues that 'we think very differently of the nature of women, if they can imagine a woman so very soon capable of returning an affection as this seems to imply' (353). Harriet knows that she 'can never make you happy, nor you me' (I. 114); Fanny, assured that Henry will make her happy, maintains as firmly that 'we should be miserable' (348). Both beg their suitors never to raise the matter again.

An appeal to Harriet's vanity, 'how many ladies ... and fine ladies too, have sigh'd in secret for Sir Hargrave! You will have the glory ... of fixing the wavering heart of a man who has done, and is capable of doing, a great deal of mischief' (I. 62), just as for

Sir Charles 'so many virgin hearts have sighed in vain! – And what a triumph to our Sex is this, as well as to my Harriet!' (III. 68), reappears in Mary Crawford's similar vocabulary and sentiments: 'And then, Fanny, the glory of fixing one who has been shot at by so many; of having it in one's power to pay off the debts of one's sex! Oh, I am sure it is not in woman's nature to refuse such a triumph'. Harriet responds with compassion for the ladies who sigh for him in secret (I. 62), nor can Fanny think well of a man who sports with any woman's feelings (363).

More attractive to both heroines is the notion that as married women they can make their suitors' fortunes a blessing to multitudes (I. 64). Fanny warms to Henry when he seems 'the friend of the poor and oppressed! Nothing could be more grateful to her' (404). His introducing of himself to tenants on his estate is worthy of the great Sir Charles Grandison himself, he who proposes 'to take a personal Survey of his whole estate. He will make himself acquainted with every tenant, and even cottager' (III. 288).

But Harriet and Fanny stand firm. Fanny shrinks from 'such an office of high responsibility' (351) as to reform a rake by marrying him, and Richardson too, asserting that reformation does not hold, said that contrite rakes prove unsociable from guilt (I. 429–30). Mary Crawford similarly fears that even if married to Fanny, Henry will grow like his wicked uncle the Admiral (296), and indeed he does feel 'vexation that must rise sometimes to self-reproach, and regret to wretchedness' (468–9). Richardson allowed his rake a brief death-bed repentance (III. 461), but the remorse of Jane Austen's is prolonged:

That punishment, the public punishment of disgrace, should in a just measure attend *his* share of the offence, is, we know, not one of the barriers, which society gives to virtue. In this world, the penalty is less equal than could be wished; but without presuming to look forward to a juster appointment hereafter, we may fairly consider a man of sense like Henry Crawford to be providing for himself no small portion of vexation and regret – vexation that must rise sometimes to self-reproach, and regret to wretchedness …

Henry's proposal like Sir Hargrave's fails, but he lives on, after losing 'the woman whom he had rationally, as well as passionately loved' (468–9).

Jane Austen's plot is a marriage quest like many another novelist's, but her working of it resembles Richardson's. Harriet Byron, who has 'a very high notion of the marriage-state', hears Sir Charles declare himself 'a great friend to the married state; especially with regard to [the female] sex'. He is 'for having everybody marry' (I. 25, 290, 428). In *Mansfield Park* however, it is Henry Crawford who says in cynical echo, 'Nobody can think more highly of the matrimonial state than myself'; Mary who makes the mercenary qualification, 'I would have every body marry if they can do it properly ... every body should marry as soon as they can do it to advantage'; and Sir Thomas Bertram who is 'an advocate for early marriages, where there are means in proportion' (43, 317). These speakers endanger the tone, but their advice to the female sex is generally good, as Richardson and Charlotte Lucas knew. In a world where women's only way to status and comfortable independence is marriage, the choice is crucial, the hazard grave. *Grandison* and *Mansfield Park* both explain how to avoid the quest's traps and difficulties, that is marriages for money, marriages as escape from parental restraint, and marriages based on physical attraction alone. Both books explore the difficulties of being the first to love, or of loving another before or after marriage, and both write sympathetically of the problem that there are few good men about.

Mercenary marriages are attacked as '*Smithfield bargains*' in *Grandison* (III. 28); Maria Bertram, whose happiness centres on a large income, causes Sir Thomas's revulsion from 'ambitious and mercenary connections' (471) and the darkest scenes in Jane Austen's work. Mercenary marriages seem almost pagan. Where Charlotte Grandison describes women marrying as 'milk-white heifers led to sacrifice' (III. 235), Maria reminds Mary of 'some of the old heathen heroes, who after performing great exploits in a foreign land, offered sacrifices to the gods on their safe return' (108).

Maria is 'prepared for matrimony by an hatred of home, restraint, and tranquillity'. 'Independence was more needful than ever; the want of it at Mansfield more sensibly felt. She was less and less able to endure the restraint which her father imposed. The liberty which his absence had given was now become absolutely necessary. She must escape from him and Mansfield as soon as possible, and find consolation in fortune and consequence, bustle and the world, for a wounded spirit' (202). Richardson had put similar sentiments into the mouth of his Charlotte Grandison. 'At that time, our life was a confined one; and I girlishly wished for Liberty – MATRIMONY and LIBERTY – Girlish connexion! as I have since thought' (I. 406). Maria, who pushes past the iron gate and over the ha-ha into the world beyond, is recognisably one of Richardson's company of women who 'marry not so much now-a-days for Love, or fitness of tempers, as for the liberty of gadding abroad, with less censure, and less controul'. She too will 'gallop over hedge and ditch; leap fences; and duty, decency, and discretion, are trodden under foot!' (II. 553, I. 343).

Grandison's third warning is about 'the foible our sex in general love to indulge for handsome men. For, O my dear, womens eyes are sad giddy things; and will run away with their sense, with their understandings, beyond the power of being over-taken either by stop thief, or hue-and-cry' (I. 182). Richardson took his own advice when he made Lord G. good though un-attractive like Hickman, but he bowed to a friend's plea for beauty to reflect worth when he made Sir Charles a rake in his address and a saint in his heart (III. 93). Jane Austen too admits the attraction of appearance when she makes Henry Crawford 'the gentleman, with a pleasing address' (44). His acting and his agreeable manners at Portsmouth affect even Fanny, while Maria is completely taken in.

Marriage themes in *Grandison* and *Mansfield Park* centre on first and second love. Charlotte Grandison attacks romantic in-flexibility as '*first* Love, *first* Flame, but *first* Folly' (III. 228) in an outspoken comment applicable to Harriet, who loves Sir Charles but may be brought to love Lord D., as well as to Clemen-tina, who loves Sir Charles but may learn to love the Count of Belvedere. If Sir Charles married Clementina, laughs Charlotte, 'Pho, pho, never fear but Harriet would have married before my Brother and Clementina had seen the face of their second boy' (III. 406). Jane Austen is equally casual when she writes,

Would [Henry] have deserved more, there can be no doubt that more would have been obtained; especially when that marriage had taken place, which would have given him the assistance of her conscience in subduing her first inclination, and brought them very often together. Would he have persevered, and uprightly, Fanny must have been his

reward – and a reward very voluntarily bestowed – within a reasonable
period from Edmund's marrying Mary.   (467)

Harriet herself doubts that she could ever learn to love Lord D.,
because Sir Charles was 'my first Love; and I never will have any
other ... is not the man Sir Charles Grandison?' (II. 542); Clementina cannot easily transfer her affections to a second love, just as
Fanny's affection is 'engaged elsewhere' (231). Richardson
advances three unsatisfactory solutions to his problems, marrying Harriet to her first love Sir Charles, postponing Clementina's
marriage beyond the confines of the book, and creating for his
third inflexible romancer Emily Jervois a 'second Sir Charles
Grandison', Sir Edward Beauchamp (I. 440). Fanny's constancy
to her first love is rewarded also, while Mary like Clementina
finds no other suitor good enough.

Even Sir Charles complains that Clementina 'was to me, what
I may truly call, a first Love' (III. 10), a selfish parade of grief before
the very person it will pain most. That selfishness reappears in
Edmund's groan, 'Fanny, think of *me*!' (446). Sir Charles's
divided heart so provoked Richardson's correspondents that they
may have forced revisions on the seventh volume[6] to prompt Sir
Charles's consciousness of 'the delicacy of my situation, with
regard to what some would deem a divided or double Love'.
Charlotte jeers at him for speaking carefully of Clementina and
Harriet as sister-excellences: 'Betwixt her excellencies and yours,
how must my brother's soul be divided! ... Ass and two bundles
of hay, Harriet. But my brother is a nobler animal: He won't
starve. But I think, in my conscience, he should have you both'
(III. 77, 195). Oblivious to Harriet's suffering both before and after
their marriage, Sir Charles has 'at *best*, a divided heart!', she
thinks bitterly (III. 52). When Edmund urges Fanny to sisterly
friendship with Mary, 'the two dearest objects I have on earth',
he is equally unaware of the 'stab' he inflicts on Fanny (264).

Harriet's hopes of marrying her first love derive in an extraordinary fashion from *Paradise Lost*, IX. 911–16, where Adam
rejects the idea of taking a second Eve. Harriet, justifying her
victory over a 'fallen' Clementina, believes that Sir Charles
would have acted differently:

if there be a fault *between* them, it must be *all* that person's; and he will
not, if it be possible for him to avoid it, be a sharer in it? Do you

think ... that had he been the first man, he would have been so com-plaisant to his Eve as *Milton makes Adam* [So contrary to that part of his character, which made him accuse the woman to the Almighty ...] – To taste the forbidden fruit, because he would not be separated from her, in her punishment, tho' all *posterity* were to suffer by it? – No; it is my opinion, that your brother would have had gallantry enough to his fallen spouse, to have made him extremely regret her lapse; but that he would have done *his own duty*, were it but for the sake of posterity, and left it to the Almighty, if such had been his pleasure, to have annihilated his first Eve, and given him a second ... (II. 609)

Milton may also have shown Richardson the way to dispense with the first Eve. His tract on divorce, especially Book I, chapter viii, which advises divorcing 'an Idolatrous Heretic' for fear of spiritual contagion, could have influenced Catholic Clementina's vision of herself as the spurned woman from the Song of Solomon (II. 247).

Whatever the sources, some complicated group of ideas about polygamy, divorce and remarriage gives rise to Sir Charles's un-comfortable awareness that he comes with a very ill grace 'to of-fer myself, and so soon after [Clementina's] refusal, to a Lady of Miss Byron's delicacy. I should certainly have acted more laudably, respecting my own character *only*, had I taken at least the usual time of a *Widower-Love'*. Yet what did he do, he cries defensively, 'but declare a passion, that would have been, but for one obstacle, which is now removed, as fervent as man ever knew?' (III. 57). Faced with the same problem, Jane Austen simply brazens her way out:

I purposely abstain from dates on this occasion, that every one may be at liberty to fix their own, aware that the cure of unconquerable passions, and the transfer of unchanging attachments, must vary much as to time in different people. – I only intreat every body to believe that exactly at the time when it was quite natural that it should be so, and not a week earlier, Edmund did cease to care about Miss Crawford, and became as anxious to marry Fanny, as Fanny herself could desire. (470)

The outspoken Olivia calls Sir Charles a 'widower-bachelor'. 'Un-worthy Grandison! Unworthy I *will* call you; because you cannot merit the Love of such a spotless heart' (II. 647). Of Edmund, fallen in love again, Jane Austen says essentially the same: 'Even in the midst of his late infatuation, he had acknowledged Fanny's mental superiority ... She was of course only too good for him' (471).

The transfer of attachments from a first love to a second is only acceptable before marriage, or so a parliament of young women in *Grandison* decides. 'Suppose, after I have vowed Love to a man quite indifferent to me, I should meet with the very one, the kindred soul, who must irresistably claim my whole heart? I will not suspect myself of any possibility of misconduct ... But must I not, in such a case, be for ever miserable?'. Harriet's grandmother Mrs Shirley quickly picks up the reference to *The Princess of Cleves*. It is not impossible, she says, that a woman could meet with 'persons in some external accomplishments superior to the deserving man' she has married, 'But will you suffer your eye to lead you into misery *then*, when an additional tie of duty forbids its wandering?'. If so, why not now? 'What think you of those girls, who blast all the hopes of their fond parents, by eloping with a well-drest captain, a spruce dancing-master, or a handsome player?' (III. 399–400). Jane Austen is equally severe on Maria's elopement with Henry, a man of external accomplishments superior to her husband, Rushworth. Henry resembles Sir Hargrave Pollexfen in many particulars, and like him ruins a young creature 'already under vows of marriage' (I. 63). 'Horrid!' thinks Harriet when Sir Hargrave claims that she is 'a runaway wife, eloped to, and intending to elope from, a masquerade, to her adulterer' (I. 166). Jane Austen uses the same emotional word or its cognates five times about her own runaway wife Maria (440–2).[7]

If the objects of first loves marry, characters must suppress adulterous passions. Emily has to be reminded, and Clementina too, that Sir Charles 'actually is, the husband of another woman' (III. 396). But when in his last volume Richardson brought Clementina to England, he may not have anticipated how it might be read. It is certainly odd to watch Clementina suddenly repudiate Olivia's 'disgraceful imputations' of '*culpable* inclinations', or Mrs Beaumont warn Clementina that 'what Olivia has hinted, the *world* will hint' (III. 414–5). Where Clementina prudently retreats to Italy, Maria, who is equally the subject of the world's talk, loses all 'on the side of character' (451). Sir Charles asks Clementina, 'will not ill-will and slander follow you into the most sacred retirements?' (III. 428); Maria withdraws to Mrs Norris, 'to a retirement and reproach, which could allow no second spring of hope or character' (464).

Such are women's difficulties in the pursuit of happiness. But the most challenging is the most pragmatic, how to find good men in a bad world. If affinity is essential to love, what is one to do in 'a great dearth of good men' (II. 348), when as Charlotte Grandison complains, 'we have our lots cast in an age of Petits Maitres, and Insignificants'? 'The men, in short, are sunk, my dear; and the Women but barely swim'. 'Women must not encourage Fops and Fools. They must encourage Men of Sense only ... But what will they do, if their lot be cast only among Foplings? If the Men of Sense do not offer themselves?' (I. 180, 230). Harriet resists her foppish suitor in self-defence, not out of intolerance. No more will Fanny give herself to Henry Crawford, not the 'man of sense' he thinks himself (297), but one whose manners, principles, and character she disapproves.

Sir Charles and Edmund are too few by three for Harriet, Clementina, Emily, Fanny, and Mary. Richardson creates another Sir Charles for Emily, and the Count of Belvedere for Clementina, but what of all the rest? He admits that Sir Charles's marriage 'would break half a score hearts' (I. 182), an image Jane Austen slyly transfers to Henry: 'Oh! the envyings and heart-burnings of dozens and dozens!' (360). As there is 'but *one* Sir Charles Grandison in the world, were his scheme of Protestant Nunneries put in execution, all the rest of womankind, who had seen him with distinction, might retire into cloisters', for 'can the woman be happy in a second choice, whose first was Sir Charles Grandison?' (III. 239, 396). So too Mary Crawford is 'long in finding among the dashing representatives, or idle heir ap-parents, who were at the command of her beauty, and her 20,000*l*. any one who could satisfy the better taste she had acquired at Mansfield ... or put Edmund Bertram sufficiently out of her head' (469).

If a good man sets intolerably high standards, so does a good woman, for as Harriet's disappointed suitors complain she is 'a perfect paragon', a 'nonsuch', a 'jewel' (I. 38, 110, 120). Edmund too is spoilt 'for common female society ... You and Miss Crawford have made me too nice' (355). He is wrong about Miss Crawford but right about Fanny Price,[8] the pearl of great price which a man must give up everything to gain. 'Fanny was worth it all', thinks Henry; 'there is not a better girl in the world', says Mary (336, 293). But Henry (like the base Indian) 'throw[s] away ... such a woman as he will never see again' (455). Just as Harriet's mind, superior to the minds of almost all other women, makes her 'an example to a world that wants it' (III.213), so Fanny, more wise and discreet than others, is 'the perfect model of a woman, which I have always believed you born for' (197, 347).

Heroines are of course ideal. Harriet's charms of person are platonically matched by her charms of mind (III.274),[9] and Fanny shows 'a youth of mind as lovely as of person' (326). Even if Harriet's features and complexion had not been as fine as they were, her 'Soul shining out in her lovely aspect, joined with the ease and gracefulness of her Motion, would have made her as many admirers as beholders' (I.12). Similarly 'Fanny's attractions increased – increased two-fold – for the sensibility which beautified her complexion and illumined her countenance, was an attraction in itself' (235).

Richardson disarms our unbelief by Cassio's trick in praise of Desdemona. 'How have I despised the romancing Poets for their unnatural descriptions of the Eyes of their heroines! But I have thought these descriptions, tho' absurd enough in conscience, less absurd (allowing something for poetical licence) ever since I beheld those of Miss Harriet Byron' (I.12). Romantic terms work their magic even while they are being disowned – Richardson places them in the mouth of a professional gallant, a device imitated by Jane Austen when she makes Henry, the most extravagant admirer of Fanny's manners and mind, 'quite the hero of an old romance, [who] glories in his chains', as Mary says (360) in echo of Sir Hargrave Pollexfen (I.85). In this romantic mode Harriet is an angel, a goddess on whom sun and world depend (I.13, 71), a divine intercessor to the rakes. Fanny too has 'some touches of the angel', which briefly make Henry a better man (344).

Fanny's sexual readiness is signalled by allusions to *The Rape of the Lock*, as in Marianne Dashwood before her. Henry notices with the eye of a lover 'one little curl falling forward' on Fanny's neck, and vies with his rival Edmund for the role of Pope's Baron over whose chain, whose marriage chain, will fit through the ring of the 'very pretty amber cross' that Fanny wears round her 'lovely throat' (296, 254, 259). This is indeed a cross that Jews might kiss and infidels adore. When Fanny visited Portsmouth, writes Mary, 'the balmy air, the sparkling sea, and your sweet looks and conversation were altogether in the most delicious harmony, and afforded sensations which are to raise ecstacy even in retrospect' (415); Belinda smiled and all the world was gay. 'The 'brisk soft wind, and bright sun, occasionally clouded for a minute; and every thing ... so beautiful under the influence of such a sky, the effects of the shadows pursuing each other ... the ever-varying hues of the sea now at high water, dancing in its glee and dashing against the ramparts with so fine a sound' (409) reflect Pope's sun-beams trembling on the flowing tides, his smooth flowing waves and gently playing zephyrs, above all his light disporting in 'ever-mingling Dies' and 'new transient Colours' shimmering around Belinda (III. 47–68). But it is Mary who plays the fatal game of cards, Mary who like a woman of spirit stakes her last. Her excitement, her pyrrhic victory when 'the game was hers, and only did not pay her for what she had given to secure it', involves like Belinda's a knave and a queen. She and Belinda may exult, but Fanny, by not parting with her queen, wins the final game and Edmund too (242–4).[10] Mary plays Pope's Clarissa when she helps 'Baron' Henry in his attempt to seduce the heroine, but scorning Edmund, she dies a maid.

The marriage plot requires that one paragon find another. Sir Charles is '*nearly* perfect' (I. 185), some fallible humanity being forced upon him by Richardson's correspondents. Jane Austen, whom pictures of perfection made sick and wicked (*Letters*, 23 March 1817), is more subtle than Richardson when she shows Edmund as pliant and self-deluding, though better than his fellows.[11] Sir Charles, above quarrelling with the world for trifles, is 'still more above making such compliances with it, as would impeach either his honour or conscience' (I. 182); Edmund descends from his 'moral elevation' over the play, worrying only that his capitulation will *look* absurd, that it will wear the *appearance* of inconsistency (158, 154). Sir Charles is always right, Edmund is often wrong. He gives in to the theatricals, he misjudges Maria and Julia, he falls for Mary Crawford, he thinks that Henry will do for Fanny, he fails to see that Fanny is suitable and available. But since he is a sensitive friend and a man of principle, we can hope that he becomes good enough for Fanny on the analogy of Dr Grant, whose own sermons made him better than he would otherwise have been.

Fanny finds not a perfect man, but one readier to learn than Sir Charles. Richardson acutely saw that men in his novels matter only as they complement or thwart the heroines' desire for liberty, which is impossible at home or in the single state. To be free they require not so much a perfect as a compatible man, loving, rich, and generous enough to enlarge their ability to do good. In the same way Jane Austen's heroines are not mercenary as some say. They need a husband's money as well as his status to change from dependents into active moral and social beings.

So much for the marriage plot. Other details in *Mansfield Park* are only to be explained in terms of *Grandison*, for instance Mary's needless jealousy of the Miss Owens (286–7) which is so similar to Harriet's of the Canterbury ladies (I. 291). Fanny's lack of strength is foreshadowed by Harriet's being easily 'over-fatigued' by long walks. On one occasion Harriet and Clementina are 'surprised by a sudden shower of rain; a violent one; a thunder-shower: No shelter: They were forced to run for it towards a distant tree; which, when they approached, they found wet thro'; as they both were. So they made the best of their way to the house; were seen at a little distance, making the appearance of frighted hares' (III. 419). Jane Austen strips this scene of unseemly farce and turns it to different ends when Fanny, 'overtaken by a heavy shower ... endeavouring to find shelter under the branches and lingering leaves of an oak', offers Mary the delightful sight of 'Miss Price dripping with wet in the vestibule' (205–6).

Harriet contributes some of her story and character to Fanny. So does Richardson's sweet enthusiast Clementina. A creation in the sublime mode, passionately religious, and given to broken hyperbole, Clementina is a kind of Mary Magdalene suffering for her love. Fanny's heightened sensibility, tears, debility, suffering, 'enthusiasm', and 'rhapsodizing' are very much like hers (113, 209). But Jane Austen alters melodrama into realism when instead of Clementina rejecting the man she loves for the sake of religion and country, Fanny rejects the man she does *not* love for incompatibilities in 'nature, education, and habit' (327). The 'kneeling father ... sighing mother; generous, but entreating brothers' (III. 326) who urge Clementina to marry the Count of Belvedere are Englished among the Bertrams, and isn't there mockery of Clementina's pathetic 'he is actually gone? Gone for

ever? No, not for ever!' (II. 127) in Sir Thomas's uncomprehending hope that 'the deserted chair of each young man might
exercise [Fanny's] tender enthusiasm, and ... the remaining cold
pork bones and mustard in William's plate, might but divide her
feelings with the broken egg-shells in Mr. Crawford's' (282)?

Grandison's shy ward Emily Jervois may have contributed to
Fanny as I have said, but her story also opens possibilities for
Fanny's sister Susan. Emily plans to live with Harriet's family
as a 'second Harriet'. 'How you would rejoice them all, my
Emily! and, if we must part, *me*', cries Harriet, 'to have my Emily
be to my dearest friends what their Harriet so happily was!'. Sir
Charles too is gratified by this 'desire to restore to Mrs Shirley,
Mrs Selby, and Mr Selby, the grand-daughter and niece I have
robbed them of' (III. 321–3). Jane Austen eases the transition in
the same way, her version flickering with irony. 'Selfishly dear
as [Fanny] had long been to Lady Bertram, she could not be parted
with willingly by *her* ... But it was possible to part with her,
because Susan remained to supply her place. – Susan became the
stationary niece – delighted to be so!' (472).

In *Grandison* Richardson sets a witty woman against his good
one, but *Mansfield Park* makes them rivals. Charlotte Grandison
and Mary Crawford share more than their dark lively eyes and
clear complexions (I. 179; 44). Both are musical, Charlotte
playing the harpsichord and Mary the harp[12] on occasions that
tell us as much about them as their skill. Both are revealed by
a card game based on trumps (II. 389; 243), both are distinguished
by vivacity, wit and teasing. For instance Charlotte teases Harriet
about her love for Sir Charles (I. 271–5) just as painfully as Mary
teases Fanny about Henry (362). 'Wit ... is a dangerous weapon',
says Sir Charles. 'I was bespeaking your attention upon a very
serious subject ... and you could be able to say something that
became only the mouth of an unprincipled woman to say' (II. 86);
'your lively mind can hardly be serious even on serious subjects',
says Edmund in rebuke to Mary Crawford (87).

Jane Austen links 'lively, agreeable manners, and probably ...
morals and discretion to suit' (450) to suggest like Richardson
that playfulness of manner can reveal the mind to be tainted
(269). Wit, though attracting and attractive at first, proves, as
Locke said, to be the antithesis of judgment, not so much
Shaftesbury's test of truth as its destruction. '*Wit* and *wisdom*

are two different things', wrote Richardson (I. 38), 'Wisdom is better than Wit', wrote Jane Austen to Fanny Knight in a letter of 18 November 1814. Neither Charlotte Grandison nor Mary Crawford may be trusted. Though Charlotte reforms, Mary stands in the door-way calling to Edmund for all the world like Spenser's singing laughing wanton Phaedria to his temperate Guyon.

At this point the Charlotte-ish lineaments of Mary Crawford merge with those of Richardson's Olivia, an heiress ruined like Mary by too early an independence. Sir Charles coolly discourages her attempt to seduce him, just as Edmund finds it the 'impulse of the moment to resist' Mary (453–60). Olivia's 'behaviour afterwards was that of the true passionate woman; now ready to rave, now in tears. I *cannot*, Dr. Bartlett, *descend to particulars*. A man, who loves the Sex; who has more compassion than vanity in his nature; who can value (even generally faulty) persons for the qualities that are laudable in them, must be desirous to *draw a veil* over the weaknesses of such' (II. 622). Over Mary's attempt Jane Austen draws as prompt a veil. 'Let other pens dwell on guilt and misery. I quit such odious subjects as soon as I can' (461).

Sentiments like those of Sir Charles to Olivia in Volume V, letter xli appear in Edmund's 'sermon' to Mary (458). Sir Charles, 'the Friend of your Fame, the Friend of your Soul', tenderly wishes her happiness in his 'friendly ... brotherly expostulation'. God and nature have done their parts by her, her own should not be wanting. 'To what purpose live we, if not to grow wiser?' he asks. 'Shall it be said, that your great fortune, your abundance, has been a snare to you? That you would have been a happier, nay a *better* woman, had not God so bountifully blessed you?' Edmund too, aware that he sacrifices a 'friendship', wants to carry away 'the right of tenderness and esteem'. Like Sir Charles he wishes her well, hoping that 'she might soon learn to think more justly, and not owe the most valuable knowledge we could any of us acquire – the knowledge of ourselves and our duty, to the lessons of affliction'. Like Sir Charles speaking of Olivia, he ascribes Mary's delightfulness to nature, her errors to nurture. 'How excellent she would have been, had she fallen into good hands earlier'.

Olivia accepts Sir Charles's criticism, though objecting to one 'officious' and 'obnoxious' passage; Mary too is angered, changing countenance and turning 'extremely red'. Olivia realises that by 'hoping to prove herself more, she made herself appear less than woman. She despised that affectation, that hypocrisy, in her Sex, which unpenetrating eyes attribute to modesty and shame'; Edmund criticises Mary for a similar lack of 'feminine' or 'modest' loathings. Olivia ridicules Sir Charles as a 'widower-bachelor', and in a delightful moment of dramatic irony Fanny and Edmund are quite agreed about 'the lasting effect, the indelible impression, which such a disappointment must make on his mind. Time would undoubtedly abate somewhat of his sufferings, but still it was a sort of thing which he never could get entirely the better of; and as to his ever meeting with any other woman who could – it was too impossible to be named but with indignation'. Olivia sends Sir Charles back to Harriet; Fanny's friendship is all that Edmund has to cling to.

The remembrance of *Grandison* clearly affects the story of *Mansfield Park* and its characters. Jane Austen also shares Richardson's belief in the power of education and of the social duties, she shows like him an ideal world shaped by ways as much religious as secular, and she uses his methods to convey her vision to the reader.

'My Tutor, my Brother, my Friend!'

Educational determinism controls both *Grandison* and *Mansfield Park*. Richardson, who quoted part of Locke's treatise in *Pamela II*, believes like him that the infant is father to the man, and that true knowledge is morality. From seven to fourteen, he says in *Grandison*, 'the foundations of all female goodness are to be laid'. From information about his characters' education, we may confidently deduce their futures. Harriet's happy fate is clear, for instance, when she is said to have been taught by her worthy grandmother and her grandfather, a man of 'universal learning' and 'as polite as learned' (I. 13). The Grandison sisters are brought up by their Roman matron of a mother, pious, patient, and loving, and though Caroline is impressed with enough virtue to last, Charlotte's flightiness results from her mother's early death. Emily is removed from her bad mother to profitable propinquity with Sir Charles, Olivia is wild and uncontrolled from early independence, and Clementina the spoilt darling is deranged by a love-crisis that Harriet has the stamina to endure.

Jane Austen's message is essentially the same as Richardson's. All that happens to her characters may be ascribed to education.[13] If Harriet and Fanny are 'natural geniuses' on whom learning and example exert their influence, Fanny's sister Susan, preserved in the midst of negligence and error by 'the natural light of the mind which could so early distinguish justly' (395), may be improved by her teacher Fanny, and a regular course of reading from the library.

Richardson and Jane Austen both acknowledge the erotic appeal of shaping young minds. Fanny's tutor Edmund is like Clementina's hero and mentor Sir Charles, as Lascelles saw (pp. 66–8). He chooses *Paradise Lost* for his text (II. 144), for Adam and Eve are the very model of the pedagogic love relationship. Walden the arrogant pedant explains that to have women 'come to their husbands, to their brothers, and even to their lovers, when they have a mind to know anything out of their way, and beg to be instructed and informed, inspireth them with ... becoming humility ... and giveth us importance with them' (I. 70). Jane Austen, appropriating these words and sentiments for Fanny's 'brother', lover, and husband-to-be Edmund, infuses them with sympathetic warmth: 'Loving, guiding, protecting her, as he had been doing ever since her being ten years old, her mind in so great a degree formed by his care, and her comfort depending on his kindness, an object to him of such close and peculiar interest, [she was] dearer by all his own importance with her' (470).

'You had rather (and I believe most men are of your mind) have a woman you could teach', says Harriet to Walden (I. 51); Edmund enjoys playing Pygmalion to his adoring Galatea. If Clementina runs mad for 'my Tutor, my Brother, my Friend!' (II. 564), in return for Edmund's educational services Fanny 'loved him better than any body in the world except William; her heart was divided between the two' (22). The comic variation in *Mansfield Park* is that Henry plans to 'excite the first ardours of her young, unsophisticated mind!' (235–6), oblivious to the fact that these ardours have already been excited at the unsophisticated age of ten. Sir Thomas thinks that her education and manners are his alone (276), and Lady Bertram imagines that she wrought the transformation by sending Chapman. But Chapman came too late, and the only advice Fanny ever received was the need to accept such a very unexceptionable offer as Henry's (333). Fanny is Edmund's creature. 'Having formed her mind and gained her affections, he had a good chance of her thinking like him' (64). On this affinity they will share a life.

Bad education causes a second fall, or even a first one if as Locke says moral qualities are not innate. Plants, like Richardson's organic metaphors for the mind,[14] flourish in Fanny's schoolroom, which is white as a *tabula rasa* (151). Mrs Norris is wrong to ascribe Fanny's beauty to 'transplantation' to Mansfield (276), for Fanny's goodness and education are complementary. But that noble tree the moor park can bear poor fruit in the garden of Mrs Norris, just as the 'promising talents and early information' of Maria and Julia do not help when Lady Bertram fails to teach them, and supply them with an example (54, 19). Mrs Norris, as much a failure at mothering as her two faulty sisters, rushes into this space, provoking Sir Thomas's wretched reflection on the damage his 'anxious and expensive education' has done (463). This false nurturer's name derives from the French 'nourrice' and English 'norris', as Hardy also notes in 'The objects in *Mansfield Park*', while 'Ward' is an equally ironic naming for sisters incapable of 'watching the behaviour, or guarding the happiness of his daughters' (163).

Mary Crawford, deprived of the parents who might more justly have educated her, is exposed rather to the example of Admiral Crawford. He is 'a man of vicious conduct, who chose, instead of retaining his niece, to bring his mistress under his own roof' (41) – Sir Thomas Grandison also kept his son abroad when he took a mistress (I. 321). Even at his most besotted, Edmund knows that '"the influence of [Mary's] former companions makes her seem, gives to her conversation, to her professed opinions, sometimes a tinge of wrong" ... "The effect of education," said Fanny gently ... "Yes, that uncle and aunt! They have injured the finest mind!"' (269). Mary, in a way to be 'cured' by *Mansfield Park*, is led astray by fashionable London companions, though Fanny thinks tartly that she is just as likely to have led *them* astray. Mary's education spoils her natural gifts, leaving her with 'faults of principle ... of blunted delicacy and a corrupted, vitiated mind' (424, 456).

Education in *Grandison* and *Mansfield Park* creates ideal womanhood, as Richardson described it in *Rambler*, no.97. 'Modesty and diffidence, gentleness and meekness, were looked upon as the appropriate virtues characteristick of the sex. And if a forward spirit pushed itself into notice, it was exposed in print as it deserved'. Maria's forward spirit is also exposed in print. Modesty is 'the characteristic of women', he repeats in *Grandison* (III.152). Women may be clever only if they are good, for as Harriet puts it, 'where modesty, delicacy, and a teachable spirit, are preserved, as characteristics of the sex, it need not be thought a disgrace to be supposed to know something' (I.102). Fanny fits this pattern to perfection. She shines like Harriet in one area of creativity permitted to women, familiar letter-writing, and perhaps in the only other one, if her assistance with Lady Bertram's needlework is anything to go by.

Fanny's looks and voice are so 'truly feminine' (169) that she cannot read a man's part. Since for Richardson and Jane Austen 'not feminine' means somehow 'masculine', both attack signs of independence they believe more appropriate to men. In *Grandison*, Richardson uses Lady Mary Wortley Montagu as his model for Miss Barnevelt, a mannish woman who makes advances to Harriet. Horse-riding especially indicates the Amazon,[15] its elevation, power, and ease of motion translating directly into psychological terms. 'The blind god sets you out, where you mean the *best*, on a pacing beast; you amble, prance, parade till your giddy heads turn round; and then you gallop over hedge and ditch; leap fences; and duty, decency, and discretion, are trodden under foot!' (I.343). In *Mansfield Park* it is Mary Crawford who excels at horse-riding: 'I cannot but think that good horsemanship has a great deal to do with the mind', comments Maria with more accuracy than she knows (69). Mary is condemned again by Richardson's criteria in Edmund's mouth. Where once he thought her faulty but 'perfectly feminine', he criticises her for lacking 'feminine – shall I say? ... modest loathings' (64, 455).

Education determines the fate of Richardson's male characters too. Sir Charles, taught on Lockean lines by his mother and his masters, easily resists the corruptions of the Grand Tour. 'Neither a learned, nor what is called a *fine* education', writes Richardson, 'has any other value than as each tends to improve

the morals of men, and to make them wise and good' (I.48).
Morals, in short, 'should take up more of the learner's attention
than they generally do' (III.249). Education can destroy natural
advantage as utterly as the Fall destroyed Adam's, but with each
child one starts anew.

Jane Austen cares as much as Richardson for the education
of her men. Edmund suffers little from his public school and
Oxford education, though critical of their inability to teach
the persuasive presentation of truths (339–40). 'Reading well',
wrote Richardson in the *Correspondence*, is 'a more uncommon
excellence than preaching well ... Why has it not entered into
the heart of some worthy benefactor, as there are professor-
ships of Greek and Latin, to establish one in each University
for lectures in the mother tongue?' (III.237). Of far greater
importance in the book is example, which in the quasi-parental
shape of the Admiral ruins Henry, the 'man of talent', made
'thoughtless and selfish from prosperity and bad example' (328,
115). Raised as a libertine, he has simply nothing to do. Like
Sir Hargrave Pollexfen he flirts, instead of fulfilling his social
duties.

Henry Crawford is very much like the protean, energetic,
Satanic Lovelace.[16] No more than his sister can he think seriously on serious subjects, because of the 'education and adviser' he
has had. His feelings (350–1), or as Richardson would say
his 'passions', have become his guides. 'Ruined by early independence and bad domestic example' (467), he loses Fanny, and
the happiness his gifts deserved. Edmund's exemplar is his
father Sir Thomas Bertram, who even his critics must admit
sacrifices time and health to his duties as a landlord. Where
Henry's plans to be an ideal landlord come quickly to confusion,
Edmund turns talents to useful ends. The reward for his human-
ism is Fanny.

'Careless as a woman and a friend'

The social duties meant duty to God, to oneself, and to one's
neighbour. The exemplary Sir Charles Grandison is pious, and
ensures that others are too. He beautifies the church and slips
away to family prayers (II.7, III.279), whereas Rushworth's
redecorated chapel remains unused:

'It is a pity,' cried Fanny, 'that the custom should have been discontinued. It was a valuable part of former times. There is something in a chapel and chaplain so much in character with a great house, with one's ideas of what such a household should be! A whole family assembling regularly for the purpose of prayer, is fine!'

[Edmund] 'If the master and the mistress do *not* attend themselves, there must be more harm than good in the custom.'   (86–7)

Sir Charles, Fanny, and Edmund are singular in an impious world. Edmund the clergyman-to-be takes on characteristics from both Sir Charles and the reverend Dr Bartlett, for where Sir Charles shows his Christian duty by his practice (II. 379), Edmund will also teach by personal example (248). In Dr Bartlett the fine gentleman is no more separable from the clergyman than it is in Edmund. 'Pity they should be in any of the function!' writes Richardson (I. 229).

In both books the Delphic advice 'know thyself' is the first requisite for fulfilling one's duties. 'I live not to the world', says Sir Charles, 'I live to myself; to the monitor within me' (I. 206). Action in *Grandison* startles by its rarity. That novel is characteristically reflective, self-questioning, anticipatory. Self-knowledge is equally important in *Mansfield Park*. The Bertram sisters, who lack it (19), fall prey to vanity and passion, but Fanny, never believing in her own worth, constantly questioning her own reactions and feelings, trying to anticipate effects from causes, estimating right and wrong, remembering, judging, reasoning, is very like Richardson's 'casuistical' characters.[17] Harriet for instance writes that 'self-partiality has suggested several strong pleas in my favour, indeed by way of extenuation only. How my judge, CONSCIENCE, will determine upon those pleas, when counsel has been heard on both sides, I cannot say. Yet I think, that an acquittal from this brother and sister, would go a great way to make my conscience easy' (I. 186). Self-examination results in the self-awareness by which reciprocal duties of parents and children, masters and servants, husbands and wives, may successfully be carried out.

Relationships between parents and children, education on the one side and grateful obedience on the other, is then thematically vital to both *Grandison* and *Mansfield Park*. Earlier readers of Jane Austen might have seen a significance now lost to us in the servants' corruption from duty and contentment by their masters' play. The third category, duties of the married state, is only anticipated for Fanny and Edmund, but they have already fulfilled other social duties compatible with those of husband and wife, the important duties of friend.

The highest friendship outside marriage is that of brother and sister, a relationship in which women can express a rare equality of feeling.[18] Jane Austen loved her brothers for reasons that I do not mean to diminish, but the intense sibling love in *Mansfield Park* is also remarkable in *Grandison*. Charlotte is proud to descant upon her brother's excellencies (I. 182). Even more strikingly, as soon as Harriet makes a friend of Fowler, Orme, or Sir Charles, she bestows upon him the valuable name of brother. Jane Austen's rhapsody about Fanny's 'unchecked, equal, fearless intercourse' with her brother and friend William, 'an advantage this, a strengthener of love, in which even the conjugal tie is beneath the fraternal. Children of the same family, the same blood, with the same first associations and habits, have some means of enjoyment in their power, which no subsequent connections can supply' (234–5), would not seem odd in a Richardsonian context. Harriet is 'adopted' as third sister to the Grandisons; Fanny, raised from youth as third sister to the Bertrams, has even longer to acquire the associations and habits of the family. By marrying her 'brother', each heroine adds conjugal happiness to fraternal.

'From the first, I called Miss Byron my sister, but she is *more* to me than the dearest sister; and there is a more tender friendship that I aspire to hold with her', says Sir Charles (II. 301); Edmund is similarly struck 'whether it might not be a possible, an hopeful undertaking to persuade her that her warm and sisterly regard for him would be foundation enough for wedded love' (470). 'How delightful the domestic connexion! To bring to the paternal and fraternal dwellings, a sister, a daughter, that shall be received there with tender love', writes Sir Charles (II. 141); Sir Thomas finds that Fanny is 'indeed the daughter that he wanted' (472).

If the relation of 'sister' provides fortuitous closeness, it also throws up barriers. 'His *third* sister! – The repetition has such an officiousness in it', says Harriet bitterly (II. 15), while Clementina, keeping Sir Charles at a distance by calling him 'BROTHER', makes him 'too clearly [see] the *exclusive* force' of the recognition (II. 615). In Jane Austen's version, Mrs Norris is wonderfully sure that no match will result if Fanny and Edmund are brought up as brother and sister (6–7). Edmund needs all the time in the novel to know that Fanny is more than a sister.

Whereas love is the Paphian stimulus, a 'narrower of the heart', a 'selfish Deity' that promotes the self-love of Hobbes or the animal lust of Swift (II. 131, I. 454, 348–9), intellectual and sexless friendship is that 'noblest, that most delicate union of souls!', wrote Richardson in *Grandison*. 'A *Friend* is one of the highest characters that one human creature can shine in to another. There may be *Love*, that tho' it has no view but to honour, yet even in wedlock, ripens not into friendship' (II. 326). Love to Richardson is selfish, isolating, hierarchical, always close to rape and possession, but friendship based on mind is re-assuringly equal. As Sir Charles says in an extraordinarily Cartesian passage,

Supposing, my Charlotte, that all human souls are, in themselves, equal; yet the very design of the different machines in which they are inclosed, is to super-induce a temporary difference on their original equality; a difference adapted to the different purposes for which they are designed by Providence in the present transitory state. When those purposes are at an end, this difference will be at an end too. When Sex ceases, ine-quality of Souls will cease; and women will certainly be on a foot with men, as to intellectuals, in Heaven.   (III. 250)

Charlotte may comment ruefully that this life is probationary indeed, but at least in friendship one can anticipate the delights of Heaven, as to intellectuals, with men.

The words 'friend' and 'friendship' recur constantly in *Mansfield Park*, and with the same weight as in *Grandison*. The lovers Henry, Mary, Maria, Julia, and Yates cause pain to themselves as to others; the friends Fanny and Edmund maintain the social bonds. Edmund thinks of himself as 'one of [Fanny's] oldest friends', but learns that Fanny regards him as her 'only friend' (261, 321). After Mary's betrayal he opens his heart to Fanny as a friend, for her friendship is all he has to cling to (453, 460). Lastly, it is to the 'two young friends' that Sir Thomas gives his blessing (471). And so to the conjugal and fraternal qualities are added those of friend.

Friendship acts through trust. 'The mutual unbosoming of secrets is the cement of faithful Friendship, and true Love', so 'can friendship and reserve be compatible? Surely, No', writes Richardson (II. 165, I. 184). When Clementina promises to tell the truth to her 'brother' and best friend Sir Charles, she cries, 'You, in imitation of the God of us all, require only the heart. My heart shall be as open to you, as if, like Him, you could look into every secret recess of it' (II. 611), and that *'godlike man'* himself *'has nothing to conceal'* (I. 290). Whereas Charlotte's secrecy about Captain Anderson briefly alienates her brother, Harriet's habitual frankness makes friends for her. Jane Austen is of Richardson's party concerning friendship, her parody of sentimental friendship in *Love and Friendship* only proving her wish to test it. Fanny is always honest at least in private, whatever she suppresses in public for the sake of modesty or peace. From their first acquaintance Edmund urges her to speak openly (15), and when she cannot, as in the play scheme or about Mary, all is misery. Conversely, insincerity damages truthful communication whether in a play or in life. Henry, who is by far the best actor, a Satanic shape-changer both on and off the stage, deceives Maria and Julia, takes Fanny in about the necklace, and convinces her his manners have improved. Acting is exhilarating for Henry and Mary, but awkward for Edmund, and impossible for Fanny.

Much has been made of that play, notably by Lionel Trilling. In his article on *Mansfield Park* he regrets the insincerity into which it draws the characters. But Jane Austen's use of the play is more complicated yet. It is simply bad – melodramatic, unrealistic, and sentimental – and Jane Austen is being her usual literary-critical self when she condemns it. Then, as Butler acutely points out (pp. 232–7), it grants characters permission to act out hidden hopes. It also confuses real and fictional worlds, so that Yates's start is called a piece of true acting (182). And when Henry continues to hold Maria's hand, she concludes that he loves her in the way that the character he plays loves hers. Finally, as Edmund complains, they are not professionals but raw amateurs (124). They act badly, they carry their own lives into the roles instead of projecting and perhaps enobling themselves.

Henry, who has no character at all, takes on other people's colouring. In a fit of naval gallantry he tries on William's character, in a fit of gravity, Edmund's, in a fit of improving, Rushworth's.

He plays lover to Fanny and benefactor to William, but briefly. As Jane Austen's favourite poet Crabbe wrote about actors in letter 12 of *The Borough*, a poem from which she had already taken the name of Fanny Price (I. 397–406), an actor can play in 'farce' or 'rant and rapture' any part, Squire Richard and King Richard, knights, queens, monarchs and heroes – like the actor Henry:

I really believe [says Henry] I could be fool enough at this moment to undertake any character that ever was written, from Shylock or Richard III. down to the singing hero of a farce in his scarlet coat and cocked hat. I feel as if I could be any thing or every thing, as if I could rant and storm, or sigh, or cut capers in any tragedy or comedy in the English language.

(123)

Henry is 'determined to take any thing and do my best' (132), just as Crabbe had said that actors 'all engage/ To take each part, and act in every age' (II. 19–20). In Crabbe's damning words he is a 'manufactured man' who plays prince and knave by turns (II. 38, 58). He may convince himself, nearly persuade Fanny, and puzzle many critics, but nothing holds.

Crabbe had also described incompetents like Rushworth, who dressed in his ridiculous blue cloak, cons his lines with pain, and sees his mistress flirt:

> Nor is there lack of labour. To rehearse,
> Day after day, poor scraps of prose and verse;
> To bear each other's spirit, pride, and spite;
> To hide in rant the heart-ache of the night;
> To dress in gaudy patch-work, and to force
> The mind to think upon the appointed course;
> This is laborious, and may be defined
> The bootless labour of the thriftless mind.   (II. 89–96)

The billiard room is not the only stage in *Mansfield Park*. The chapel, its crimson velvet recalling the theatre where Jane Austen had recently looked for Crabbe (*Letters*, 15 September 1813), provides a setting for characters to rehearse a marriage. The Restoration set of diverging paths in the wilderness, too, allows groups of characters to emerge, regroup, and disappear, with one still small spectator vainly trying to control them from centre stage.

People destroy communication by acting falsely. Even Mary

admits the advantages of plain dealing when she says that 'you have all so much more *heart* among you, than one finds in the world at large. You all give me a feeling of being able to trust and confide in you; which, in common intercourse, one knows nothing of'. In fact she is willing to deceive and deceive again, whether about the necklace or in covering up her brother's actions. She claims to be Fanny's friend, flinging the word around with an abandon worthy of the heroines in *Love and Friendship* (359), but her imprecise usage reveals like Isabella Thorpe's a corrupt understanding of the word. 'Complaisant as a sister, [she] was careless as a woman and a friend', thinks Fanny (260).

Mansfield Park, writes Lascelles, is 'a comedy, with grave implications, of human interdependence numbly unrealized or wilfully ignored until too late' (p. 164). Richardson knew how miserable it was to be friendless:

> what a solitariness, what a gloom, what a darkness, must possess that mind that can trust no friends with its inmost thoughts! The big secret, when it is of an interesting nature, will swell the heart till it is ready to burst. Deep melancholy must follow – I would not for the world have it so much as thought, that I had not a soul large enough for friendship. And is not the essence of friendship communication, mingling of hearts, and emptying our very soul into that of a true friend?
>
> (*Grandison*, II. 165)

Fanny is bereft when Edmund cannot speak to her, when she cannot hope for 'a renewal of such confidential intercourse as had been' (453). Indeed almost every chapter ends with Fanny suffering from lack of openness or the excess of it, usually Mrs Norris's. Where comedy balances tragedy in *Grandison*, Fanny's solitary deep melancholy darkens her book unbearably.

From the honesty of true friendship arises communication, and from communication comfort in its richest degree. Richardson did not use 'comfort' so pointedly as Jane Austen does,[19] but I believe that her meaning is very like his ideal of mutual understanding grown of communication and friendship, like the 'comfortable words' of the Communion service. Comfort is neither the bustle that Mrs Norris thinks it, nor the indolence of Lady Bertram, but a trusting contentment, a marriage of true minds.

Friendship governs the domestic and marital relationship,

and more. 'To call a man a good FRIEND', says Sir Charles, 'is indeed comprizing all the duties in one word. For ... a man cannot be defective in *any* of the social duties, who is capable of it, when the term is rightly understood' (II. 43). The benevolent friend, by relieving pain, prompts gratitude in the mind that knows what it owes to God and to those who imitate his example. Jane Austen, who repeated Harriet's cry of gratitude (I. 167) in a letter of 11 October 1813, reveals in *Mansfield Park* an idea as august as Richardson's. Fanny again heads the hierarchy of sensibility with her eager gratitude, while Mrs Norris comes in very low for her perversion of the word. To be grateful is to be within the pale. Gratitude's reciprocity, its binding and communicating power, makes up a movement that weaves a community together, as Richardson says: 'There is a kind of magnetism in goodness ... trust, confidence, love, sympathy, and a reciprocation of beneficent actions, twist a cord which ties good men to good men, and cannot be easily broken' (II. 45). The dance of duty performed, gratitude returned, and duty reciprocated, unifies souls as far as it is possible for individual sensoria.

Gratitude is especially evoked by memory. The characters of *Grandison* constantly recollect past events: 'what a *rememberer*, if I may make a word, is the heart!', says Harriet (II. 299). By renewing gratitude, they learn from their own histories or biographies in a book called the *History* of Sir Charles Grandison. Such 'reflecting and doubting, and feeling' also characterises Fanny Price, a woman constantly 'wondering at the past and present, wondering at what was yet to come ... in a nervous agitation' (260, 329). Such a state, Richardson claimed in his Preface, was evoked by familiar letters, 'written, as it were, to the *Moment*, while the Heart is agitated by Hopes and Fears, on Events undecided'.

Fanny educates herself from history and biography in a manner at worst sentimental, at best experiential beyond her own narrow life.[20] For the history of her own biography she has the most acute memory in the book. Whereas she recollects scenes or accurately recreates emotions,[21] characters inferior to her suffer lapses in memory. Lady Bertram remembers nothing of the ball; Henry cannot recall whether he saw Henry VIII acted; Mary only remembers the rehearsal when she returns to the school-room; and Mr Price soon quite forgets his daughter (283, 338,

358, 380). Memory is a touchstone for character, and requires strenuous exercises of retention and comparison to ensure that it accurately guides character. As Fanny says,

If any one faculty of our nature may be called *more* wonderful than the rest, I do think it is memory. There seems something more speakingly incomprehensible in the powers, the failures, the inequalities of memory, than in any other of our intelligences. The memory is sometimes so retentive, so serviceable, so obedient – at others, so bewildered and so weak – and at others again, so tyrannic, so beyond controul! – We are to be sure a miracle every way – but our powers of recollecting and of forgetting, do seem peculiarly past finding out.

Constantly recalling, interpreting, assessing her own actions, writing in effect her own history, Fanny is recognisably the sister to Richardson's heroines. And from one who remembers and reflects we can expect a consistency not found in Mary, 'untouched and inattentive' to the didactic dialogue of the mind (209). No wonder that Fanny should admire the evergreens.[22]

Friends relieve friends but also judge. Judgment is a duty, not a privilege. When Harriet is offered 'an intimate friendship' with Sir Charles, 'that of a brother to a sister', she desires to be 'intitled to tell you your faults, as I see them. In your sister *Harriet* you shall find, tho' a respectful, yet an open-eyed monitor' (I. 194). *Grandison* is full of occasions where characters act as respectful yet open-eyed monitors one to the other, a 'liberty ... such as constitutes the essence of true friendship' (II. 137). In 'The vocabulary of *Mansfield Park*', David Lodge calls the scene where Fanny and Edmund sit in judgment at the Crawfords (63–4) 'entirely representative of the tone and preoccupations' of that novel. It is also entirely representative of *Grandison*. Right, ought not, wrong, indecorous, ungrateful, impropriety, reflection, faults, justified – such 'vocabulary of discrimination', as Lodge calls it, shows like Richardson's the mind at work.

The epistolary form grants limitless opportunities to judge. Since writing to the moment is writing to the moment just past, record and assessment occur together sentence by sentence, paragraph by paragraph, interleaved, interwoven. So too in *Mansfield Park*. Mary Crawford's letter provides proof of her vitiation, which freed from the distraction of her presence, could stand in a court of law. Jane Austen may have largely rejected the epistolary method, but still uses it to advantage.

Letters in Jane Austen provide fruitful if rare opportunities of assessing character − they reveal more than conversation. For the most part however the judging mind works through appearances, or manners. Lodge, who defines her sense of 'manners' as moral conduct, shows briefly how the sense alters in value depending on the speaker. Austen and Richardson were both alert to the need to discriminate. 'Refined! what meant the man by the word in this place?' worries Richardson characteristically (I. 85). Their good characters use important words with a full moral weight; bad ones mis-use and debase them as in the case of 'friend' and 'comfort'. Since the whole value of the novel depends upon delicate discrimination, we learn something important about Edmund when he defines manners in its richest connotation as '*conduct* ... the result of good principles; the effect, in short, of those doctrines which it is [the clergy's] duty to teach and recommend' (93).

Manners of the lesser kind, 'good breeding ... refinement and courtesy ... the ceremonies of life' (93), may deceive, for they may be learned.[23] The pleasing manners of the Crawfords are dangerous in ways that Richardson would have understood, he who 'with his brilliant Grandisonian ... mistrust of worldliness', as Angus Wilson puts it,[24] drew rakes with deceiving airs or agonized about whether to endow his hero with a fine address. Good manners which like acting mislead, are only to be trusted in trustworthy characters. Where Fanny's manners are an accurate 'mirror of her own modest and elegant mind', Henry only *appears* 'the gentleman, with a pleasing address', while Mary believes that varnish and gilding hide many stains (294, 44, 434). Sir Thomas Bertram the 'courtier and fine gentleman' (439) embodies gentle conduct just as the hero of Richardson's novel, originally and within the book called *The Fine Gentleman* (II. 181), derives from feudal and Christian codes. Sir Thomas's selflessness in asking after the heroine's health, though tired and fatigued himself, is for instance like Sir Charles's in similar circumstances (178; II. 654, 659).

Concern with mere appearance may lead to foolish punctilio. 'Wicked Politeness! Of how many falshoods dost thou make the people, who are called *polite*, guilty!' writes Richardson (II. 388).

Jane Austen's Julia is equally discomfitted when 'the politeness which she had been brought up to practise as a duty, made it impossible for her to escape; while the want of that higher species of self-command, that just consideration of others, that knowledge of her own heart, that principle of right which had not formed any essential part of her education, made her miserable under it' (91). At the other extreme 'there is more indelicacy in delicacy, than you *very* delicate people are aware of', laughs Charlotte (II. 350), just as Tom Bertram complains of 'scrupulousness run mad' (128). Both authors know that 'etiquette' (203) is mere parade.

People concerned with appearances are passionate, self-willed, liable to produce confusions, bustle, agitation, disorder, noise, distress, exhaustion, fatigue, change, and suchlike signs of a world out of joint and upside-down. (Butler writes of 'a developing theme of stillness opposed to bustle' in the novel, p. 241.) People of true manners are candid, scrupulous to judge and to relieve, concerned always to strengthen the social bonds. They are, in short, true friends. The implications of these ideas are not just secular. Hints of the great themes of Christianity echo from *Grandison* to *Mansfield Park*, as I shall show.

The paradisal park

Grandison Hall is built in an H, as Sotherton is 'built in Elizabeth's time' (56). Here direct imitation stops, for Jane Austen now turns everything in Richardson's account (Volume V, letters v–vii) to criticism of her own characters. 'The situation is delightful', writes Lucy Selby; 'the situation of the house is dreadful', says Maria Bertram (82). From the windows of Sir Charles's spacious house, the gardens and lawn seem to be 'as boundless as the mind of the owner, and as free and open as his countenance', but the situation of Rushworth's house reveals *his* mind by excluding 'the possibility of much prospect from any of the rooms ... Every room on the west front looked across a lawn to the beginning of the avenue immediately beyond tall iron palisades and gates' (85). Jane Austen, having observed that Sotherton is furnished 'in the taste of fifty years back', that is, with the crimson velvet and wealth of the mid-eighteenth century when *Grandison* was published, develops her theme of outmoded and tasteless grandeur in this 'ancient manorial residence of the family' (84, 82).

Harriet enters Grandison Hall as the rightful possessor and bride, but Maria at Sotherton is too precipitate by far. 'The whole house, my dear ... and every person and thing belonging to it, is yours', says Sir Charles; 'Mr. Rushworth's consequence was hers', writes Jane Austen of Maria, who feels a mercenary 'elation of heart' in pointing out his property (81–2). Harriet justifiably exclaims, 'here I am! The declared mistress of this spacious house, and the happiest of human creatures!', but when Maria's spirits are 'in as happy a flutter as vanity and pride could furnish' (83), she anticipates too much. Harriet is shown the house by the housekeeper, and the family portraits by Sir Charles, her heart exulting at the thought that she will take her place among them; at Sotherton, Maria views portraits 'no longer any thing to any body but Mrs. Rushworth, who had been at great pains to learn all that the housekeeper could teach, and was now almost equally well qualified to shew the house' (85). Grandison Hall has an 'elegant little chapel, neatly decorated'; Sotherton's ostentatious but unused chapel provides awkward revelations for Mary.

Richardson describes two gardens, Sir Charles's and Clementina's. At Grandison Hall the flourishing garden with its stream, fish, vineyards, flowers, fruit, contented gardener, and busy wife, looks markedly paradisal. Semicircles of fruit trees planted in a natural slope, 'all which in the season of blossoming, one row gradually lower than another, must make a charming variety of blooming sweets to the eye', are laid out as in Paradise. Rows of pine, cedars and firs shelter the garden, as in *Paradise Lost*:

> ... and over head up grew
> Insuperable highth of loftiest shade,
> Cedar, and Pine, and Firr, and branching Palm
> A Silvan Scene, and as the ranks ascend
> Shade above shade, a woodie Theatre
> Of stateliest view.
> ... a circling row
> Of goodliest Trees loaden with fairest Fruit,
> Blossoms and Fruits at once of golden hue
> Appeerd, with gay enameld colours mixt.   (IV. 137–49)

Sir Charles's garden 'being bounded only by sunk fences, the eye is carried to views that have no bounds'. So too 'our General Sire', says Milton, had 'prospect large/Into his neather Empire neighbouring round' (IV. 144–5). Jane Austen, who had already observed details of the Grandison house, could not fail to notice the garden in which it is set. But I think rather that she was alerted by the Miltonic allusions to remember Eden for herself[25] – she alludes to *Paradise Lost* on page 43. Only this would explain why features of her garden in Volume I, chapters ix–x are closer to the similar account in Milton.

Her 'lawn, bounded on each side by a high wall [which] contained beyond the first planted aerea, a bowling-green, and beyond the bowling-green a long terrace walk ... commanding a view ... into the tops of the trees of the wilderness immediately adjoining', her apparently locked door, her 'knoll', all seem to echo Milton's 'verdurous wall', his 'enclosure green', his lines,

> As with a rural mound the champain head
> Of a steep wilderness, whose hairie sides
> With thicket overgrown, grottesque and wilde,
> Access deni'd ... (IV. 133–7)

In spite of the levity of its continuing inversions – the characters, unlike Adam or Sir Charles complacently surveying their domains, find the view over Sotherton's sunken fences and ha-ha's a 'good spot for fault-finding' – Jane Austen's garden is surely as symbolic as Richardson's. The difference is that where his garden is prelapsarian, hers is not. Significant allusions to the Fall occur in her wilderness, and although she needed no reminder of what happened in Paradise, she must have been struck by the theological implications of the second garden in *Grandison*, Clementina della Porretta's.

Clementina's relationship with Sir Charles is portrayed in images from Milton. Here in a fertile garden of alleys and winding walks she meets her lover, here they sit and read *Paradise Lost* in 'happy times', when 'I was innocent, and was learning English!' as she laments (II. 144, 482), here her innocent admiration of Sir Charles becomes guilty awareness of erotic love. If Sir Charles is a type of Adam and a kind of Christ, and if Clementina is the first Eve supplanted by a second, Richardson invites us to view a Fall.

If the wilderness at Sotherton is then as fully symbolic as Richardson's Italian garden or Milton's Paradise, details take on

new resonance.[26] Mary and Edmund speak of the wilderness as
an emblem of deception just as Richardson wrote of the heart
misleading Harriet 'into what a labyrinth! ... a maze of bewilder-
ing fancy, in which she may else tread many a weary step, that
ought to be advancing forward in the paths of happiness and duty'
(II. 546) – of Mary it will be said that she has 'a mind led astray
and bewildered, and without any suspicion of being so' (367). The
company at Sotherton, tempted by 'all the sweets of pleasure-
grounds', finds the door to the wilderness unlocked, and passes
through. 'Winding in and out ever since we came into [the
wood]', Mary and Edmund take a 'very serpentine course' that
takes them away from 'the first great path'. Mary in her 'feminine
lawlessness' leans Eve-like on Edmund's arm and defies his
rational arguments. 'She would only smile and assert'. Sir
Thomas Grandison had already found that the man who con-
descends to argue with a woman, especially on certain points 'in
which *nature*, and not *reason*, is concerned, must follow her
through a thousand windings, and find himself farthest off when
he imagines himself nearest; and at last must content himself,
panting for breath, to sit down where he set out; while she
gambols about, and is ready to lead him a new course' (I. 339–
40). This theme of disobedience and fall is repeated by Maria, who
confronted with the iron gate, cries out, 'Prohibited! nonsense!',
and 'I certainly can get out that way, and I will'. She will not wait
for the key and Rushworth, who is posting away 'as if upon life
and death' (101), but pushes hastily by.

Not only the Fall is re-enacted in Clementina's garden, so too
is the primal sin: she dreams that Sir Charles lies dead and
bleeding in the orange grove, killed in revenge by a Porretta
'brother', linked in another dream to Cain (II. 241, III. 149). Something of the same idea may survive in Mary Crawford's appalling
eagerness for Tom Bertram to die that his brother may inherit
(434), for this episode, like the scene in the wilderness, carries
more emotional weight than is easily to be explained.

Sotherton's iron palissades and gate appear neither in Milton
nor in Richardson. But here Jane Austen's mind leapt I think to
another favourite author, Samuel Johnson, whose Happy Valley
is also paradisal with its abundant water, fertile verdure, fish,
fowl, trees, flowers, and millennial mingling of animals. She
quotes from *Rasselas* on page 392. An iron gate like Sotherton's

makes it a prison to Rasselas, just as Rushworth says that Sotherton is like a prison (53). Johnson's Nekayah complains like Maria of 'tasteless tranquility', while Rasselas in the Happy Valley is 'impatient as an eagle in a grate', or barred cage (pp. 2–3, 41, 13). This fuses with Sterne's very similar 'I cannot get out, as the starling [in the Bastille] said', Maria's restless cry before she pushes past the iron gate at Sotherton. Even the ha-ha, a fence sunk into a ditch, hints at hidden social enclosures that will exclude her forever from the paradise at Mansfield Park, and trap her in hideous confinement with Mrs Norris.

The distinction of false Edens from true leads inevitably to traditional debates about art and nature. Sir Charles, said Richardson, did not aim to 'force and distort nature; but to help it, as he finds it, without letting art be seen in his works, where he can possibly avoid it'. This hint Jane Austen opens out into her important theme of improvement by means of Rushworth, Mrs Norris, and Henry Crawford. Sir Charles would 'rather let a stranger be pleased with what he sees, as if it were *always* so; than to obtain comparative praise by informing him what it was in its former situation' (II. 160–1). 'Contenting himself to open and enlarge many fine prospects' by cutting a few trees, he thinks it 'a kind of impiety to fell a tree, that was planted by his father' (III. 273). But Rushworth boasts to his visitors that 'there have been two or three fine old trees cut down that grew too near the house, and it opens the prospect amazingly' (55). Only Fanny regrets his plan to cut more avenues.

Where Sir Charles has 'a great taste ... yet not an expensive one',[27] Mrs Norris chatters, 'Such a place as Sotherton Court deserves every thing that taste and money can do'; 'The expense need not be any impediment. If I were you I should not think of the expense' (53). Sir Charles 'studies situation and convenience; and pretends not to level hills' or to force and distort nature (II. 160); though Mary remembers the dirt and confusion of previous alterations, Henry casts an improver's eye over Sotherton, and plans preposterous metamorphoses for Thornton Lacey (242).

Milton's 'happy rural seat' is controlled not by 'nice Art' but by 'Nature boon' (IV. 241–2), and Spenser too sets art and nature in opposition. Richardson's Harriet appears as a kind of Una (I. 285), while Clementina corresponds enough to Fidessa in her

Catholicism and seductive beauty to render inevitable the
return of the Red Cross Knight/Sir Charles to Una/Harriet,
to religion and quiet truth. Edmund abandons his Una for the
alluring Mary Crawford, not just a laughing Phaedria but a
Fidessa in her worldliness, her artful attractions, and her abrupt
revelation of evil to her sometime suitor. The dangerous am-
bivalence of Spenser's Bower of Bliss, where 'that, which all
faire workes dost most aggrace,/The art, which all that wrought,
appeared in no place' (*The Faerie Queene*, II.xii.58), reappears
in Sotherton. With its little wood, winding walks and false
enchantments, it too proves a house of pride and deception,
a place to be shunned.[28]

Like Richardson then, Jane Austen writes of two gardens,
Sotherton the false, fallen, deceptive Paradise created by art, and
Mansfield Park the true Paradise born naturally of time and
tradition. In a bravura display, her quick combining mind
expands Richardson's hints to link her wilderness with the great
topoi of Renaissance epics, and make her characters re-enact the
Christian history of humanity. She does so lightly, for her art
conceals art.

'If not Authors, Carvers'

If Jane Austen and Richardson share some of their main ideas, and
if they employ similar plots, characters, dialogue, and commentary to express them, their aims too may be alike. The novel
represents to them both, I think, an agent of moral change
operating on a fictional world that then doubles back into reality.
Reformation is effected in both books by means of education, the
marriage choice, exhortation, and example.

The power of education to sustain or corrupt has already been
seen, but good characters can exclude the bad by their marriage
choice. Charlotte Grandison plays a genteel Lysistrata in refusing
to sit with the rakish Everard, saying, 'let him be good then. –
Till when, may all our Sex say, to such men as my Cousin has
been – ''Thus let it be done by the man, whom, if he were good,
good persons would delight to honour'''. A good man may redeem
faulty women the same way. 'Let the envious, the censorious,
malign our sex, and charge us with the love of rakes and liber-
tines, as they will, if all men were like my brother, there would

not be a single woman, and hardly a bad one, in the kingdom' (I. 235, 291). The 'angel' Fanny temporarily converts Henry, Edmund creates in Mary a 'better taste' that she carries into her exile. Good women recognise good men, men become good in order to be recognised, good men make it worth while for a woman to be good. In a moment of complacency Sir Charles alters Dryden's 'None but the Brave deserves the Fair' to 'None but the *good* deserves the fair' (II. 345), but Henry's like boast, 'They will now see what sort of woman it is that can attach me, that can attach a man of sense' (297), is hubristic, shadowed by dramatic irony.

Both novels show characters acting as teachers and preachers to one another, the highest office of a friend. Sir Charles for instance reforms almost every faulty person in the book, including the Jew Merceda, which proves that the millennium is near. Mary Crawford rightly sees Edmund's reproaches as a 'sermon'. Ordination only institutionalizes an act that the characters already perceive as their duty. Like clergy they teach by exhortation the conduct that results from good principles, conscious of their charge of 'all that is of the first importance to mankind, individually or collectively considered, temporally or eternally ... the guardianship of religion and morals, and consequently of the manners that result from their influence', as Edmund puts it. Or they teach by personal example, for 'as the clergy are, or are not what they ought to be, so are the rest of the nation' (92–3). When Fanny goes from the house of order to the house of misrule at Portsmouth, she teaches, she judges candidly, she tries to reform. In Richardson's terms she is a friend, amending out of love. Education creates good principles, good principles appear in conduct, right conduct promotes harmonious social bonds, and social bonds make up a Christian nation. 'Families are little communities ... there are but few solid friendships out of them; and ... they help to make up worthily, and to secure, the great community, of which they are so many miniatures', he explains (I. 25).

These orderly fictional worlds are not however self-contained. Their debates lure readers to make up their own minds, to 'carve', in Richardson's word. When characters bring rewards and punishments upon themselves, when plots are animated through the moral choices of characters, when event is subsumed in moral action, reaction and relationship, we observe, listen, and judge for ourselves. Such invitations to share the characters' self-examination, aided and invoked by memory, make touchstones of the books, lifelike substitutes for life on which to test our moral capacity. And if the larger world is thus reached, Richardson's pride in *Grandison* is pardonable. 'The whole Story abounds with Situations and Circumstances debatable. It is not an unartful Management to interest the Readers so much in the Story, as to make them differ in Opinion as to the Capital Articles, and by Leading one, to espouse one, another, another, Opinion, make them all, if not Authors, Carvers'.[29]

I cannot agree with Trilling that *Mansfield Park* is intolerant of dialectic, as he writes in *Sincerity and Authenticity* (pp. 77 – 80), for what Jane Austen learnt from *Grandison* was just this skill in making her story abound with debatable situations and circumstances that make her readers if not authors, carvers. At every moment of the novel we are forced to decide upon a multiplicity of issues, from fine discrimination of usage to larger choices of moral and social philosophy. The characters of *Grandison* and *Mansfield Park* dramatize these issues, the intervention of 'real' personalities making various options as variously winning as they are in Milton. Jane Austen's provocative narrative voice provokes even more debate, as Watt saw in *The Rise of the Novel* (p. 309), for her tone, her ironies, encourage yet more fruitful irresolutions, more options to judge. The demands upon the reader become much more satisfyingly complex. With what glee she must have gathered up those wildly conflicting 'Opinions' of friends and family about the capital articles of *Mansfield Park*.

The method of both authors is ultimately Socratic. It lures the reader to predetermined ends.[30] If Richardson explains in the concluding note that his book shows 'by a series of facts in common life, what a degree of excellence may be attained and preserved amidst all the infection of fashionable life and folly', Jane Austen does the same by Fanny's 'excellence' in a vitiated world (473). Richardson's bad characters serve to warn, for 'is not vice crowned with success, triumphant, and rewarded, and perhaps set off with wit and spirit, a dangerous representation? And is it not made even *more* dangerous by the hasty reformation, introduced in contradiction to all probability, for the sake of patching up what is called a happy ending?'. No more will Jane Austen diminish the moral of her work by patching up happy endings for the witty Crawfords, for the spirited Maria.

Only Christ combines idealism with real existence in a fallen world, as Richardson points out in his note. Good characters who imitate him are tested by trial and suffering. True heroism is 'meekness, moderation, and humility, as the glory of the human nature', for 'Is not virtue to be proved by tryal? Remember you not who says, ''For what glory is it, if, when ye be buffeted for your faults, ye shall take it patiently? But if, when ye do well, and suffer for it, ye take it patiently, this is acceptable with God'' ' (I. 263, 333–4). So speaks Sir Charles, and so too Sir Thomas at the end of *Mansfield Park* acknowledges 'the advantages of early hardship and discipline, and the consciousness of being born to struggle and endure' (473). Sir Charles, Harriet, Edmund, and Fanny survive. They prove themselves heroic,[31] they invite the reader to do likewise. The secularity of this new genre, the novel, has often been remarked, but here in a Christ-like sufferer rewarded by almost transcendental happiness, religious teaching combines with realism. We may no longer be able to admire the conjunction, but it proves that 'only a novel' can serve the highest offices of art.

Mansfield Park is not *Grandison*, nor may any book be fully explained in terms of another. But it is something to watch Jane Austen, involved in *Grandison* to the extent of knowing it as a living thing, select, adapt, and rearrange elements from Richardson's long diffuse novel. She weaves a tighter mesh that forms the substance of her own.

The concept of utter newness strains credulity. Like Shakespeare transforming Holinshed or Plutarch, Jane Austen ran variations on themes she found elsewhere. Sometimes Richardson's words must have risen naturally to her creating mind, sometimes the admiring imitation must surely have been conscious. Sometimes too a concept may have tugged at her work and made it not entirely hers, sometimes undoubtedly there was allusion of a private kind to be caught by those who knew *Grandison* as well as she. She always indulged in private signalling as Richardson had done himself. And sometimes she develops a hint from *Grandison* into something very much larger in scope.

Jane Austen saw the worth of *Grandison* not just I think for its storehouse of characters, scenes, and ideas, but for its self-referential method, its debate both serious and vivacious upon itself. In the same spirit she tests Richardson's fiction for herself, though her ear for tonal uncertainty is finer. If the object under scrutiny is *Grandison*, burlesque, as in the episode of the cold pork bones, may result. If the object is her own work, there occurs that subtler form of commentary that we call irony. Richardson wants us to take everything at face value, Jane Austen definitively does not. By dispensing with the tyranny of linear time, she creates habitual gaps between what we see and what we are critically meant to see. In *Grandison* we live with the characters in time present; in *Mansfield Park* we are encouraged to range, to recollect judgments from time past, and bring them to bear upon the moment. That the situation of Grandison Hall is delightful is a fact, but when Maria says that 'the situation of Sotherton is dreadful', she meddles before she should, her cant word 'dreadful' wonderfully confirming the shallowness of her nature. Richardson had often presented both sides of a case. What is new in Jane Austen is the compression of two opinions, Maria's and the one we are to take, simultaneously into the same sentence.[32]

In these ways Jane Austen complicates what she finds in *Grandison*, making that which was single, double, and often multiple. Out of all possible meanings we choose one, guided by the playful directive voice that Richardson the epistolary novelist had been forced to exclude from his work. Thus stands free a group of 'just and lovely words' as Tave calls them (p. 30), tested by wit and proved superior to it, words such as 'comfort', 'brother', 'friend', that survive untainted by any ironic possibility. Such steadiness of values is an eighteenth-century goal, and it makes more sense to look at *Mansfield Park* with eighteenth-century eyes[33] than to gaze from a distance. In Jane Austen, Richardson would have recognised one he always sought, a truly distinguished 'Daughter of my own Mind'.[34]

6

Emma

In *Emma* and *Persuasion* Jane Austen reaches back to Shakespeare and to Chaucer. She calls on Richardson now only to solve particular problems, for where almost every page of *Sense and Sensibility*, *Pride and Prejudice*, and *Mansfield Park* bear traces of him, he does not much matter in the last two novels. She who had already drawn on Locke, Milton, Richardson, and others, now places herself even more firmly in the main line of English literature, proving the truth of Dryden's contention that poets too have a heritage, 'our Lineal Descents and Clans, as well as other Families' (*Poems*, IV. 1445).

When Emma asserts in defiance of Shakespeare that the course of true love can run smooth at Hartfield, she reveals not only her enchanting hubris but a hint that Jane Austen had at least a scrap of *Midsummer Night's Dream* in her head when she wrote *Emma*.[1] I believe one can say more. Just as predecessors provided her with controlling designs and inspiration in earlier works, so this comedy, even more thoroughly, lies behind *Emma*. Emma says smugly that 'a Hartfield edition of Shakespeare would have a long note on that passage' (75). The following discussion might serve as that long note.

A Midsummer Night's Dream is a play about the imagination, which Theseus commonsensically derides. He dismisses all the events of the night as mere fiction, because the seething brains of lunatics, lovers and poets are alike in their apprehending of more than cool reason comprehends. The tricks of strong imagination begin with some joy, associating with it the bringer of that joy. Night fears easily make the imaginer suppose a bush a bear (V. i). So too in *Emma* imagination is consistently creative, pushing beyond observation to planning and then to an actual provision of the outcome. It moves from passive spectating to

169

active meddling. Jane Austen here turns into one continuous process Samuel Johnson's two senses for the word 'imagine', '1 to fancy; to paint in the mind. 2 to scheme; to contrive'. That is, you paint a picture, then take events into your own hands, which is exactly what Emma does.

Emma is an 'imaginist' (335), a word that Jane Austen made up just for her.[2] She is herself creating what she saw, for to her way of thinking, 'what is so evidently, so palpably desirable – what courts the pre-arrangement of other people ... immediately shape[s] itself into the proper form' (344, 75). She is blessed, or cursed, by the shaping spirit of imagination, a word that turns up again and again in the novel. Intelligent and quick, she prizes herself for penetration and understanding. But when she goes further and makes her ideas of what things are into notions of what things should and will be, she exercises over other people an unwarranted licence to change their lives.

Emma's first exercise in fantasy and shaping is the notion that she made the match between Miss Taylor and Mr Weston, although Mr Woodhouse warns her against making matches and foretelling things, 'for whatever you say always comes to pass' (12). Emboldened by what she sees as her success, she presses on to more elaborate and dangerous schemes. She will work on Mr Elton, and Pygmalion-like try to make of Harriet what she wants her to be. Her efforts are presented literally in the episode of Harriet's picture, when she tries to 'throw in a little improvement to the figure, to give a little more height, and considerably more elegance'. 'You have made her too tall, Emma', says Mr Knightley, as commonsensical as Theseus (47–8). Emma goes on unabashed to dissuade her from marrying Martin, and then persuades her that she is loved first by Mr Elton and then by Frank Churchill. When Mr Elton and Emma are clapped together into the coach in the snow, she must admit that she has blundered most dreadfully, that she has been grossly mistaken and misjudging in 'all her observations, all her convictions, all her prophesies for the last six weeks'. She regrets her 'error, her active part in bringing two people together, her making a trick out of what ought to be simple'. Her resolution is that of 'repressing imagination all the rest of her life' (141–2). But when Frank rescues Harriet from the gipsies, how could she not exercise her imagination?

Such an adventure as this, – a fine young man and a lovely young woman thrown together in such a way, could hardly fail of suggesting certain ideas to the coldest heart and the steadiest brain. So Emma thought, at least. Could a linguist, could a grammarian, could even a mathematician have seen what she did, have witnessed their appearance together, and heard their history of it, without feeling that circumstances had been at work to make them peculiarly interesting to each other? – How much more must an imaginist, like herself, be on fire with speculation and foresight! – especially with such a ground-work of anticipation as her mind had already made.

Here is Theseus's very comparison between seething brains and cold reason. She may think it a 'mere passive scheme. It was no more than a wish. Beyond it she would on no account proceed' (334–5). But activity is as irresistible to this imaginist as to Theseus's poet. She teaches her pupil all too well. Harriet becomes an imaginist too, first about Mr Elton and then about Mr Knightley. The schemer's schemes are all blown up.

With insufferable vanity had she believed herself in the secret of everybody's feelings; with unpardonable arrogance proposed to arrange everybody's destiny. She was proved to have been universally mistaken; and she had not done quite nothing – for she had done mischief. She had brought evil on Harriet, on herself, and she too much feared, on Mr Knightley. (412–3)

It has all been the result of her own conniving, of an imagination active in Johnson's second sense of indefensible schemes against other people. Only at the end does it work for her, when her mind 'with all the wonderful velocity of thought' is able to 'catch and comprehend the exact truth of the whole' that Mr Knightley loves her, and her only (430).

Harriet is scarcely tragic, but Jane Fairfax could easily become so. We find it harder to forgive Emma for hurting her, just as Emma herself finds it harder. Emma builds up edifices of speculation out of vanity and jealousy which do her little credit. Mr Knightley, striving to avoid her 'errors of imagination', perceives an understanding between Jane and Frank, but Emma answers with 'a confidence which staggered, with a satisfaction which silenced, Mr. Knightley', laughing at him for allowing his 'imagination' to wander (350–1). The news that Jane and Frank are indeed engaged undermines Emma in her proudest part, her perception. She sees wretchedly into a future where Harriet is married to Mr Knightley, Hartfield comparatively deserted, and Mrs Weston occupied with her child (422), but just when she plans never to make plans again, all is clarified with Mr Knightley, and her future will be very different from the one she had imagined. She makes one last projection for herself, that she will be humble and circumspect for the future. With her record one wonders, but Jane Austen takes all prophecy out of her hands and ours when she tells us with the full authority of her narrative voice that 'the wishes, the hopes, the confidence, the predictions of the small band of true friends who witnessed the ceremony, were fully answered in the perfect happiness of the union' (484).

Emma is not the only imaginist in the book, for she has undoubtedly inherited her imaginative tendencies from Mr Woodhouse. He like his daughter projects visions of the present into the future, and exerts persuasive powers to bring his wishes about. Marriage is to him a kind of death, and sensual indulgence, even eating, suggests intimations of mortality. In a book where so many are hoist by their own petards, it is nice to see Mr Woodhouse being hoist by his. Confronted with the news of the turkey-thief, he exchanges the prospect of 'wretched alarm every night of his life' for the protection of a son-in-law. To him 'pilfering was *housebreaking*' (483), for as Theseus had said, 'Or in the night, imagining some fear,/How easy is a bush suppos'd a bear?' (V.i.21–2). His other daughter Isabella shares his imagination of disaster when they are snowed in – Mr Knightley answers like Theseus that there is 'nothing to apprehend' (128) – and John Knightley is her perfect mate in his gloomy relish when things go as badly as he had prophesied. Mrs Churchill has 'imaginary complaints', one of which carries her off (387), the Westons are imaginists in their hopes for Frank and Emma. 'I have been making discoveries and forming plans, just like yourself', says Mrs Weston (222). Mr Elton is an imaginist when he sees himself as a languishing lover of the wealthy and beautiful heiress. So too is the charming Augusta Hawkins, whose attempts to shape Jane's life make her Emma writ large. Maple Grove and Selina and the barouche landau exist entirely in her imagination for all we know, and she projects a florid glamour in her imaginings about herself and the donkey and her *caro sposo*. Once again it is Mr Knightley who disconcertingly calls imagination's bluff. He offers a donkey, and cold meat indoors.

The best joke is that Mr Knightley, for all his claims to cold reason, is an imaginist too. He is like Emma not only in his plans for Robert Martin, but in his will to bring them to pass. Robert is his creature, whether he is advising him to marry Harriet or manoeuvering to bring them together again in London. He too proves himself a schemer. When he thinks Emma is in love with Frank, he exercises his imagination, he builds jealous fantasies about them very much as she does, from slender scraps of evidence and hasty and uncharitable conclusions. Even before Frank arrives he anticipates jealously what a chattering coxcomb Frank will be (145 – 51), and he fears that Frank will usurp him just as Emma fears that Jane will usurp her. Mr Knightley will require a whole novel to unblind him. His jealous crossness about the ball might remind us that he is John Knightley's brother. Better indeed that he spend his time with that old grouch William Larkins, his agricultural *alter ego*. Comically enough, for a man who likes to control things, he stumbles into the proposal pretty much by accident and with a little help from Emma. Emma might not have known that she loved Mr Knightley, but neither did he until recently know that he loved Emma. Both have been so busy initiating and elaborating their fantasies, both have been so literally carried away by their own imaginations, that they miss what actually goes on in their own hearts.

And so the book, typically for Jane Austen, accumulates clusters of words to do with the concept of imagination. Some words describe the creative faculty itself, like picture, image, fancy, idea, suspect, speculate, perception, penetration, conjecture, guess, invent, and think. Some project imagination into the future, like wish, hope, plan, design, foresight, foresee, apprehend, confidence, and prophesy. Some show the imagination exercising a possibly dubious power, like scheme, plot, contrivance, connivance, meddle, interfere, and prevent. Some show the limits of imagination, like riddle, puzzle, conundrum, acrostic, secret, mystery, surprize, and confuse, and some show its capacity for evil, such as mistake, error, trick, lead astray, deceive, and blind. The book gradually moves away from this fifth group to another which includes natural, simple, artless, sincere, and truthful. 'Mystery; Finesse – how they pervert the understanding! My Emma, does not every thing serve to prove more and more the beauty of truth and sincerity in all our dealings with each other?', says Mr Knightley (446). Jane hated having to be so 'cold and artificial! – I always had a part to act. – it was a life of deceit!' Emma speaks for them all when she says, 'oh! if you knew how much I love every thing that is decided and open!' (459–60).

True love runs smooth in neither *A Midsummer Night's Dream* nor *Emma* because of the blind self-delusion of love. As Theseus says, imagination can act positively or negatively, seeing Helen in a brow of Egypt or becoming quite mad. The words 'blind' and 'madness' turn up again and again in *Emma*, only vanishing towards the end when truth, sincerity, openness, and reason take their place. Blindness and deception cause madness and pain, anger and bitterness, in the play as in the novel when characters are irritated beyond bearing, driven to do things uncharacteristic of their best selves. Jane lives a life of deceit, Frank is dangerously indiscreet and cruel, Mr Knightley sulks, and Emma lashes out at Miss Bates. Comedy in these works need not necessarily triumph.

A Midsummer Night's Dream and *Emma* are alike in a number of things, the hot pursuit by lovers through a midsummer landscape, the matching and mismatching of two couples, female friendship and its betrayal, and the movement towards tolerance, forebearance, and generosity at the end. The principal stories of *A Midsummer Night's Dream*, the quarrel of Titania and Oberon over the changeling child together with the use of the love-potion on the two loving couples and the rustics' play for the wedding of Theseus and Hippolyta all take place on Midsummer's Night. In *Emma* too the main events take place in Midsummer, a time when young people traditionally discover who they will marry. Mr Knightley, as Jo Modert notes in 'Chronology within the novels', actually proposes on Midsummer's Day, Old Style.

Irritability and fatigue are worsened by the midsummer weather, in *Emma*. The visit to Donwell Abbey takes place 'under a bright mid-day sun, at almost Midsummer' (357), where under the glaring sun Mrs Elton is the first to succumb. She badgers Jane Fairfax into taking the superior position until Jane escapes in exhaustion. Immediately Frank Churchill appears, hot in pursuit and hot in body. He has met Jane running away, and Emma thinks that he is cross because he is hot:

had he known how hot a ride he should have, and how late, with all his hurry, he must be, he believed he should not have come at all. The heat was excessive; he had never suffered any thing like it – almost wished he had staid at home – nothing killed him like heat – he could bear any degree of cold, &c. but heat was intolerable – and he sat down, at the greatest possible distance from the slight remains of Mr. Woodhouse's fire, looking very deplorable. (363–4)

Midsummer Day at Box Hill is ominously very fine, even hotter than the day at Donwell. Frank's and Emma's flirtation grows more hectic as the day proceeds, ending with Emma's unforgiveable remark to Miss Bates, Mr Knightley's rebuke, and Emma's exhausted and heartfelt remorse. The last hot walker in the novel is Mr Elton. Thinking to meet Mr Knightley, he has made himself hot and tired. 'Such a dreadful broiling morning! – I went over the fields too – (speaking in a tone of great ill usage) which made it so much the worse. And then not to find him at home! I assure you I am not at all pleased' (457). These hot walks, these fruitless pursuits, these desperate escapes, these followings after false objects and misleading hopes, are as much a part of *A Midsummer Night's Dream* as they are of *Emma*. So too are the 'odd' meetings that resolve all, like Harriet's encounters with Robert Martin at Randalls, or at Ford's (32, 178–9). 'Madness in such weather!', says Frank, 'absolute madness!'; 'what blindness, what madness had led her on!', thinks Emma (364, 408). As in Shakespeare's play, these characters speak constantly of midsummer madness, of the blunders and blindness of love.

In *A Midsummer Night's Dream* the matching and mismatching of the lovers is brought about by Puck's love-potion. Hermia and Lysander love each other, but Lysander is made to love Helena. Helena loves Demetrius but he loves Hermia, and when the love-potion forces him to dote on Helena, she can only think it cruel deception. Everything works out in the end, though not before much bitter anger is felt by all. How like this is to *Emma*. Harriet loves Robert Martin but is made to think she loves Mr Elton and then Mr Knightley. Emma, who thinks Harriet loves Frank Churchill, is equally deceived in thinking that Jane Fairfax, who does love Frank, loves Mr Dixon. Mr Elton rebuffs the doting Harriet and makes love to the reluctant Emma, while she herself, in love with Mr Knightley, persuades herself she could love Frank and flirts with him excessively at Box Hill (368). Mr Knightley, in love with Emma, appears to be falling in love first with Jane Fairfax and then with Harriet. In other words Jane Austen throws everything into confusion much as Shakespeare does, so that she may have the pleasure of sorting it all out again.

The course of true love never did run smooth, says Lysander (V. i), for either it was different in blood, a theme worked out through Harriet: 'what a connexion had she been preparing for Mr Knightley ...!' thinks Emma. Or else misgraffed in respect of years: Mr Knightley has to realise that the sixteen years separating himself and Emma do not matter (482, 99). Or else it stood upon the choice of friends: so Emma, as 'friend', forces couples together. Harriet takes such difficulties as a sign of true love, repeating over and over Emma's romantic and foolish remark that '*more* wonderful things had happened' (406). Mr Knightley turns out to be 'in every respect so proper, suitable, and unexceptionable a connexion ... so peculiarly eligible' for Emma, just as Jane and Frank's match has an 'equality of situation' (467, 428). The weight of the book thus comes down upon those matches where the partners are truly suited by rank, taste, and mutual knowledge. 'Every man should take his own/... Jack shall have Jill; / Nought shall go ill; (The man shall have his mare again, and all shall be well', sings Puck, ending a story in which three couples are to marry and 'ever true in loving be', as in *Emma* (III. ii. 459–63). But for one brief moment it did not seem possible. At the very instant that Emma knew she loved Mr Knightley, she foresaw as a result 'such a burst of threatening evil, such a confusion of sudden and perplexing emotions' (409). In similar words Lysander sees that even when there is 'a sympathy in choice', love can be as brief as lightning. And so 'quick bright things come to confusion' (I. i. 141–9). The same image of love as lightning appears in *Romeo and Juliet*, another play about thwarted love which shows how dark *A Midsummer Night's Dream* and *Emma* could easily become. But day succeeds night in the play as it does in the novel (421–4). The last sentence of Jane Austen's book promises a 'perfect happiness' for the heroine and hero, just as Hippolyta sees that the story of the night told over, and all their minds transfigured together, is more than fancy, for it grows to 'something of great constancy,/ But howsoever strange and admirable' (V.i. 26–7). As Harriet says, 'the strangest things do take place!' (74).

The two sets of loving couples may be even more precisely compared. Jane is like Helena in her height, her pallor and her 'wan, sick looks' (167–99, 443), for of Helena it is said, 'All fancy-sick she is and pale of cheer/ With sighs of love that costs the fresh blood dear' (III. ii. 293, 96–7). Jane and Helena both have good reason to complain of the hard usage from which they run away; Jane, whom Frank treats with 'shameful, insolent neglect' (441), might say to her lover as well as Helena, 'Use me but as your spaniel, spurn me, strike me,/ Neglect me, lose me ... I am sick when I look not on you' (III. ii. 343, II. i. 205–12). Helena dotes on the 'spotted and inconstant man' Demetrius. He now loves Hermia and hates his betrothed Helena. But with the help of the love-potion he gladly returns to Helena, explaining, 'To her, my lord,/ Was I betroth'd ere I saw Hermia' (IV. i. 168–9). Of his newly recovered love he declares,

> But, as in health, come to my natural taste,
> Now do I wish it, love it, long for it,
> And will for evermore be true to it.   (IV. i. 171–3)

Frank also returns to his original betrothed, promising 'we are reconciled, dearer, much dearer, than ever, and no moment's uneasiness can ever occur between us again' (443). At the end he praises Jane extravagantly for her pale skin, calling her 'a complete angel' (478–9); Demetrius, awakening, calls Helena goddess, nymph, perfect, divine, a 'princess of pure white' (III. ii. 137–144). But Frank like Demetrius is a spotted and inconstant man who has flirted with Emma/Hermia and laid Jane/Helena open to mockery and derision. The knowledge preserved in the family that Jane's marriage would be brief is not surprising. 'He is a disgrace to the name of man', says Mr Knightley; 'Jane, Jane, you will be a miserable creature' (426). That Emma should see her in a context of *Romeo and Juliet* certainly suggests a tragic potential in her life, an idea already introduced when she imagined Jane 'unconsciously sucking in the sad poison' of Mr Dixon's presence (400, 168).

Mr Knightley is like Lysander who loves Hermia/Jane, even though he says sturdily that he has no 'charm thrown over my senses' (37). Emma is like Hermia in loving Lysander/Knightley, but she is pushed towards marrying Frank/Demetrius by the agency of her friends the Westons. Looking back she marvels at how Jane managed to withstand the agony of that time, and she blames Frank:

What right had he to endeavour to please, as he certainly did – to distinguish any one young woman with persevering attention, as he certainly did – while he really belonged to another? ... And how could *she* bear such behaviour! Composure with a witness! to look on, while repeated attentions were offering to another woman, before her face, and not resent it.   (396–7)

But Jane's worst moment at Box Hill is caused as much by Emma as by Frank, and the issue of the ruptured friendship between two women is as crucial to the novel as to the play. Helena, complaining that Hermia and Demetrius 'make mouths upon me when I turn my back,/Wink each at other, hold the sweet jest up' (III. ii. 238–9), could just as well be Jane speaking to Emma after the word game or at Box Hill. Jane might turn on Emma thus:

> Injurious Hermia! most ungrateful maid!
> Have you conspir'd, have you with these contriv'd,
> To bait me with this foul derision? ...
> And will you rent our ancient love asunder,
> To join with men in scorning your poor friend?
> It is not friendly, 'tis not maidenly;
> Our sex, as well as I, may chide you for it,
> Though I alone do feel the injury.   (III. ii. 195–219)

Emma similarly doubts whether she has not 'transgressed the duty of woman by woman', for 'it was hardly right' to betray her suspicions to Frank Churchill (231). Mr Knightley rebukes her for her joke against Jane, 'so very entertaining to the one, and so very distressing to the other'. 'A mere joke among ourselves', protests Emma. 'The joke', he replies gravely, 'seemed confined to you and Mr. Churchill' (349–50). 'If you have any pity, grace, or manners, / You would not make me such an argument', says Helena (III. ii. 241–2), rather as Mr Knightley at Box Hill points out Emma's lack of compassion, lack of feeling, and insolence (374–5). 'This sport, well carried, shall be chronicled', says Helena bitterly (III. ii. 240); the news of the flirtation at Box Hill will be carried by letters to Maple Grove and as far as Ireland, not that Frank cares. 'Let my accents swell to Mickleham on one side, and Dorking on the other', he says (368–9).

Helena reproaches Hermia most of all for the loss of their 'ancient love', their bond of female friendship. Emma stands accused of betraying someone who was not her childhood friend, but should have been. Helena recalls how she and Hermia sat on one cushion, singing and embroidering together, but Emma remarks, 'I have known [Jane] from a child, undoubtedly; we have been children and women together, and it is natural to suppose that we should be intimate, – that we should have taken to each other whenever she visited her friends. But we never did' (203). The break between Shakespeare's heroines is caused by the love-potion, while that between Jane Austen's is plausibly accounted for by Emma's envy. Jane runs away from Emma's uncomprehending cruelty as Helena does from Hermia's, and when Frank tries to stop her, as he later reveals, she in 'the agony of a mind that would bear no more' breaks off the engagement and accepts the superior position at Mrs Bragge's, tears standing perpetually in her eyes (362, 440–1, 421, 379). Helena, running away from Demetrius – 'Stay, gentle Helena, hear my excuse;/ My love, my life, my soul, fair Helena!' – weeps too for the mockery and hatred she has received (III.ii.245–6, 158). Emma should have been Jane's friend and she was not. When at last she is kind to Jane, Jane is in no condition to accept her friendly overtures. Emma thinks she understands. 'She was sorry, very sorry. Her heart was grieved for a state which seemed but the more pitiable from this sort of irritation of spirits, inconsistency of action, and inequality of powers; and it mortified her that she was given so little credit for proper feeling, or esteemed so little worthy as a friend' (391). The revelation of the secret engagement clarifies everything. 'Jealousy. – In Jane's eyes she had been a rival ... An airing in the Hartfield carriage would have been the rack, and arrow-root from the Hartfield store-room must have been poison' (403). Only at the end can Emma 'compress all her friendly ... sensations into a very, very earnest shake of the hand' (453).

Emma betrays not just one woman but two, and she does so more than once. She claims an intimacy with Harriet like that of Hermia and Helena, but she uses it falsely to prevent her friend's happiness with Mr Martin. Jane Austen even copies

Shakespeare's phrase, 'your poor friend', when Emma's resolution to keep Harriet's secret about Mr Knightley is 'all the service she could now render her poor friend'. 'You have been no friend to Harriet Smith', Mr Knightley had said, but Emma defines friendship as the right to control other people. Her last service is her best – 'she had led her friend astray, and it would be a reproach to her for ever' (63, 431). But she is neither so romantic nor so heroic as to insist that her friend have Mr Knightley instead. When Emma gives preference to reason, her friendly treachery is at an end.

Hermia at the start of the play will never marry if she may not have Lysander. Theseus asks her unsympathetically,

> Whether, if you yield not to your father's choice,
> You can endure the livery of a nun,
> For aye to be in shady cloister mew'd,
> To live a barren sister all your life,
> Chanting faint hymns to the cold fruitless moon.
>
> (I. i. 69–73)

Far happier is the rose distilled, he says, than that which withers on the virgin thorn, and 'Grows, lives, and dies, in single blessedness' (I. i. 78). Emma also gives way to the gentle tyranny of her father when she declares she will never marry (41). Her hymns take the form of carpet-work, and to supply the barrenness of her declining life she imagines the visits of nephews and nieces (85–6). By the end of the book Emma accepts with as much alacrity as Hermia the marriage option recommended by Theseus, and her solemn resolution of never quitting her father (435) is made redundant by the turkey-thief. Jane Austen typically repeats this theme of foolish self-denial. 'I shall never marry', says Harriet in her devotion to Mr Knightley, while Jane, her engagement apparently impossible, has resolved 'with the fortitude of a devoted noviciate [like Shakespeare's nun] to complete the sacrifice, and retire from all the pleasures of life ... to penance and mortification for ever' (341, 165).

In *A Midsummer Night's Dream* the alternations and reversals in the plot are caused by Puck's potion, love-in-idleness – one idle day, Emma began her imaginative schemes for Miss Taylor (12–13). Magic makes them arbitrary, they happen in a wink. Changes in *Emma* can be just as swift. They result not from magic, but from the understandable results of unblinding caused by better knowledge of oneself or others. Most obvious is the occasion when she realises that she loves Mr Knightley. 'It darted through her, with the speed of an arrow, that Mr. Knightley must marry no one but herself!' (408). That arrow must be the arrow of the blind boy Cupid, the golden arrow of happiness which in *A Midsummer Night's Dream* fell upon the little flower and made it potent. Images of the blinding power of love occur frequently in *Emma*. Frank Churchill for instance admits to blinding the world about his engagement, while Emma knows she has been doomed to blindness, though not about his attention to herself (441, 425–7). Jane Austen's world is realistic not magical, and yet the words luck, fortune, strange, extraordinary, wonderful, odd, amazement, alteration, and change recur in the novel as they do in Shakespeare's play until the wonderful moment when all delusion is past, and she knows that 'Harriet was nothing; that she was every thing herself' to Mr Knightley (430).

Emma is a kind of Hermia, but she is also a Titania to Mr Knightley's jealous and quarrelling Oberon.[3] At the Crown Miss Bates thinks indeed that 'This is meeting quite in fairy-land! – Such a transformation!', and they plan to open windows much as the rustics plan to open theirs to let in moonlight (323, 251). Both *A Midsummer Night's Dream* and *Emma* begin with a meeting by moonlight – 'a beautiful, moonlight night', says Mr Knightley on his first entrance into the story (10). He and Emma are as ill met as the fairy king and queen when they begin to quarrel over Harriet, the changeling child. Both become angry, indignant, and vexed, and their discordancies make them want to part (65). They are briefly reconciled to each other when Mr Knightley takes the child out of Emma's arms with 'all the unceremoniousness of perfect amity' (98). One might say too that Emma falls in love with an ass, or at least Mr Knightley thinks she has. 'I must to the barber's', says Bottom, and Frank pretends that he has gone to London for a haircut (IV.i.23; 205). Mr Knightley's tender anxiety for her when he knows that Frank will marry Jane is like Oberon's pity when the fairy queen dotes on Bottom: 'Time, my dearest Emma, time will heal the wound' (426). But Titania has never really been in love with the rustic actor Bottom, nor has Emma really loved the shape-changing Frank Churchill.

When the King and Queen of Fairy fall out through 'the forgeries of jealousy', like Emma and Mr Knightley (II. i. 81; 432), the weather becomes unseasonable, the green corn rots in the field, the nine men's morris is filled with mud. Frost falls at midsummer, rain and fog obliterate the proper season. The weather in Emma also changes according to Emma's mood, or rather her relationship with Mr Knightley.[4] When she thinks that he will marry Harriet and contemplates what she has done to Jane, winter comes unseasonably at midsummer:

The evening of this day was very long, and melancholy, at Hartfield. The weather added what it could of gloom. A cold stormy rain set in, and nothing of July appeared but in the trees and shrubs, which the wind was despoiling, and the length of the day, which only made such cruel sights the longer visible.

The next morning is just as melancholy, until a change in the weather promises comedy again. 'In the afternoon it cleared; the wind changed into a softer quarter; the clouds were carried off; the sun appeared; it was summer again. With all the eagerness which such a transition gives, Emma resolved to be out of doors as soon as possible. Never had the exquisite sight, smell, sensation of nature, tranquil, warm, and brilliant after a storm, been more attractive to her' (421–4). She walks out to the shrubbery, and there is Mr Knightley.

The insistent Englishness of this scene in *A Midsummer Night's Dream* is echoed in the English landscape of *Emma*. Robert Martin, who works it, is not the gross, clownish, awkward, uncouth, vulgar farmer thinking of nothing but profit and loss that Emma imagines him to be, but a true pastoral swain out of Shakespeare or Spenser with whom Harriet enjoys moonlight walks and merry evening games, a man who will go three miles round in order to bring her some walnuts, who brought the shepherd's son on purpose into the parlour to sing to her, who sings himself, and keeps a very fine flock (28–33). Not for him the empty sheep-fold and murrained sheep of Shakespeare's play, but prosperity and beauty, spreading flocks, an orchard in blossom, and a light column of smoke ascending that may well have come out of Fanny Price's transparency of Tintern Abbey. 'English verdure, English culture, English comfort' provide a practical prosperity anchored firmly in drains, fruit-bearing trees, and eight cows (360, 27). Here is an Eden won by labour as in Virgil's Golden Age or Milton's Paradise.[5] It is more realistic, more English simply, than Marianne's. Even after her brother commented pedantically on the apple trees in bloom in July,[6] Jane Austen never corrected them, perhaps because there are frosted summer buds in the midsummer night of Shakespeare.

When the King and Queen quarrel the very basis of English society is ruined. But with the pretty rustics settled at Martin's farm and the king and queen on Donwell ruling together as they ought, sympathetic magic ensures the prosperity of the land – Kirkham points out how 'George Knightley' echoes the name of England's patron, Saint George (p. 128), and Modert remarks on insistent references to the pagan and Christian festivals of Michaelmas, Christmas, Valentine's Day, Easter, and Mid-summer or May Day. This ancient theme is reinforced by William Larkins, the stock figure of the comic rustic who like the gardeners in *Richard II* sees rulers come and go, but the land go on for ever. His name should by rights be Hodge, a name Jane Austen gave to Mr Knightley's housekeeper Mrs Hodges. Her passionate celebration of her native land may well have been inspired by John of Gaunt's dying speech in the same play.

Mr Knightley and Emma may profitably be compared to Oberon and Titania. They can equally be seen as Theseus and Hippolyta – traditionally the two couples are portrayed by the same actors. Fanny Burney could call a woman Amazonian for her powers of mind as well as of body (see p. 148 above), and Emma's powers of penetration certainly compete with Mr Knightley's. Theseus says to his Amazonian Queen that he 'won thy love doing thee injuries' (I. i. 17); 'I have blamed you, and lectured you, and you have borne it as no other woman in England would have borne it', says Mr Knightley, 'I have been a very indifferent lover' (430). Most important of all the comparison illuminates the climactic scene at Box Hill. Like Hippolyta, Emma queen of Highbury 'presides' over the revels, and expects

something very entertaining from each of you, in a general way. Here are seven of you … and she only demands from each of you either one thing very clever, be it prose or verse, original or repeated – or two things moderately clever – or three things very dull indeed, and she engages to laugh heartily at them all.

Just so Theseus runs through the various possibilities for the wedding plays, dismissing the ones he knows already and fixing on the play of the six rustics (one less than in Jane Austen). The play of Pyramus and Thisbe will be 'tedious and brief'. When Miss Bates offers to say three dull things, Emma's response is swift. 'Pardon me – but you will be limited as to number – only three at once' (369–70). This is brief tedium indeed. Mr Knightley's rebuke to Emma appears in the same terms as Theseus's to Hippolyta in Act V scene i of *A Midsummer Night's Dream*. When she jeers at the actors' lack of ability, complaining 'I love not to see wretchedness o'ercharged, / And duty in his service perishing', Theseus replies,

> The kinder we, to give them thanks for nothing.
> Our sport shall be to take what they mistake;
> And what poor duty cannot do, noble respect
> Takes it in might, not merit.

'Never anything can be amiss / When simpleness and duty tender it', he explains. True courtesy will prevent the nobles from despising their inferiors, who say themselves that 'if we offend it is but with our good-will. That you should think we come not to offend, but with good will'. These words are used of Miss Bates almost every time she appears: 'she knows I would not offend for the world', or 'her own universal good-will' (176, 21). Hippolyta is courteous at last. 'Well shone Moon', she says appreciatively, and Emma goes off willingly to visit Miss Bates.

Emma and Hippolyta must learn that their superiority in rank and intelligence do not give them rights to laugh at those who offend only with their good-will. On the contrary, their *noblesse* obliges them to be encouraging and supportive to their inferiors. When Mr Knightley rebukes Emma for her insolent wit, Emma like Hippolyta at first shrugs it off, explaining 'you must allow, that what is good and what is ridiculous are most unfortunately blended in her'. Mr Knightley will not allow her excuse. 'Her situation should secure your compassion. It was badly done, indeed!' (375). Compassion, generosity, forbearance, toleration, and graciousness form another cluster of words towards which the book steadily works. Miss Bates may be a figure of fun like Bottom, but her minutiae and her digressions show her relishing life as much as he. Emma has indeed done badly in this scene of tragical mirth.

This novel proceeds by comparison, as John Burrows saw in his book. We forgive and understand along with the characters by a kind of extenuating relativism. This growing mood of toleration and forgiveness is signalled by the words blunder, forgive, and pardon. Most obviously in the puzzle game (347–9) Frank picks out the secret message 'blunder', but in the agony of the moment Jane pushes the letters forming 'pardon' angrily away, a detail recorded again in family tradition (*Memoir*, p. 158). 'Blunder' occurs over and over in the book associated with blindness, as when Emma amuses herself by thinking how John Knightley blunders in thinking her blind and ignorant, or at last recognises the 'blunders, the blindness of her own head and heart!' (112, 411–12). We are back with the vocabulary of *A Midsummer Night's Dream*, its repetitions of 'blind' and 'ignorant' and 'delusion' and 'dream'. Indeed Frank has been a kind of Puck as Emma realises. 'I do suspect that in the midst of your perplexities at that time, you had very great amusement in tricking us all ... I am sure it was a source of high entertainment to you, to feel that you were taking us all in' (478). He may not put a girdle round the earth in forty minutes (II. i. 175–6), but he does cover sixteen miles twice over on his restless errand to London (205).

Even for Frank there is forgiveness. Once she is safe with Mr Knightley, Emma is in perfect charity with Frank, and even he, if he could have thought of Frank Churchill as they returned to the house, 'might have deemed him a very good sort of fellow' (436, 433). The book moves from the pity that conceals a desire to possess and manipulate, as in Mr Woodhouse's 'poor Miss Taylor', to the compassion of genuine friendship. Friendship and forgiveness spread out, marked by the earnest shaking of hands. Mr Knightley presses Emma's hand when he knows she has been to see Miss Bates, and when Jane longs to apologise to Emma, Emma cries warmly, taking her hand, 'you owe me no apologies ... all the apologies should be on my side. Let us forgive each other at once' (386, 459). All her friendly feelings are compressed in that earnest shake of the hand. Frank thanks her for her forgiveness, hoping that 'time has not made you less willing to pardon'. 'No indeed', says Emma, 'I am particularly glad to see and shake hands with you' (476). Emma and Mr Knightley apologise to each other, for each has much to forgive (432). Emma too has been something of a Puck, as Tave sees in his book (p. 212) – she has done mischief, as she admits to Frank. 'Perhaps I am the readier to suspect [you of meddling], because, to tell you the truth, I think it might have been some amusement to myself in the same situation. I think there is a little likeness between us' (413, 478).

A Midsummer Night's Dream ends likewise in perfect reconciliation. Puck's last act is to ask that this amity be extended further, to the relationship between actors and audience. He begs for friendship as well as applause when he says in the last lines of the play,

> Give me your hands, if we be friends,
> And Robin shall restore amends.

Shakespeare implicitly asks for understanding to be extended to himself as author, just as the Jane Austen who shows us a world of strife restored to friendship by the earnest shaking of hands might reasonably expect sympathy and understanding for her own imaginative heroine, for her own imaginative self. The strange events of *Emma* were just 'the fierce vexation of a dream' – 'vex' is a word used often in *Emma*, from the first sentence on. Jane Fairfax's memory may however well be longer. 'What an air of probability sometimes runs through a dream!', cries Mr Woodhouse, wiser than he knows. 'And at others, what a heap of absurdities it is! ... Emma, you are a great dreamer, I think?' (345). Indeed she is. At the very end of the book Emma thinks that she dreams again, and the 'dread of being awakened from the happiest dream' is perhaps her most prominent feeling (430). So too the lovers in *A Midsummer Night's Dream* question in their newfound happiness, 'Are you sure/ That we are awake? It seems to me/ That yet we sleep, we dream' (IV. i. 189–91). Emma's good fortune, like the lovers' good fortune, is that dream and reality are one. Theseus is wrong and Hippolyta is right. By the devices of the imagination a Shakespeare, a Jane Austen, can create illusions to rival life itself.

In her first three published novels Jane Austen's attitude to the books that inspired her may be called impatiently affectionate, like Emma's to Miss Bates. To some extent I think she wanted her readers to recognise her allusions and see what she had done. By the time she writes *Emma* the case seems different. John Dryden would instantly have recognised what she does with *A Midsummer Night's Dream* in *Emma*, he who wrote, 'I take Imitation of an Authour ... to be an Endeavour of a later Poet to write like one who has written before him on the same subject: that is, not to Translate his words, or to be Confin'd to his Sense, but only to set him as a Pattern, and to write, as he supposes, that Authour would have done, had he liv'd in our Age, and in our Country' (I. 184).

Jane Austen is indeed a 'translator' of Shakespeare. She imitates him by involving his characters, events, and ideas in a new and contemporary context. But where I see literary criticism of her sources everywhere in those first three works, as if she were aware of them all the time, here the variations are much more loose and free. Less closely tied to her original, less immediately referential, she creates a new province of fiction with an expansiveness not seen before. Elizabeth's world has limits and Fanny's certainly has ha-ha's, but Emma's world goes on through family and friends and absent characters, for ever. Much too must be ascribed to the maturity of her gift, but something might also be suggested from the fact that she has moved in her 'translating' to the greatest master of them all, Shakespeare. She meets him in *Emma* as an equal.

7

Persuasion

Debate fills the penultimate chapter of *Persuasion*. Anne Elliot, faced with Captain Harville's accusations about the inconstancy of women, his threat to call up 'fifty quotations in a moment on my side the argument' from histories, stories, songs, and proverbs, replies firmly, 'if you please, no reference to examples in books'. They are all written by men, who, she says, 'have had every advantage of us in telling their own story. Education has been theirs in so much higher a degree; the pen has been in their hands. I will not allow books to prove any thing'. But the one who said this first was Chaucer's Wife of Bath.[1] Driven distracted by Jankyn's collection of stories and proverbs about wicked women, she insisted that all depends upon who tells the story:

> By God! if wommen hadde writen stories,
> As clerkes [learned men] han withinne hire oratories,
> They wold han writen of men moore wikkednesse
> Than al the mark of Adam may redresse! (ll. 693–6)

Anne Elliot and the Wife of Bath might seem a capricious, even ludicrous pairing, but the similarity suggests that Jane Austen read Chaucer with attention.

What are we to do with this allusion? It does seem that Jane Austen often knew novels, plays, or poems virtually by heart, entering into their imagined worlds until they were as real to her as life itself. And if, as I have suggested, her books are often transformations of Shakespeare, Milton, Locke, or Richardson, why not other authors that she knew? It is safe enough to note echoes from books owned by herself or her family, but where evidence is circumstantial, should one necessarily be more cautious? Complete lists survive neither of her collection nor of her borrowings from circulating libraries, only those she mentions or those that happen to turn up in sales (see Gilson, section K). An apparent allusion like this one to the Wife of Bath may be more than a scrap of the kind by which Edmund says most people remember Shakespeare (*MP*, 338). If her own book seems to be deeply informed by the same issues and ideas, we can pursue the seam as long as it will hold.[2]

Chaucer she could scarcely miss, just as if we had no proof of her reading Shakespeare we could safely invent it. Thomas Tyrwhitt's important edition of the *Tales* (1775–8), reprinted in 1798 and widely anthologised, made Chaucer familiar reading in the latter part of the century.[3] Illustrators promptly seized on the pilgrims as a topic. One was Thomas Stothard, who also illustrated Richardson, and another was William Blake, whose painting of 1809 was published as an engraving in 1810. She is unlikely to have read Blake's rare *Descriptive Catalogue* which calls the Wife a blight and a scarecrow, but did she know Stothard and Hoppner's prospectus where, says Blake disgustedly, they 'think that the Wife of Bath is a young, beautiful, blooming damsel, and H--- says, that she is the Fair Wife of Bath, and that the Spring appears in her Cheeks'?[4] These are conventional images enough, but Jane Austen used both 'bloom' and 'spring' to characterise her own fair woman of Bath. If she had read for instance this, or Crabbe's careful account of Chaucer as a coarse but meticulous writer in the Preface to his *Tales*, or Dryden's affectionate and generous praise of 'the Father of *English* poetry' prefacing his *Fables Ancient and Modern* (*Poems*, IV. 1452), she could well have been fired to read Chaucer for herself. Dryden's version of the Wife's Tale and Pope's of her Prologue were widely available in early nineteenth-century collections of poetry, but whenever Jane Austen seems to draw on Chaucer for *Persuasion*, she seems closer to the original than to those distinguished, but often free, translations. It is intriguing to think of her reading Chaucer in the original, especially a Prologue too licentious, thought Dryden, to translate.

How far may the Wife be pursued into *Persuasion*? I believe that from the Tale she drew not only the story of the Loathly Lady herself but themes of 'gentillesse' defined as rank, wealth, outward finery, and deeds. The Wife's Prologue may similarly have prompted her discussion of 'maistrie', and her defence of constancy in women.

The Loathly Lady

In the Wife's Tale, a knight marries a repellent old woman in exchange for her help. Forced to choose whether his wife will be old and faithful or young and untrue, the knight, sighing deeply, says the decision is hers. He is instantly rewarded when she becomes fair and young, and promises to be ever faithful.

Anne Elliot likewise changes from a loathly lady to a lovely young woman in the course of *Persuasion*, but instead of magic to do the trick, Jane Austen uses loss of health and its restoration. This idea she could have found in *Sir Charles Grandison*, the book from which she had already derived so many good ideas. Richardson's heroine Harriet Byron pines away in the course of the novel because Sir Charles seems about to marry Clementina. His return restores her health. Jane Austen's heroine Anne Elliot pines away after losing Captain Wentworth eight years before, and she too must watch him court another. Harriet's heart being a 'wedded heart', she refuses another suitor (II. 289); Anne refuses Charles Musgrove out of faithfulness to Wentworth (28). Anne is Harriet's sister, for their cases are similar and their symptoms are the same. In particular, the comprehensive account of Harriet in *Grandison*'s second letter contains details corresponding to Anne's being a model of female excellence, with an elegance of mind and sweetness of character, an original bloom, prudence, and mild eyes (159, 5 – 6). When Harriet believes she has lost Sir Charles, her cheek fades, and her health languishes, to the grief of her loving family. 'And must Harriet Byron, blessed with beauty so unequalled; health so blooming; a temper so even; passions so governable; generous and grateful, even to heroism! – Superior to every woman in frankness of heart, in true delicacy; and in an understanding and judgment beyond her years – Must *she* be offered up, as a victim on the altar of hopeless Love!' (II. 546, 542). Harriet's faded cheeks, pale lips, and changed complexion all give the impression that she is not built for duration. She remains cheerful for fear of giving concern, playing the harpsichord as soon as she is asked and joining in any private ball that her grandmother decides to give (II. 659, 516).

Anne at the start of *Persuasion* seems foul and old like the Loathly Lady; Sir Walter thinks her haggard (6). Twenty-seven years old, and she bloomed at fifteen, she is 'faded and thin', her bloom vanished early (153, 6, 28). She sighs as she walks along her favourite grove (25) but like Harriet conceals her grief, not out of concern for a loving family, but in the knowledge that they are too selfish to care. At any 'unpremeditated little ball' Anne also plays for as long as she is wanted, her eyes sometimes filling with tears (47, 71).

Anne like Harriet alters from loss of love into a Loathly Lady by the time *Persuasion* begins. How she is restored to youth and beauty, like Harriet, like the Loathly Lady, is the story of the novel. Chaucer's knight had been appalled that his lady looked so 'foule', and she had chidden him for being 'dangerous', disdainful, not courteous (ll. 1082, 1090). Wentworth is equally 'not very gallant' when he thinks Anne so altered he should not have known her again, confirming Anne's sense of the destruction of her youth and bloom. 'He had thought her wretchedly altered', says the narrator, while Anne imagines him looking at her 'altered features', at the 'ruins of the face which had once charmed him' (60–1, 72). Those features are restored, as for Harriet, by the restoration of affection. After Sir Charles Grandison proposes to Harriet and compliments her on her 'restored complexion [I did indeed feel my face glow]' (III. 76), her health is never again in doubt. 'Glow' is also Jane Austen's word for a blush, a sensibility, an erotic awareness, with 'complexion' used again and again as a sure indicator of Anne's condition. At Lyme the narrator repeats the same words. Her features, 'having the bloom and freshness of youth restored by the fine wind which had been blowing on her complexion', instantly impress Mr Elliot, while Wentworth's look seems to say, 'even I, at this moment, see something like Anne Elliot again' (104). Anne's remarkable improvements in plumpness and looks raise hopes that she may be blessed with a second spring of youth and beauty (124). Even her father thinks her 'less thin in her person, in her cheeks; her skin, her complexion, greatly improved, – clearer, fresher' (145). Although the baronet puts it down to Gowland, he is not all wrong. Complexion is the key to beauty. Soon she is generally acknowledged to be very pretty, and encouragement about Wentworth's feelings makes her eyes brighten and her cheeks glow (177, 185). After the proposal Anne is 'glowing and lovely' (245). When Wentworth in the forgetfulness of his love earnestly asserts that 'to my eye you could never alter', Anne lets it pass, knowing that 'it is something for a woman to be assured, in her eight-and-twentieth year, that she has not lost one charm of earlier youth' (243). When Chaucer's knight sees how fair and young the lady is, 'for joye' he seizes her in his arms, 'his herte bathed in a bath of blisse'. And, says the Wife, they lived to their lives' end 'in parfit joye' (ll. 1252–8). So too Anne and Wentworth, exquisitely happy, their 'spirits dancing in private rapture', pace the gradual ascent, the author promising them a future in which to number this moment among their happiest (240). Thus Jane Austen turns her lady from a loathly to a lovely one as Chaucer did, and calls on Richardson's realistic method to do so. But first she layers her story with images of autumn and spring drawn, I think, from Thomson and from Shakespeare.

Jane Austen, who owned Thomson's works, quotes from *The Seasons*, one of the major poems of the century, in *Northanger Abbey* (15). She also mentions him in *Sense and Sensibility* (92). She may for instance have found there Wentworth's exemplum of the 'glossy' hazel-nut which he catches down to Louisa from 'an upper bough' (88), because in Thomson's 'Autumn' another lover finds hazel-nuts 'where they burnish on the top-most Bough', a 'glossy Shower' (ll. 617–20). Among the 'some few of the thousand poetical descriptions extant of autumn, that season of peculiar and inexhaustible influence on the mind of taste and tenderness, that season which has drawn from every poet, worthy of being read, some attempt at description, or some lines of feeling' (84) must surely be included Thomson's 'Autumn'. Like Milton's protagonist in *Il Penseroso* on which it draws, the poet there describes himself as walking solitary and pensive 'through the sadden'd Grove' (l. 972), just as Anne walks sighing and thinking through the grove at Kellynch (25). These autumnal reflections are countered, however, by the fact that as in Thomson the seasons revolve and spring returns again. She sees 'the ploughs at work, and the fresh-made path spoke the farmer, counteracting the sweets of poetical despondence, and meaning to have spring again'. She herself has put aside the 'sweet scenes of autumn' unless 'some tender sonnet, fraught with the apt analogy of the declining year, with declining happiness, and the images of youth and hope, and spring, all gone together, blessed her memory' (85). The obvious sonnets are Shakespeare's. In Sonnet 73 yellow leaves like Anne's tawny ones (84), ruined quires like the 'ruins' of Anne's face, and autumn identified with the speaker's state of mind, suggest that this is indeed what Jane Austen thought of. Her autumn is replaced by 'a second spring of youth and beauty' (124), for Anne, overleaping winter, comes round to spring again, blooming like the Countess of Hertford to whom Thomson addressed his song.[5]

In 'Spring', the maiden's attractive bloom leads to love, but absence can 'Chill the warm Cheek, and blast the Bloom of Life' (1. 1006). 'Sad amid the social Bands [the lover] sits, / Lonely, and inattentive' (ll. 1017–18). Thomson seeks out sympathetic scenes in nature, falling into the melancholy so well described in 'Autumn':

> He comes! he comes! in every Breeze the POWER
> Of PHILOSOPHIC MELANCHOLY comes!
> His near Approach the sudden-starting Tear,
> The glowing Cheek, the mild dejected Air,
> The soften'd Feature, and the beating Heart,
> Pierc'd deep with many a virtuous Pang, declare.
>
> (ll. 1004–9)

Melancholy real and imaginary is a major theme in *Persuasion*, as McMaster notes in her book. Anne has genuine cause for hers, even though she laughs at herself for feeding it with quotations. When Captain Benwick does exactly the same thing, she recommends some fortifying prose (101). Her self-indulgence in 'grieving to forego all the influence so sweet and so sad of the autumnal months in the country' (33) is forgiveable compared to Mary's imaginary agitations and her claim that she suffers more than anyone else. Mrs Musgrove's large fat sighings for a son she hardly recalls is melancholy artificially invoked, and Captain Benwick's turns out to be just as manufactured (66–8, 96–7). Intimately acquainted 'with the tenderest songs of [Scott], and all the impassioned descriptions of hopeless agony of [Byron], he repeated with ... tremulous feeling, the various lines which imaged a broken heart, or a mind destroyed by wretchedness'. He doubts the efficacy of more heartening books 'on grief like his' (100–1). His carefully nourished melancholy is comically reminiscent of Jacques in *As You Like It* sucking melancholy out of songs 'as a weasel sucks eggs', or of the Duke in *Twelfth Night*, a play known to Darcy and Elizabeth Bennet (44), who feeds his love-melancholy through the 'sweet pangs' of the Clown's lugubrious songs.

Rain in both 'Autumn' and *Persuasion* accompanies melancholy, natural enough for autumn, and traditional for lost love, as in the anonymous sixteenth-century poem:

> Western wind, when wilt thou blow,
> The small rain down can rain?
> Christ, if my love were in my arms,
> And I in my bed again!

Persistent rain falls in *Persuasion*. When Anne leaves Kellynch a 'small thick rain' almost blots out all she loves; when she is newly separated from Wentworth, Bath is 'smoking in rain' (123, 135) deceptively like the 'smoky rayn' that keeps Chaucer's inconstant Criseyde under Pandarus's roof, with Troilus (III. 628). It rains again when Wentworth comes back to Bath, but he has bought an umbrella as though he means to stay (177). Although rain keeps everyone aside while the last vital conversation takes place, the lovers' slow and rapturous walk together must be made possible by a magical clearing in the weather (240). As Thomson had said in both 'Autumn' and 'Spring', rain is not only destructive but regenerative; it promotes growth, fertility, and spring. Like the Flood it promises new beginnings, as Griffin sees (p. 193). Rain, at first the correlative to melancholy in *Persuasion*, becomes the agent for spring, and a mirror to Anne Elliot's renewal.[6]

If autumn promises spring, melancholy contains hope. 'Exquisite', a word often applied to 'the English malady', melancholy,[7] occurs often in this book about intense feelings. Sometimes it means torture, excruciating pain, as when Anne and Wentworth remember the first meeting in Milsom-street and the concert as 'made up of exquisite moments' (244). At other times it means a different kind of acute sensibility, as when they return again into their past 'more exquisitely happy, perhaps, in their re-union, than when it had been first projected' (240).[8] Most typically though for this heroine of a 'thousand feelings' (59), 'exquisite' means a happiness mixed with pain which to Burke represented the sublime, and to the Romantics the whole soul of man brought into activity. When Doody writes in *The Daring Muse* that in mid-Augustan poetry the truly fine experience is intense, painful, 'uncertain, mingled and strenuous', she might just as well be speaking of *Persuasion* (p. 175).

Anne's 'exquisite' gratification when Wentworth is jealous of Mr Elliot is for instance quickly succeeded by 'misery' when she cannot communicate the truth to him (191). Characteristically she lives in 'the happiness of such misery, or the misery of such happiness', and Wentworth too must find out what it means to be in 'half agony, half hope' (229, 237). Pain and pleasure mingle in this book (184), to mark a fineness of sensibility that creates not only intensity but anxiety in the reader as to how it will be resolved. When Reginald Farrer writes in his 'Jane Austen, *ob.* July 18 1817' that 'the sensitised reader is left fairly staggering in the gale of Anne's emotion', he captures exactly one's sense of Anne as a vulnerable and responsive Eolian wind-harp, like Coleridge's. The 'lively pain' attendant upon 'strong felicity' at the end of *Persuasion* is characteristic of the whole (251). Anne's feelings of sunshine and glory at being a sailor's wife, mixed with a tax of quick alarm, are exquisite, intense, sublime.

In the same kind of way the extravagant melancholy of Thomson, Scott, and Byron points to their energetic Romanticism. To the list of poets that Jane Austen had fresh in her mind when she wrote *Persuasion*, we may I think add Coleridge.[9] There is a distinct echo of *Kubla Khan*, published the summer she finished her first draft, in the 'green chasms between romantic rocks', the 'luxuriant growth' of the wonderful Pinny at Lyme (95). Anne is no woman wailing for her demon lover, but the sense of bursting out, of release from restraint everywhere evident in that extraordinary dream poem, parallels closely the exhilaration of spirits after Anne's escape into a world of purpose, energy, and radiant life.

Gentillesse as rank, wealth, and beauty

Chaucer's knight, wallowing and tossing in his bed beside his new wife, complains bitterly of her age, her ugliness, her low degree. She responds briskly, attacking the notion that 'gentillesse/ As is descended out of old richesse' inevitably makes men noble: 'Swich arrogance is nat worth an hen' (ll. 1109–12). The greatest gentleman, she says, is he who does all the gentle deeds he can, for 'gentillesse' comes from Christ alone. She quotes from Dante's *Purgatorio* (VII. 121–3) to the effect that true goodness comes from God, not through the 'branches' of a family (l. 1128). Virtuous living is not to be bequeathed like wealth: indeed the fact that man may hurt and maim temporal things proves in another way that 'gentereye / Is nat annexed to possessioun' (ll. 1146–7). A lord's son may do shame and villainy even if born of a gentle house and noble, virtuous elders. Conversely, if he does not do gentle deeds, 'he nys nat gentil, be he duc or erl; / For vileyns synful dedes make a cherl' (ll. 1157–8). She concludes with the proverb, 'he is gentil that dooth gentil dedis' (l. 1170). As Dryden sums it up, the Wife's Tale shows 'the silly Pride of Ancestry and Titles without inherent Vertue, which is the true Nobility' (IV. 1460).

How like this is to *Persuasion*. Jane Austen is as forthright as Dryden or the lady when she talks of Anne's 'conceited, silly father' (5), his belief in the importance of beauty and inherited rank, his attachment to his 'possessioun' Kellynch Hall, his vanity in thinking that he deserves his position in life. Captain Wentworth by contrast does noble deeds by land and sea in a profession distinguished in its domestic virtues as well as in its national importance, and thus proves himself a gentleman (252); the Lady praises deeds 'pryvee and apert', private and public (l. 1114). Though of noble blood Mr Elliot proves a churl, an undutiful 'branch ... dismembered ... from the paternal tree' (136) exactly as Chaucer in echo of Dante had said. Commentators agree that Chaucer's translation of him is not altogether clear. Jane Austen, who knew something of Italian (*Memoir*, p. 88), and read, thinks Bradbrook (p. 79), the *Inferno*, the *Purgatorio*, and the *Paradiso* in translation, might well have checked for herself what Dante actually said, for in Dante the stanza is indeed made up of 'inverted, transposed, curtailed Italian lines' such as William Elliot admires Anne for being able to translate (186).

Pride of descent is linked in *Persuasion* as in the Tale with wealth and with vanity of outward appearance. All three are embodied in Sir Walter Elliot, admiring, as the book opens, his own ancient and respectable lineage. Jane Austen's tone is consistently attacking whenever she speaks of Sir Walter:

Vanity was the beginning and the end of Sir Walter Elliot's character; vanity of person and of situation ... Few women could think more of their personal appearance than he did; nor could the valet of any new made lord be more delighted with the place he held in society. He considered the blessing of beauty as inferior only to the blessing of a baronetcy; and the Sir Walter Elliot, who united these gifts, was the constant object of his warmest respect and devotion.　　　　　　　　　　　　　　　　(4)

Pride of descent made Sir Walter forbid the 'degrading' alliance of Anne to the base-born Wentworth, 'a stranger without alliance or fortune' (26–7).[10] Lady Russell and the Musgrove girls provide variations on the theme of 'rank, people of rank, and jealousy of rank', Mrs Clay flatters Sir Walter, and Sir Walter is proud to walk behind the broad back of privilege belonging to the dowager Viscountess Dalrymple (11, 46, 185). She and her daughter Miss Carteret splendidly prove the Tale's contention that to be born of noble blood is not necessarily to be noble. 'There was no superiority of manner, accomplishment, or understanding. Lady Dalrymple had acquired the name of "a charming woman," because she had a smile and a civil answer for every body. Miss Carteret, with still less to say, was so plain and so awkward, that she would never have been tolerated in Camden-place but for her birth' (150). When the little flea Mrs Clay deserts Sir Walter, he finds that 'to flatter and follow others, without being flattered and followed in turn, is but a state of half enjoyment' (251).

Anne is the only Elliot to stand out against pride of rank. '"Well," said Anne, "I certainly am proud, too proud to enjoy a welcome which depends so entirely upon place"' (151). Charles Musgrove's warm outburst that he will not fawn on the Dalrymples and Mr Elliot, 'I am not one of those who neglect the reigning power to bow to the rising sun. If I would not go for the sake of your father, I should think it scandalous to go for the sake of his heir' (224), allows Anne to show Wentworth that she agrees.

'Possession' is to Sir Walter the second sign of a gentleman, after rank. Wentworth's brother had no property and so is nobody, but Charles Musgrove, for being the eldest son of a man of landed property and general importance, is somebody (23, 28). As the Lady says, however, nobility must deserve its riches. Sir Walter is foolish and spendthrift, without 'principle or sense enough to maintain himself in the situation in which Providence had placed him' (248). So distressed for money that he must retrench (9), his response is all the funnier for being a swift and accurate parody of that other proud old man, King Lear.[11] 'What! Every comfort of life knocked off! Journeys, London, servants, horses, table, – contractions and restrictions every where. To live no longer with the decencies even of a private gentleman! No, he would sooner quit Kellynch-hall at once, than remain in it on such disgraceful terms' (13). Sir Walter stalks off not to the tempestuous heath, but to rainy Bath, and his daughters are not so much his tormentors as companions in vanity. But Anne does resemble Cordelia, for her voice too is gentle and low, an excellent thing in a woman, and even when it harms her she does her duty, obeying Lady Russell and clearing away the claims of creditors (12). Like Cordelia she is the true defender of her father's honours when William Elliot, like Shakespeare's Edmund, plots to gain the very ranks and titles he despises in their present owner (206). Anne/Cordelia's true worth is recognized in the midst of her self-seeking family by Wentworth/France, and although Sir Walter 'could give his daughter at present but a small part of the share of ten thousand pounds which must be hers hereafter', he recognizes her at the end, though a very fond and 'foolish' old man (248).

Sir Walter never knows how much his importance depends upon Kellynch Hall. Anne alone grieves that

her father should feel no degradation in his change; should see nothing to regret in the duties and dignity of the resident land-holder; should find so much to be vain of in the littlenesses of a town; and she must sigh, and smile, and wonder too, as Elizabeth threw open the folding-doors, and walked with exultation from one drawing-room to the other, boasting of their space, at the possibility of that woman, who had been mistress of Kellynch Hall, finding extent to be proud of between two walls, perhaps thirty feet asunder.   (138)

By contrast, the naval officers cut through dependence upon place by having no home at all. The Crofts are happy to be tenants of Kellynch Hall, Captain Harville by 'ingenious contrivances and nice arrangements' turns the small rooms of their lodgings to 'excellent accommodations', and Mrs Croft says that women on ships may be 'as comfortable on board, as in the best house in England' (98–9, 69). It is not the nature of the accommodation that matters, but the busyness and merit of the occupants. Anne's 'raptures of admiration and delight on the character of the navy – their friendliness, their brotherliness, their openness, their uprightness ... they only knew how to live, and they only deserved to be respected and loved' (99), have much to do with the fact that their characters, not their quarters, give them consequence.

Most important of all, the seafaring people are ennobled by their hospitality. Hospitality, as a mark of gentility, one finds in Pope rather than in Chaucer's Tale, pervading his *Odyssey* as well as his verse about his own hospitable house at Twickenham. *The Second Satire of the Second Book of Horace Paraphras'd*, which shrugs off the loss of property into other hands, is a particularly apt rebuke for Elizabeth Elliot:

> My lands are sold, my Father's house is gone;
> I'll hire another's; is not that my own,
> And yours my friends? thro' whose free-opening gate
> None comes too early, none departs too late;
> (For I, who hold sage Homer's rule the best,
> Welcome the coming, speed the going guest).   (ll. 155–60)

Elizabeth, knowing she ought to ask the Musgrove party to dine with them in their hired lodgings, is restrained by her awareness that she must betray a difference from the style at Kellynch Hall. She rationalizes to herself, 'Old fashioned notions – country hospitality – we do not profess to give dinners – few people in Bath do' (219). But even in hired lodgings the Harvilles are 'kindly hospitable'. Anne, who sees 'such a bewitching charm in a degree of hospitality so uncommon, so unlike the usual style of give-and-take invitations, and dinners of formality and display' and 'heartless elegance' (98, 226) – like that of Pope's Timon – might well conclude with Pope,

> Let lands and houses have what Lords they will,
> Let Us be fix'd, and our own masters still.   (ll. 179–80)

Anne alone of all her family has never believed that property makes the gentleman. She easily resists the temptation of being mistress of Kellynch and William Elliot's wife, and when she does visit it again, 'could not but in conscience feel that they were gone who deserved not to stay; and that Kellynch-hall had passed into better hands than its owners'.' She has 'no power of saying to herself, ''These rooms ought to belong only to us. Oh, how fallen in their destination! How unworthily occupied! An ancient family to be so driven away! Strangers filling their place!'' No, except when she thought of her mother, and remembered where she had been used to sit and preside, she had no sigh of that description to heave' (125–6). Instead of gaining their importance from the 'richesse' of property, naval men, forever on the move, derive their nobility from noble deeds, national importance, and domestic life. For them, 'gentereye / Is nat annexed to possessioun' (ll. 1146–7).

Poverty, says the Loathly Lady, is not to be despised. Answering the knight's complaint that she is not only old and ugly but poor, she argues from the example of Jesus that whoever is content with his poverty is in fact rich, even if he is without a shirt. He who is poor but not covetous is rich indeed, for all that the knight may think him a menial. Poverty is a hateful good, she says, being a great incentive to a livelihood. It improves the wisdom of those who take it patiently, for the poor man discovers both God and himself and finds out who his true friends are (ll. 1177–98). Similar arguments inform the Mrs Smith episode in *Persuasion*. Sir Walter, like the knight in reviling women for being ugly, old, and poor, particularly attacks Anne's friend for being a 'poor widow, barely able to live,' 'old and sickly'. This is choice, because he, who frittered away his own fortune, does not recollect that Mrs Smith is 'not the only widow in Bath between thirty and forty, with little to live on' (157–8). He has forgotten his toady, Mrs Clay.

To this ungentle knight Anne makes the same reply as the Loathly Lady to hers. She observes that Mrs Smith has allowed neither sickness nor sorrow to close her heart or ruin her spirit. Although she has lost everything, husband and influence both, and has neither child, relations, nor health (like Chaucer's 'al hadde he nat a sherte'), poverty *has* been a hateful good to her, for it has set her upon a livelihood making and selling knick-knacks through her friend Nurse Rooke. As Anne says, expanding upon Chaucer's lady, 'a submissive spirit might be patient, a strong understanding would supply resolution, but here was something more; here was that elasticity of mind, that disposition to be comforted, that power of turning readily from evil to good, and of finding employment which carried her out of herself, which was from Nature alone'. This, thinks Anne, is the choicest gift of Heaven (compare *Paradise Lost*, V. 18), an instance where 'by a merciful appointment, it seems designed to counterbalance almost every other want' (154). And if poverty is as the Lady says 'a spectacle' through which 'he may his verray freendes see' (ll. 1203–4), Mrs Smith from the vantage of her poverty sees that there is 'little real friendship in the world' (156). William Elliot, once a most intimate friend of her husband, betrayed him in his poverty. Like Antonio in *Twelfth Night* who complains that his friend Sebastian, as he thinks, denies him his own purse freely lent, Mr Smith had treated Mr Elliot like a brother; having the 'finest, most generous spirit in the world, [he] would have divided his last farthing with him; and I know that his purse was open to him' (199–200). Mr Elliot's 'cold civility' and 'hard-hearted indifference' make up for Anne as for Amiens in *As You Like It* 'a dreadful picture of ingratitude and inhumanity'. No flagrant open crime could have been worse, she thinks (209–10).

Mrs Smith finds one friend in Anne and another in Wentworth, who takes on the executorship relinquished by Mr Elliot, and brings her financial relief. But, says the narrator, 'these prime supplies of good', her 'cheerfulness and mental alacrity', were still as they had been when she found contentment in the Wife's 'glad poverte'. Indeed she says, giving it one final turn, 'she might have been absolutely rich and perfectly healthy, and yet be happy' (252).

Gentillesse as outward appearance

Sir Walter Elliot believes that nobility inheres in rank, wealth, and beauty, but he is not himself ennobled by any of them. In the fixity of his conviction he is easy prey to those who fasten on the vulnerable vanity of place, to a Mr Shepherd, shepherding his client wherever he likes, or a Mrs Clay, common and malleable as clay, who changes allegiance – a bold political reference for Regency Bath – from the old king to the new.[12] Vain himself, he is readily deceived by nobility of outward appearance. To develop her characterisation of the theme in Mr Elliot, Sir Walter, and Captain Wentworth, Jane Austen turned again to Richardson.

William Elliot seems at first to be like Sir Charles Grandison as described in Volume I, letter xxxvi. His manners are polished and easy (143), just as Sir Charles shows 'ease and freedom of manners'. 'Though not handsome, [William Elliot] had an agreeable person' (105); Sir Charles is 'thought (what is far more eligible in a man, than mere beauty) very agreeable'. Like Richardson's hero, William Elliot claims to have 'strong feelings of family-attachment and family-honour', living with the 'liberality of a man of fortune, without display'; Sir Charles dresses 'rather richly ... than gaudily'; his equipage 'not so much to the glare of taste, as if he aimed either to inspire or shew emulation'. Mr Elliot judges 'for himself in every thing essential, without defying public opinion in any point of worldly decorum' (146); Sir Charles lives 'to himself, and to his own heart; and ... tho' he had the happiness to please every-body, yet made the judgment or approbation of the world matter but of second consideration'.

Like Sir Charles, Mr Elliot claims to value all the felicities of domestic life, for his first marriage has produced 'no unhappiness to sour his mind' (147); the good sense of Sir Charles is not 'rusted over by sourness, by moroseness'. His 'air of elegance and fashion' produces a 'very gentlemanlike appearance', where Sir Charles 'dresses to the fashion'; his 'good shaped face' is like Sir Charles's, 'in shape .. a fine oval', his 'sensible eye' is also like Sir Charles's, which shows 'sparkling intelligence'. No wonder, when he looks the perfect hero, that everyone should be fooled. Everyone except Sir Walter, who laments that he is very much under-hung (141).

Sir Walter for once is right. William Elliot is not Sir Charles Grandison – and this is actually the *fourth time* that she has used this revelation in her novels – but his rake Sir Hargrave Pollexfen. When Mr Elliot claims longer acquaintance with Anne than is physically possible, and argues that 'I knew you by report long before you came to Bath. I had heard you described by those who knew you intimately. I have been acquainted with you by character many years. Your person, your disposition, accomplishments, manner – they were all described, they were all present to me' (187), he is particularly like Sir Hargrave seeking to ingratiate himself with Harriet Byron. 'And are at last my eyes bless'd with the sight of a young Lady so celebrated for her graces of person and mind? Much did I hear, when I was at the last Northampton races, of Miss Byron: But little did I expect to find report fall so short of what I see' (I.43). No more than Harriet does Anne wish to marry her unwelcome suitor. He is nothing to her, she says (196), just as casually as Harriet says 'he does not hit my fancy'. She provokes Mrs Smith's accusation of cruelty in pretending to delay, much as Harriet, accused of cruelty by Sir Hargrave, decides not to indulge in 'female trifling' (I.83).

The abrupt discovery of Mr Elliot's villainy has puzzled many readers. It seems an uncharacteristically clumsy resolution, and one wonders what she might have done with it if she had revised it as she did the ending. It is then interesting to know that Mrs Smith's melodramatic sketch of William Elliot's true character closely echoes Richardson's scene in which a character arbitrarily appears to warn Harriet about Sir Hargrave. Harriet knows of the rake's ungentle deeds before she ever meets him; Anne though likes the man before she knows him. Sir Hargrave, says Harriet's informant, is 'a cruel man', 'a very dangerous and enterprising man ... malicious, ill-natured, and designing; and sticks at nothing to carry a point on which he has once set his heart'. He has 'ruined' three young creatures (I.63). Mr Elliot, says Mrs Smith, is a man 'without heart or conscience; a designing, wary, cold-blooded being, who ... would be guilty of any cruelty', one who leads others into 'ruin' (199). Once again Jane Austen conflates Richardson's hero with his villain, and so unfolds a plot.

Sir Walter ought by his station in life to be a Sir Charles Grandison, but Admiral Croft makes a better landlord than he, a better example to the parish, and kinder to the poor (125).[13] Sir Walter resembles Sir Hargrave in vanity. Whereas the admiral remarks, 'he must be rather a dressy man for his time of life. – Such a number of looking-glasses! oh Lord! there was no getting away from oneself' (128), Sir Hargrave

forgets not to pay his respects to himself at every glass; yet does it with a seeming consciousness, as if he would hide a vanity too apparent to be concealed; breaking from it, if he finds himself observed, with a half-careless, yet seemingly dissatisfied air, pretending to have discover'd something amiss in himself. This seldom fails to bring him a compliment: Of which he shows very sensible, by affectedly disclaiming the merit of it; perhaps with this speech, bowing, with his spread hand upon

his breast, waving his head to and fro – By my Soul, Madam (or Sir) you
do me too much honour.   (I. 45)

Just so Sir Walter forces a compliment. 'Modest Sir Walter! He
was not allowed to escape, however. His daughter and Mrs. Clay
united in hinting that Colonel Wallis's companion might have
as good a figure as Colonel Wallis, and certainly was not sandy-
haired'. The watch from *The Rape of the Lock* might well strike
eleven with its silver sounds for Sir Walter's sacred rites of pride
(142–4) – as H. J. C. Grierson pointed out in a letter to the *TLS*.

Taken to extremes, concern for outward appearance actively
disables. As Fielding wrote in the *Covent-Garden Journal*, no. 4
(14 January 1752) the word 'fine' in phrases such as '*fine*
Gentleman, *fine* Lady' is to be understood 'in a Sense somewhat
synonymous with useless'. Convention's power to fetter is what
Mrs Croft protests about to Wentworth. 'I hate to hear you
talking so, like a fine gentleman, and as if women were all fine
ladies, instead of rational creatures' (70), that is, sensible women
who cope like her, like Anne, with adversity and hardship.

Captain Wentworth alone is a true Sir Charles Grandison,
for only in him appears that Platonic correlation between outward beauty and inner worth, the fine appearance that neither
deceives the spectator nor disables the possessor. Sir Charles
is 'a real fine gentleman' valued 'not so much for being an
handsome man; not so much for his birth and fortune' as 'for
being, in the great and yet comprehensive sense of the word,
a *good man*' (I. 182). Richardson here struggles to characterise
realistically the Christian Hero. The Wife's public and private
spheres of action recur in the remark that Sir Charles is 'one of
the busiest men in the kingdom ... and yet the most of a family-
man' (I. 279). He rescues the heroine, he delivers his friends, he
performs all the relative and social duties. Captain Wentworth's
deeds are conditioned by their setting in Regency not Arthurian
England, but his rescue of Anne from the suffocating embraces
of the child or his concern for her fatigue are knightly and gentle
enough. His dashing naval career displays the martial hero. In
private he is like Sir Charles when he helps the Harville family,
succours his friend Benwick, or acts as executor for Mrs Smith.
The 'domestic virtues' and 'national importance' of his profession are the last resounding words of the novel, the summary

of Wentworth's true standing as a Christian Hero. Sir Walter, eyeing his new son-in-law more closely by daylight, is 'very much struck by his personal claims', and feels that such superiority of appearance might be not unfairly balanced against Anne's superiority of rank (248). He ennobles Wentworth as he ought when he enters the marriage in the volume of honour, for here is a man gentle not for rank or wealth, but for deeds, as the Loathly Lady prescribed.

Maistrie

Whether or not Chaucer originally designed the Wife's Tale for her, it deals like her Prologue with 'maistrie', or control in marriage. The Loathly Lady and the Wife, both older women married to young men, have lost the power once granted them by youth. As soon as sovereignty is returned to them they become loving, and young as well in the case of the Lady. Both stories are self-referential, self-fulfilling. The knight, by acting out his theoretical knowledge that what women love best is 'maistrie', wins a wife miraculously restored to youth; Jankyn, by giving the Wife the reins, ensures she will be loving and true.

But the Wife must fight to gain her power. Violence ends her Prologue when she attacks Jankyn for gloating over his book. She tears out a leaf (or three), throws it into the flames, and hits him backwards into the fire. He smites her on the head so that 'in the floor I lay as I were deed' (l. 796). Suddenly the story looks very like that of the determined Louisa Musgrove jumping down from the Cobb at Lyme in Volume I, chapter xii. She too falls down on the pavement, severely bruising her head, to be 'taken up lifeless!' 'Her face was like death ... "She is dead! she is dead!"' screamed Mary'. The Wife feigns to wake out of her 'swogh' (l. 799); Louisa 'once opened her eyes, but soon closed them again, without apparent consciousness ... a proof of life'. Jankyn, who is 'agast' when he sees 'how stille that I lay' (ll. 797–8), kneels beside her stricken with remorse; Wentworth, seeing Louisa's closed eyes, her lack of breath, her pallid face, 'knelt with her in his arms, looking on her with a face as pallid as her own, in an agony of silence'. Jankyn asks forgiveness of his 'Deere suster Alisoun', promising 'as help me God! I shall thee nevere smyte'. But he adds, 'that I have doon, it is thyself to wyte [blame]' (ll. 804–6). In very similar words Captain Wentworth says, 'Oh God! that I had not given way to her at the fatal moment! Had I done as I ought! But so eager and so resolute! Dear, sweet Louisa!'. Like Jankyn he blames himself, but the woman too.

The Wife wins mastery over Jankyn, but Jane Austen, by giving her story to Louisa, shows Anne and Wentworth that one-sided 'maistrie' will not do. And yet just as the Wife 'condescended to be pleas'd', in Pope's version, when she gains 'by maistrie, al the soveraynetee' (l. 818), Anne feels a 'pleasure ... a great pleasure' that Wentworth shows a 'deference for her judgment' in the emergency at Lyme. Jane Austen's first volume ends just where the Prologue ends, with the woman's point of view triumphant. That the Wife's Prologue belongs to Anne as well as Louisa is shown when Mary, dimly perceiving that something is up, assures herself 'with some anxiety, that there had been no fall in the case; that Anne had not, at any time lately, slipped down, and got a blow on her head' (238). Anne too is a woman of Bath after all.

Admiral Croft seizes on the creative possibilities of the exciting event. 'A new sort of way this, for a young fellow to be making love, by breaking his mistress's head! ... This is breaking a head and giving a plaister truly!'[14] Because of similarities to Dryden's Preface to the *Fables*, Jane Austen may be actually revealing her opinion of Chaucer when she adds that his 'manners were not quite of the tone to suit Lady Russell, but they delighted Anne. His goodness of heart and simplicity of character were irresistible' (126–7). An 'uneducated' woman herself, she praises Nurse Rooke, Mrs Smith's friend, as a shrewd, intelligent, sensible woman, with

a line for seeing human nature; ... a fund of good sense and observation which, as a companion, make her infinitely superior to thousands of those who having only received 'the best education in the world,' know nothing worth attending to ... she is sure to have something to relate that is entertaining and profitable, something that makes one know one's species better.

Nurse Rooke's advantage is to witness 'varieties of human nature' (155–6); Chaucer, said Dryden, was 'a perpetual Fountain of good Sense', and knew 'the various Manners and Humours ... of the whole *English* Nation' (IV. 1452–4). One can certainly see why an author denied formal education might admire Chaucer, whose art is based on human nature. Indeed Dryden's comments on Chaucer might be extended to her own characters. Where Dryden thought Chaucer 'a rough Diamond' who 'must first be polish'd e'er he shines' (IV. 1457), Sir Walter thinks naval men 'rough and rugged to the last degree', but allows that he might not be ashamed to be seen with Admiral Croft if his own man might have had the arranging of his hair (20, 32).

If the Wife's last struggle pertains to Louisa and to Anne, her appearance as Chaucer describes it in the General Prologue is transferred rather to Mrs Croft. The Wife, bold and red-faced, with wide-set teeth and broad hips, has 'passed many a straunge strem' in her wanderings (ll. 458–72); Mrs Croft, though neither tall nor fat, had a 'squareness, uprightness, and vigour of form, which gave importance to her person'. She has 'good teeth' and a 'reddened and weather-beaten complexion, the consequence of her having been almost as much at sea as her husband' (48). 'In felaweshipe' the Wife was well able to laugh and talk (l. 474); Anne delights to watch the Crofts talk together, or to see 'their eagerness of conversation when occasionally forming into a little knot of the navy, Mrs. Croft looking as intelligent and keen as any of the officers around her' (168). Jane Austen seems though to protect Mrs Croft from being thought too like the Wife when she adds of her open and decisive manner that it is 'without any approach to coarseness, however, or any want of good humour' (48). Mrs Croft does not seek for sovereignty, but goes 'shares with him in every thing' (168). And where the Wife in her Prologue gets 'al the bridel in myn hond' (l. 813), or as Pope translates it, 'Receiv'd the Reins of Absolute Command', Mrs Croft only takes the reins to save them both from danger:

> 'My dear admiral, that post! – we shall certainly take that post.'
> But by coolly giving the reins a better direction herself, they happily passed the danger; and by once afterwards judiciously putting out her hand, they neither fell into a rut, nor ran foul of a dung-cart; and Anne [felt] some amusement at their style of driving, which she imagined no bad representation of the general guidance of their affairs ...   (92)

Such equality is what Anne and Wentworth seek. Not sovereignty, not weakness, but a sense that both are 'more equal to act'. Wentworth has learnt at Lyme 'to distinguish between the steadiness of principle and the obstinacy of self-will, between the darings of heedlessness and the resolution of a collected mind' (241-2), he has learnt to criticise Louisa, and to appreciate a more balanced equality like the Crofts'. Like the Admiral he will hand over the reins to Anne on important issues. He can forgive Lady Russell and be in charity with her, and in spite of her 'former transgressions, he could now value [her] from his heart. While he was not obliged to say that he believed her to have been right in originally dividing them, he was ready to say almost every thing else in her favour' (251). He comes as close as can be expected to admitting that Anne was right when he says, 'perhaps I ought to have reasoned thus ... but I could not. I could not derive benefit from the late knowledge I had acquired of your character' (244-5). Jane Austen at least seems to think that Anne did right when she suggests that they are 'more exquisitely happy, perhaps, in their re-union, than when it had been first projected; more tender, more tried, more fixed in a knowledge of each other's character, truth and attachment; more equal to act, more justified in acting' (240-1). The Wife and Jankyn never quarrel again, she being as loving and faithful to him as he to her. Anne too is 'tenderness itself, and she had the full worth of it in Captain Wentworth's affection' (252). By deferring to her judgment at Lyme and at the end, Wentworth like the knight, like Jankyn, exchanges some sovereignty for happiness with his wife.

The constancy of women

True valour, sings Bunyan, may be seen in one who is constant, come wind, come weather. So too Jane Austen in *Persuasion* celebrates the real heroism of constancy. Anne's relationship with Wentworth is a contest in constancy for which the revised ending provides a soaring cadenza. Anne, who has consistently turned to literature to illustrate her feelings, does so here more than ever in the contemplation of constancy and alteration. The density of allusion of the penultimate chapter is remarkable. Speakers take on the voices of characters in other literary works, voices to make up a 'book' of constant women that answers Jankyn's collection of treacherous women, in the Wife of Bath's Prologue.

Early on Anne guesses that Wentworth may be constant (30), and she is right. The clues which point to his 'eternal constancy'[15] allow her to hope that 'Surely, if there be constant attachment on each side, our hearts must understand each other ere long' (192, 221). Wentworth can write with some justice, 'Dare not say that man forgets sooner than woman ... I have loved none but you. Unjust I may have been, weak and resentful I have been, but never inconstant' (237). Proof of their true constancy in love lies in the refusal of each to see alteration in the other. Eight or nine years have not robbed him of one personal grace, thinks Anne; when Wentworth, anxious to discover if Anne has changed, remarks pointedly, 'time makes many changes', Anne cries out, 'I am not yet so much changed' (179, 225). The change in Anne is of course only temporary. Wentworth rapidly observes as little alteration in her as she in him. Both in effect say that love is not love when it alteration finds, like Shakespeare in Sonnet 116. Impediments to the marriage of these true minds disappear. The crowds that cluttered their meeting-places transform to an animated frieze, their power to hurt gone.

Opposed to this constant couple stands the fickle pair Benwick and Louisa. Benwick's inconstancy to the dead Fanny Harville appals Captain Wentworth when he has his portrait reset for Louisa (183). Captain Harville defends the constancy of men, but when he thinks of Benwick, his tongue is tied (236). The resolute and determined Louisa alters to suit this new lover, sitting quiet all day, and starting and wriggling like a dab chick when the door shuts a little hard (218).

Jane Austen wrote two different endings for *Persuasion*. The discarded one is dull, functional, bathetic, with the lovers' *éclaircissement* occuring almost comically through the agency of Admiral Croft. But the revised ending astonishes with its power to move. This is partly because Anne and Captain Harville debate issues central to the whole book, the openness to persuasion of men and women, and their constancy or alteration, but also because its rich and persistent allusiveness expands these issues out into the much larger world of Jane Austen's literary predecessors.

Shakespeare's Katherine in her final speech implicitly praises the 'painful labour' of men above the passivity of women who lie 'warm at home, secure and safe'; Anne, arguing that women forget less, turns the distinction another way. 'We cannot help ourselves. We live at home, quiet, confined, and our feelings prey upon us. You are forced on exertion. You have always a profession, pursuit, business of some sort or another, to take you back into the world immediately, and continual occupation and change soon weaken impressions' (232).[16] Katherine argues that the 'soft conditions' of women's external parts make them 'unapt to toil and trouble in the world', a point repeated by Sir Charles Grandison in Volume VI, letter lv. 'Why gave [nature] delicacy, softness, grace, to ... the woman ...; strength, firmness, to men; a capacity to bear labour and fatigue; and courage, to protect the other?'. This, he says, is a 'temporary difference' in the 'design of the different machines' that enclose our souls. Captain Harville similarly argues in return to Anne for a 'true analogy between our bodily frames and our mental; and that as our bodies are the strongest, so are our feelings; capable of bearing most rough usage, and riding out the heaviest weather'. Anne replies generously in the language of Sir Charles Grandison, who had said that men 'travel and toil for them; run through, at the call of Providence, or of our King and Country, dangers and difficulties', but adds that to comprehend both men's and women's suffering at once would be intolerable:

Your feelings may be the strongest ... but the same spirit of analogy will authorise me to assert that ours are the most tender. Man is more robust than woman, but he is not longer-lived; which exactly explains my view of the nature of their attachments. Nay, it would be too hard upon you, if it were otherwise. You have difficulties, and privations, and dangers enough to struggle with. You are always labouring and toiling, exposed to every risk and hardship. Your home, country, friends, all quitted. Neither time, nor health, nor life, to be called your own. It would be too hard indeed ... if woman's feelings were to be added to all this.

Anne maintains that man's nature made Captain Benwick inconstant. Her 'authority' could be the Duke in *Twelfth Night* admitting to Viola,[17]

> For, boy, however we do praise ourselves,
> Our fancies are more giddy and unfirm,
> More longing, wavering, sooner lost and won,
> Than women's are. 		(II. iv. 31–4)

An even more likely source is the song in *Much Ado* about men being deceivers ever, one foot on sea and one on shore, to one thing constant never, particularly when Anne is ready to blame Benwick's business at sea for weakening impressions, and Captain Harville retorts that the peace has in fact turned him on shore.

But it is to their own experience rather than to the authority of books that the Wife and Anne return. Harville's list of inconstant women, *mulieres mutabiles*, no doubt included more recent examples than Jankyn's, for instance the Wife of Bath herself, Chaucer's own Criseyde, Shakespeare's Cressida, and Hamlet's response to Gertrude, 'frailty, thy name is woman'. But it is Benwick who hastens to new sheets, though so young a mourner (108). Anne is no Cressida, no Wife of Bath. Against them she sets circumstances in favour of her own sex such as may be found 'within our own circle', many of which 'may be precisely such as cannot be brought forward without betraying a confidence, or in some respect saying what should not be said'. She means of course her own. Generous to the last, she allows all that Captain Harville says for the sensibilities and sufferings of men, with her 'God forbid that I should undervalue the warm and faithful feelings of any of my fellow-creatures', but argues still as Penelope might have, that men are constant only 'so long as you have an object ... All the privilege I claim for my own sex (it is not a very enviable one, you need not covet it) is that of loving longest, when existence or when hope is gone'. 'We men may say more, swear more', says the disguised Viola, but men 'prove / Much in our vows, but little in our love' (II.iv.115–17). Like Harriet (II.158), like Viola, Anne like Patience on a monument allows concealment like a worm in the bud to feed on her damask cheek, and sits smiling at grief. When at last Viola tells her love, she is with Desdemona or any of Shakespeare's heroines more than half the wooer. So too Anne in the revised ending actively promotes her fate, for Wentworth hears like Duke Orsino her admission of love, and acts with the same swift certainty as he.

Now we can see why the second ending is so incomparably better than the first. Resonant and allusive, it gives Anne a chance to exert herself like her sisters in Shakespeare, it lends her voices with which to speak. They throng about her, they add their testimony to hers, they provide layers of argument about women's sphere and women's constancy that gather and convince. Like the steadfastness of Shakespeare's ideal women, Anne's constancy corresponds to divine love and truth.[18]

This is Jane Austen's answer to Captain Harville's list, her reply to Jankyn's book. Above all she makes Anne like the Wife plead for the authority not of books but of experience. She herself has been constant, and her example is written out for us to read.[19] Her reward is to escape from the deadening confines of class, age, and sex into a world of doing instead of being. By adding the story of Anne Elliot to all the rest, Jane Austen uses the fact of its real existence as the Wife of Bath used hers to 'prove' the worth of women. It is the same neat trick as Shakespeare's at the end of Sonnet 116. Unless she never writ (and she has), and unless no one ever loved (and they have), there is no such thing as constancy (so there is).

In the juvenilia, Jane Austen taught herself through parodic play. Even in *Sense and Sensibility*, *Pride and Prejudice*, and *Mansfield Park* the same literary-critical impulse is often to be seen. In *Northanger Abbey*, *Emma*, and *Persuasion*, she makes other authors new, by new and contemporary contexts. The parodic impulse rarely appears, nor does she offer so frequently the special pleasure of recognizing allusions. She rewrites without irony for the most part, and although protecting Mrs Croft from being thought as coarse and ill-humoured as the Wife, seems to subscribe to a view more comparable to Hoppner's favourable one than to Blake's. That she dares to associate Anne with the Wife certainly suggests so.

Such verbal echoes, such similarities of characterisation and event and theme, cannot be random. They go well beyond coincidence to the likelihood of Jane Austen having read and used other authors. Her synthesizing and creative mind contained more than we shall ever know, but in Chaucer especially, she found energy and ideas to inspire her shaping of *Persuasion*.

'Nothing can come of nothing'

To look through the spectacles of books reveals Jane Austen's mind. Locke in *Northanger Abbey*, Richardson and Milton in *Sense and Sensibility*, *Pride and Prejudice*, and *Mansfield Park*, Shakespeare in *Emma*, and the whole range of English literature from Chaucer to Coleridge in *Persuasion*, were to Jane Austen as the classical authors to Fielding, a rich common where every person with a tenement in Parnassus has the right to fatten his muse (*Tom Jones*, XII. 1). Member as well as inaugurator of the great tradition of English literature, as F. R. Leavis saw, she steps outside fiction to fill that tradition in.[1]

Jane Austen's relationship to her predecessors is always changing. Sometimes she bounces off them as if unable to resist rewriting or commenting upon them; sometimes the relationship looks much more open and free. Locke, Shakespeare, and Chaucer are more generally invigorating in *Northanger Abbey*, *Emma*, and *Persuasion* than Richardson and Milton in the first three published books. As in Dryden's idea of imitation, Jane Austen the translator now 'assumes the liberty not only to vary from the words and sence, but to forsake them both as [s]he sees occasion: and taking only some general hints from the Original, to run division on the ground-work, as [s]he pleases' (*Poems*, I. 182). Nor does she any longer pause to criticise or rewrite authors so obviously companionable to her. *Emma* and *Persuasion* do not continually check themselves as if they lived part of their lives in other books. Still profitably and poetically 'book-built', they look more free, more unattached.

Jane Austen's memory was clearly vital to her invention. As Sir Joshua Reynolds explains it, the artist must first collect a stock of ideas to be combined and varied as occasion requires. Once he had learnt all that has been known and done before, he may dispense with instructions from a particular master and consider the art itself as his master. The third and last period, says Reynolds, emancipates the student from subjection to any authority. Now he may confide in his own judgment.[2]

In her first stage, Jane Austen sometimes incorporates material directly from other books. To know that the spunging-house and death-bed scenes of Eliza Brandon come from *Clarissa* is to understand why they sit there so uneasily. They belong, rather, in the books of Richardson her master. Bloom, in a debate on plagiarism, nicely calls such copying 'idolatry'. Sometimes she may have hoped for the allusion to be picked up. For instance, to know that Darcy proposes in the unlovely style of Sir Hargrave and Mr Collins makes Elizabeth's instinctive revulsion to him more comprehensible. Sometimes Jane Austen opens up differences between her version and her source in what Rogers in the same plagiarism debate calls 'discrepancy'; 'You alluded in order not to copy: you imitated, that is, at a conscious distance'. It is pleasant to know for instance that foolish Mrs Bennet inverts Sir Charles's solemnities on duels. Readers familiar with Richardson may also admire Jane Austen's trick of splitting and recombining different aspects of his characters, her technique of revealing one Richardsonian character to be another, and her manner of rewriting Harriet Byron's entry into Grandison Hall four completely different ways. Of course you need not know Richardson to appreciate Jane Austen, but there are bonuses if you do.

Sometimes her books derive from criticism. The first three published novels, and perhaps *Northanger Abbey* too, begin in the literary-critical style of the juvenilia. But burlesque and parody do not necessarily mean rejection, as Litz points out (p. 14). They represent rather experimentation, understanding, and even assimilation, for to use the very accents of other people is to prove how well you know them. Parody is the competitive, the friendly mastery characteristic of eighteenth-century confrontations with literary predecessors, as Griffin shows (pp. 233–5). Jane Austen was no passive reader; she was simultaneously both critic and creator, like Chaucer, Shakespeare, Dryden, Pope, Wordsworth, Arnold, or T. S. Eliot. She sharpened skills in those early works, even as she read and wrote.

In the third stage of her imaginative development, Jane Austen gives predecessors a local habitation and a name. Elinor's encounter with Willoughby, word by word 'translation' though it is of an episode in *Clarissa*, becomes its own self. Although some readers fret at Elinor's seeming inconsistency, few deny the scene's extraordinary power. And in *Emma* and *Persuasion* particularly, Jane Austen no longer looks so constantly to other books. Neither doting disciple nor cheeky adolescent, she takes older writers into 'partnership', as Doody puts it (p.97). She moves too fast, too confidently now, for even the slightest check to be imaginable. Close verbal correspondence gives way to the spirit of another work, freeing her mind to run variations on themes, develop them, and make them her own. She is not so much inspired as in a heightened state of inspiration. If as Henry Crawford said, Shakespeare is simply part of an Englishman's constitution, he is familiar with him from his earliest years (*MP*, 338), the same is surely true of all the authors that Jane Austen knew so well.

To speak of Jane Austen's literary heritage may seem to confirm John Bayley's claim in 'Life-enhancing world-views' that she is unoriginal in her world view. It is true that though critical of her world, she does not try to change it. Lydia is Lydia still. But by demonstrations in her own person and in those of her heroines, she proves women capable in a world controlled by men. She demonstrates the potential of women even within the restricted lives that censors of Jane Austen call 'narrow', and if one does not use faculties in daily life, it is hard to imagine where one might. From Catherine Morland the ignorant girl-child to Anne Elliot, her woman's mind enriched by years of reading and experience, Jane Austen shows that women can think and feel. The freedom they gain by marriage is no wish-fulfilment. They deserve it.

By contrast, Henry behaves irresponsibly and ungenerously to Catherine, Willoughby follows his own selfish way, Edward falls feebly for Lucy's ploy, Darcy must learn what citizenship truly means, Edmund is imperceptive, Mr Knightley is jealous, mistrustful, and unaware, and Wentworth, who flung suicidally away from the woman he claimed to love, mistakes obstinacy for constancy. Heroes as well as heroines have much to learn, in Jane Austen.

Jane Austen was not, though, a sociologist, but a maker. She was a true poet, not tied like historians to things as they are. As George Whalley says in 'Jane Austen: poet', 'the test of "reality" is not whether the episodes and personas represent ... actual events and persons, but whether the symbolic transformation into real persons and events occurs or not'. He calls it 'resonance' when Jane Austen names rather than describes, for 'describing is a matter of exhaustive delineation: naming is a matter of selective and allusive symbolising' which creates 'an aura of implication'. I would argue that literary references are to Jane Austen's prose as metaphors are to poetry. They invite us to link disparate things; they thicken the possibilities of what we read.

Jane Austen takes elements from other books, grounds them in observation, and complicates them by repetition, variation, and full orchestration. Here is one last example of her poetic making. Fanny's impression of Portsmouth may be compared to Crabbe's scene of poverty in *The Borough*, letter 18:

> The sun was yet an hour and half [sic] above the horizon ... and the sun's rays falling strongly into the parlour, instead of cheering, made her still more melancholy; for sun-shine appeared to her a totally different thing in a town and in the country. Here, its power was only a glare, a stifling, sickly glare, serving but to bring forward stains and dirt that might otherwise have slept. There was neither health nor gaiety in sun-shine in a town. She sat in a blaze of oppressive heat, in a cloud of moving dust; and her eyes could only wander from the walls marked by her father's head, to the table cut and knotched by her brothers, where stood the tea-board never thoroughly cleaned, the cups and saucers wiped in streaks, the milk a mixture of motes floating in thin blue, and the bread and butter growing every minute more greasy than even Rebecca's hands had first produced it.   (439)

The battered table may come from Cowper's 'Tirocinium', 'The bench on which we sat while deep employ'd, / Though mangled, hack'd, and hew'd, yet not destroy'd', which Crabbe quotes as his epigraph to letter 24 of *The Borough*, 'Schools', and which Fanny quotes when she identifies with the homesickness described in that poem (431). But other details seem close to Crabbe:

> That window view! – oil'd paper and old glass
> Stain the strong rays, which, though impeded, pass,
> And give a dusty warmth to that huge room,

> The conquer'd sunshine's melancholy gloom;
> When all those western rays, without so bright,
> Within become a ghastly glimmering light,
> As pale and faint upon the floor they fall,
> Or feebly gleam on the opposing wall ...
> That wall, once whiten'd, now an odious sight,
> Stain'd with all hues, except its ancient white ...
> (ll. 354–61, 364–5)

Here Jane Austen makes the unspecific actual among the Prices, and proves Crabbe's thesis that poverty degrades. Typically too she weaves it into her plot, for the sun lights up a wretchedness that Fanny cannot call home, the dirt is ignored by a mother she cannot love, and the stains are caused by her father's lolling, drunken head.[3] Jane Austen starts with an abstraction, then makes character, event, and setting consequential one upon the other. By complicating and connecting, she makes them symbolic, metaphorical, poetic, in short, imagined.

Georg Christian Lichtenberg said that though everyone is a genius once a year, the bright ideas of real geniuses come closer together (*Aphorisms and Letters*, p. 55). A great deal *happens* at any moment in Jane Austen. Scientists and historians make one word correspond to one thing, whereas poets make everything work very much harder than that. Each of Jane Austen's words react in a multiplicity of relationships with other words, phrases, and sentences, each word complicated by observation and criticism compressed within the same verbal event. She fills every rift with ore – not in Keats's sense of lavishness, for her books are very lean – but because everything is alive and reacting to everything else.

To try to account for what Jane Austen did at such a speed that it seems unconscious, effortless, is to take a flight at folly. But we can guess how she did it, if we cannot match her pace. Memory is obviously essential to the creating mind. It is clear that Jane Austen, who knew many books virtually by heart (the proof is in the ease of the allusions), accumulated thus a vast stock of ideas. Reynolds, writing that a great part of every artist's life must be employed in 'collecting materials for the exercise of genius', argued that invention 'is little more than a new combination of those images which have been previously gathered and deposited in the memory: nothing can come of nothing: he who has laid up no materials can produce no combinations' (pp. 22–3).

If we knew exactly what Jane Austen did next, we should know a great deal about the storage and retrieval of human memory. T. S. Eliot adds suggestively to Reynolds in 'Tradition and the individual talent' when he describes the poet's mind as a catalyst, 'a receptacle for seizing and storing up numberless feelings, phrases, images, which remain there until all the particles which can unite to form a new compound are present together'. When we watch Jane Austen sometimes following, sometimes diverging from, almost always reworking that material, we learn a little more about the operations of the mind.

Some who love Jane Austen understandably want all the credit to be hers. Chapman writes for instance that '*Pride and Prejudice* is like Pallas Athene, who sprang full-armed from her father's head' (p. 207), while Wilson believes her knowledge of *Grandison* to have been 'timorous and disabling'. But *Grandison* is better than he thinks, and Jane Austen more various in her use of it. When Bayley writes that 'it is in fact hard to touch the bottom of Jane Austen's lack of originality', his assumptions about the mind are quite untenable. Everything inevitably has origins. F. R. Leavis was right to say in *The Great Tradition* that 'Jane Austen, in her indebtedness to others, provides an exceptionally illuminating study of the nature of originality' for exemplifying 'beautifully the relations of "the individual talent" to tradition' (p. 5). Jane Austen's recollections of books gave her languages to speak with, the 'paradigmatic word-hoards' that Pope also, says Robert Scholes,[4] heaped up:

his verbal resources included not only a command of the English language of his own time but also in a very precise manner a command of certain poetic languages of the past. He knew Dryden, Milton, and Shakespeare, among others, superlatively well, and had in his mind not only their words but countless contexts in which they used these words. Thus he could produce words of his own in contexts of his own, which nonetheless reverberated and took on meaning from their previous incarnations in the utterance of his great predecessors. It is precisely this diachronic context which enables poetic utterances to survive the temporal decay of any merely poetic diction and remain contemporary far beyond their own time.

Utter originality cannot be. Claims to originality may be, in fact, more political than true. Even the natural geniuses beloved of the eighteenth century were conversant with books in English, and Edward Young, that early apostle of original genius, depended upon other people for his influential tract. Shakespeare himself often began with Plutarch and Holinshed, Bacon, the greatest of the moderns, turned naturally to his predecessors when he wrote *The Advancement of Learning*, Wordsworth could scarcely have written without the liberating knowledge of Milton, and nor could Coleridge, if deprived of a wide range of literary and extra-literary sources. Austen does what all poets do when she remembers literary friends. We accept that poetry is made out of poetry, but the novel too, in spite of the insistent realism by which we identify the genre, may have complex origins in other people's books that make it allusive, even symbolic. Edward Said seems to believe so, when he writes in his *Beginnings* (p. 152), 'Each new novel recapitulates not life, but other novels'. Jane Austen, for one, tunnels through the stratifications of her reading to call up 'sequences' of texts, such as *Sense and Sensibility* back to *Clarissa* back to *Paradise Lost*. On a binary principle of similarity or difference she then constructs her books. The burden of the past is to her creative, not destructive. She does not sink under a great tradition which in any case she picked out for herself, although Bloom is right to say, 'know each poem by its *clinamen* [swerve], and you will "know" that poem in a way that will not purchase knowledge by the loss of the poem's power' (p. 43).

How theoretically conscious is she of what she does? Henry James decides with a confidence that staggers and an ingratitude that stuns that Jane Austen was scarcely conscious at all. We are hardly more curious of her process, he says, or of the experience in her that fed it, than the brown thrush who tells his story from the garden bough. He allows she may have been 'enviably unconscious' as all women writers are, but 'for signal examples of what composition, distribution, arrangement can do, of how they intensify the life of a work of art, we have to go elsewhere'.[5] But her practice often looks to me like 'imitation', an eighteenth-century theory which, says Howard Weinbrot, 'fosters literary borrowing and encourages modernization'.[6] If imitation involves conscious choice, as Griffin and Doody

(p. 97) so confidently say,[7] then Jane Austen knew exactly what she did.

Modern terms like 'allusion', 'influence', and 'source' are imprecise for Jane Austen. Her 'allusions', neither casual nor temporary, resonate so widely that fully annotated editions of the novels seem almost unthinkable. 'Influence' implies subservience to another tutor, whereas Jane Austen persistently and sceptically investigated other people's books. 'Source' implies a wholesale transference of one book into another, whereas Jane Austen was almost always selective and critical. With rare exceptions she dismantled and altered all she found. Her book rather than another's is typically in charge.

'Sub-texts', 'adjacency', and 'intertextuality' also will not do. 'Sub-text' suggests a *hierarchy* of significances, whereas all texts and discourses work as one in Jane Austen. 'Adjacency' fails to convey the dynamic, complex connections between her books and those of her predecessors, while the insistent modernity of 'intertextuality' misleads. But if it means simply a complex *vraisemblance* in which 'one work takes as its basis or point of departure and must be assimilated in relation to it', as Culler says (p. 140), then intertextuality is simply imitation, which has always been essential to creation.

'Layering' is finally the only helpful term, for it suggests the reworking and enriching I have observed in Jane Austen. Life gave her experience, but literature turned life into art, literature made life multiple, causal, metaphorical, poetic. And if literature was life-like in her mind, life was transformed there into literature. Already in the *Letters* observations are shaped, at one remove from mimesis. *Sanditon* too looks like quick sketches from the life before their layering by literature, the materials for genius assembled, but not yet organised by art. As in the cancelled chapter of *Persuasion*, the language of *Sanditon* still needs to be foregrounded, that is made resonant and damascened by literary allusion. Jane Austen, remembering the topaz crosses her brother brought home, created one more suitable to modest and meditative Fanny. It is made of amber, a symbol of memory in its capacity to preserve. That cross conspicuous on Fanny's neck challenges Edmund and Henry to link their lives with hers. Fanny's smiles make Portsmouth gay to Henry Crawford, but her choice of Edmund's plainer chain, like that of the leaden casket in *The Merchant of Venice*, already prefigures her fate.

Like any other genius, like any other reader, Jane Austen lived as vividly in books as in life. Imitating books is often thought to be inferior to imitating life, but she must have valued equally the life of books and the book of life. For women especially, poring over books at home, the boundary might be no consequence at all, while to work from life already shaped by books is to give oneself an immediate creative advantage. What does matter, and crucially, is what she did with it, for that is what made it hers. Her generous appreciation of other authors is a benign, a fruitful friendship that hurts the reputation of no-one. Authors as well as characters were her 'living friends', a phrase to settle the dust between those who want her to be realistic, and those who condemn her as bookish. Literature was surely life to her, and life the stuff of literature. Richardson puts it more simply of Pamela,

I'll tell you what has been a great advantage to you: It is this love of scribbling ... So that reading constantly, and thus using yourself to write, and enjoying besides the benefit of a good memory, every thing you heard or read became your own; and not only so, but was improved ...

(III. 46–7)

We are to be sure a miracle every way, says Fanny Price, but if any one faculty of our nature may be called *more* wonderful than the rest, it is memory. Even if Jane Austen's powers of recollecting and of forgetting have proved peculiarly past my finding out, it does seem that reading, writing, scribbling, and improving were stages vital to her invention. Jane Austen's true muse was Memory, mother to all the rest. In memory she found origins for art.

APPENDIX 1

The History of Sir Charles Grandison

Harriet Byron, a woman of beauty and principle, arrives in town at the start of *Grandison*, leaving behind her two disappointed suitors, the rakish Greville and the humble Mr Orme. In London new admirers spring up. Mr Fowler is so timid that his eccentric Welsh uncle Sir Rowland Meredith must propose to Harriet on his behalf, but the fop Sir Hargrave Pollexfen, struck with her beauty and untutored wit in a sharp debate on languages and learning with the pedant Mr Walden, proposes and is promptly refused. His morals do not suit her, she says. Enraged and insulted, Sir Hargrave abducts her from a masquerade which she had attended out of politeness to friends. Just when all seems set for another *Clarissa*, Sir Charles Grandison rescues her from Sir Hargrave's coach. Without even drawing his sword, he flips the villain under his own wheels, for as he explains later in a dramatic rencounter with him, he abhors all violence and duels.

Harriet is received at their London home by Sir Charles's vivacious sister Charlotte, a woman who dispenses with the minor punctilios. Out of gratitude and admiration Harriet falls in love with her handsome preserver, the very paragon of a Christian hero: Sir Charles, naturally attracted to another paragon, is mysteriously prevented from declaring an affection that Harriet is frankly prepared to own to Charlotte, to her family, or to disappointed suitors such as Lord D., offered her by his mother.

With matters thus in suspense, Charlotte narrates the family history. After the death of their saintly mother, their father Sir Thomas Grandison had made life intolerable for Charlotte and her sister Caroline, threatening to throw them out of the house when Caroline said that she loved Lord L. Upon the death of this patriarchal rake, Sir Charles had returned from his Grand Tour,

222

its duration abnormally prolonged by a father only too conscious of his son's superior virtue. Sir Charles had moved swiftly to dispense justice to his father's mistress, clarify the finances of friends, and arrange the marriage of Caroline, now Lady L., and a model wife to a model husband.

Meanwhile Sir Charles has unaccountably declined a number of offers from wealthy and titled ladies. Harriet still loves him without hope, and Charlotte confesses that her entanglement through a secret correspondence with a military fortune-hunter, Captain Anderson. She cannot therefore marry the man Sir Charles proposes to her, Lord G. The Anderson affair resolved, she still treats the mild-mannered Lord G. high-handedly.

Sir Charles has other responsibilities yet. His gambling rake of a cousin Everard Grandison, his adoring but garrulous maiden aunt Eleanor Grandison, and his rich, adoring ward Emily Jervois, together make up a family that extends into the larger community of obligation. He detaches his gouty uncle Lord W. from a termagant mistress and marries him to an impoverished gentlewoman, Miss Mansfield. Abruptly these activities are broken off. Letters from Sir Charles and the pious Dr Bartlett, ex-tutor to the vicious Lorimer and now mentor to Sir Charles, reveal the cause of his pupil's coolness to be the lovely Italian, Clementina della Porretta. When Sir Charles saved her brother from bravoes, and taught her English using *Hamlet* and *Paradise Lost* as texts, she naturally fell in love. Faced with a Racinian choice between love and duty, her mind is breaking beneath the strain. Sir Charles must go at once to Italy, taking with him a humane English surgeon, Mr Lowther, to minister to the hurts of the two young Porrettas.

The third and fourth volumes tell of agonising indecision in Italy, balanced at home by Harriet's patient endurance and the whimsical matrimonial behaviour of Charlotte, now Lady G. Sir Charles carefully leaves the resolution of his fate to Clementina. Her affliction worsened by the cruel and unscientific treatment of her proud family, she foregoes the man she loves on grounds of religion and country. Sir Charles returns to England and Harriet.

Amid long debates on love and esteem in the marriage choice, the success of second attachments following romantic first ones, and the proper spheres of men and women, the nuptials of

Sir Charles and Lady Grandison are celebrated with a grandeur and a gladness which allay Harriet's anxiety about marrying a man with only half a heart. She gains rightful possession of Grandison Hall by means of a ceremonial tour of its gardens, rooms, and portrait-gallery.

In the seventh and final volume the last strands of the story are tied up. Charlotte, 'matronized' by the birth of a daughter, is reconciled to her husband Lord G. Using herself as proof, she delivers a lecture on the desirability of second attachments for the benefit of Emily and Clementina, both of whom have seen their first love Sir Charles marry someone else. Emily, though persuaded by Harriet that her love for her guardian is merely filial, wisely accepts the offer to replace Miss Byron as companion to her grandmother, Mrs Shirley. Sir Charles's friend Sir Edward Beauchamp, a 'second Sir Charles Grandison', begins to appeal to her.

In a dramatic last-minute twist Clementina flees to England to escape the importunities of her devoted suitor the Count of Belvedere. She wants to enter a nunnery, but her family urges her to marry. Shaken by the unkind interpretation put upon her flight to Sir Charles by Lady Olivia, an independently wealthy Italian whom he had earlier rejected and rebuked for unwomanly forwardness, Clementina eventually accepts a compromise with her parents, who have followed her to England. She will give up the nunnery if her parents promise to use persuasion only. Clementina and Harriet become close friends, but when a walk in the rain threatens Harriet with a miscarriage, Clementina resolves to return to Italy. The novel ends with the departure of the Italians and considerable uncertainty about Clementina's future. No wonder readers demanded more resolution yet; no wonder Richardson felt compelled to write a testy letter of resistance to point out that having brought the characters up to the present, he could hardly write of events yet to come. How many generations must he follow before being allowed to stop? In fact, he held open the possibility of a continuation for several years more.

As Alvin C. Metcalfe shows in his thesis, 'Sense and Sensibility: a study of its similarity to The History of Sir Charles Grandison', Richardson's book and Jane Austen's are essentially alike. He also provides a useful list up to 1967 of earlier insights.

Details should be sought in Metcalfe's thesis, which he has generously allowed me to summarize. Metcalfe writes that Jane Austen's habit is to construct 'composites' made up of character traits from the early novels out of which she builds a self-controlled woman and a self-indulgent woman, a self-controlled man and a self-indulgent man. Both Harriet Byron in *Grandison* and Elinor Dashwood in *Sense and Sensibility* must suppress their love for a man who is bound to another; both suffer in silence, both resist listening to information improperly gained – Harriet when Charlotte Grandison finds one of Sir Charles's letters, Elinor when Nancy Steele eavesdrops. Both must only esteem, not love, the man to whom they are attracted. Each heroine thinks that the hero openly praises her, each must put up with hearing about the plans of the heroes' relatives for them, each rejects a brotherly relation with the hero, each believes that the hero really loves her and so pities him instead, each believes that the hero is married and must hide her strong feelings all the more under the guise of politeness and cheerfulness, each treats her rival honourably, each breaks down weeping with relief when the hero finally declares himself, and each marries rapidly once all is resolved.

Marianne Dashwood, says Metcalfe, is like Charlotte Grandison in appearance and in her disregard for what the world thinks. She, like Harriet and Charlotte, looks for an ideal man whom she finds in Willoughby, not at first in Edward Ferrars or Colonel Brandon. Like Harriet she is rescued by the hero. Both heroines, unable to walk and carried in the arms of their rescuers, are impressed by such rapidity of thought and action. Naturally they fall in love.

Marianne also contains aspects of Richardson's spoilt heiress Olivia whom Sir Charles is forced to rebuke for her lack of reserve and her forward self-indulgence. Like Olivia, Marianne must travel to London to hear the truth of her rejection from the hero's own lips, leaving her as free as Charlotte to accept a second suitor more worthy of attachment after a first entanglement born of secret correspondence and private promises. Like Harriet she flees the city, like Harriet and her tragic rival Clementina she becomes ill as a result of thwarted affections. Like Clementina she at first plans to withdraw from society, then changes her mind under family pressure. But she is like Charlotte most of all when she is 'matronized' by the duties of her married life. To be released, Marianne like Clementina needs to know that she was indeed once loved by the man who seemed the obvious hero.

Edward Ferrars and Colonel Brandon are composites too, at times taking on aspects of Sir Charles Grandison, at others those of Charlotte Grandison's mild-mannered suitor and husband, Lord G. Edward is like Sir Charles in loving one heroine while being bound to another, so that he and Sir Charles must depart, Sir Charles to Canterbury and Italy, Edward to London, without having declared themselves. What each woman senses is that despite obligations of honour to a rival, each hero does in fact love her. Both Edward and Sir Charles allow women they no longer love to decide their fate. Meanwhile their real loves wait patiently. The belief that both men are married provokes similar strong reactions in the heroines; both men are released from obligations under conditions which preserve their honour and in no way lessen the high regard in which they are held. Lucy's letter, for instance, bears a strong resemblance to Clementina's when she abrogates her claims on Sir Charles forever, though Lucy is scarcely the high-minded enthusiast Clementina, one might remark. With identical alacrity each hero secures the hand of the woman he really loves. Thus Edward, while taking most of his character from Lord G., follows the life story of the exemplary Sir Charles Grandison.

Colonel Brandon is hurt, like Lord G., by the very vivacity that attracts him. Like Sir Charles he is benevolent, acting as guardian to Eliza Williams, helping Edward Ferrars to a living, making himself praised and generally beloved. Like Sir Charles again he must suppress his true feelings, preferring to see the women he loves happy even if it brings sorrow to himself. Willoughby, thinks Metcalfe, has no close parallel in *Grandison*, although he looks like the hero on his first entrance because of the rescue. When he leaves Marianne his halting speech is like Sir Charles's when he leaves Harriet for Italy – although Willoughby's motives for going away are more dishonest than Sir Charles's. At other times Willoughby, whose name derives from Sir Clement Willoughby in Fanny Burney's *Evelina*, is more like the mercenary fortune-hunter Captain Anderson who entangles Charlotte in a secret correspondence, or Sir Charles's rakish cousin Everard when he marries a woman of fortune for the sake of survival. He seems here to take on characteristics of Richardson's two rakes Greville and Sir Hargrave Pollexfen, especially in his self-indulged immorality which leads to his repentance and misery. Marianne, however, forgives him as Harriet forgives the man who has treated her so ill.

Thus Metcalfe argues convincingly that almost all the characters, events, and themes of *Sense and Sensibility* have counterparts in *Sir Charles Grandison*.

Sir Charles Grandison
in the juvenilia[1]

The family members to whom Jane Austen dedicated her early works knew *Grandison* almost as well as she did. We may share their pleasures of recognition if we track the allusions down.

The young Jane Austen learned her craft by play when she attacked conventions established over fifty years of novel-writing, as B. C. Southam in *Literary Manuscripts* especially has seen. But it was Richardson who originally gave power to these worlds of peerless heroes, matchless heroines, unspeakable villains, domineering fathers, elopements, recognition scenes, and alarming manifestations of sensibility. Other authors only 'tread in Richardson's steps, so far as Man's determined pursuit of Woman in defiance of every opposition of feeling & convenience is concerned', as Jane Austen herself acknowledged in *Sanditon* (*Minor Works*, 404).

Many of her targets, summarised in their purest form in *Plan of a Novel*, are not therefore *Grandison*'s alone, but I shall distinguish those which I think are. She was thoroughly conversant with *Grandison* when she wrote these early works. Two direct references prove it. Lady Williams who 'like the great Sir Charles Grandison scorned to deny herself when at Home, as she looked on that fashionable method of shutting out disagreable Visitors, as little less than downright Bigamy' (*Minor Works*, 15; *Grandison*, II. 388) takes a nice hit at Sir Charles, in love with two women at once. Jane Austen's remarking on 'that favourite character of Sir Charles Grandison's, a nurse', again shows her grasp of even minor detail (186; II. 90). Even where no specific tagging occurs, her mind is obviously filled with *Grandison* in the tales from which these examples come.

Richardson's hero is always praised in the highest terms. He is so fine in person, face, complexion, mouth, and teeth, that were 'kings to be chosen for beauty and majesty of person, Sir Charles Grandison would have few competitors', says Harriet Byron. His eye sparkles with intelligence, and the grandeur of his person and air is accompanied with 'ease and freedom of manners'. He is valued for his goodness rather than his beauty, as his sister points out (I. 181–2). Good humour sweetens his lively features, 'majesty and sweetness are mingled in every feature of his face' (I. 359, II. 29). Welcome everywhere in Europe, he 'has travelled we may say, to some purpose' (I. 182). Jane Austen places similar praise in Mr Johnson's own mouth, and she undoes him:

I look upon myself to be Sir a perfect Beauty – where would you see a finer figure or a more charming face. Then, sir I imagine my Manners & Address to be of the most polished kind; there is a certain elegance, a peculiar sweetness in them that I never saw equalled & cannot describe – . Partiality aside, I am certainly more accomplished in every Language, every Science, every Art and every thing than any other person in Europe. My temper is even, my virtues innumerable, my self unparalelled ... I expect nothing more in my wife than my wife will find in me – Perfection. (25–6)

Richardson works typologically to make Sir Charles a prince of the Almighty's creation, a Solomon, a god-like man whose face as in emblematic representations of Apollo, of Christ, of Louis XIV, emits light like the rays of the sun. He can thus write, 'a sun-beam from my brother's eye seemed to play upon his face, and dazle his eyes. The fine youth withdrew behind Lady W's chair' (III. 213). Jane Austen pushes this notion *ad absurdum*. Her hero Charles Adams is an 'amiable, accomplished & bewitching young Man, of so dazzling a Beauty that none but Eagles could look him in the Face'. At the ball he represents the sun, to the admiration of all:

The Beams that darted from his Eyes were like those of that glorious Luminary tho' infinitely superior. So strong were they that no one dared venture within half a mile of them; he had therefore the best part of the Room to himself, its size not amounting to more than 3 quarters of a mile in length & half a one in breadth.

The fierceness of his beams proving 'very inconvenient to the concourse by obliging them to croud together in one corner of the room', the gentleman 'half shut his eyes by which means, the

Company discovered him to be Charles Adams in his plain green Coat, without any mask at all' (13).[2]

The dazzling Sir Charles Grandison proves irresistible to women: 'Five Ladies ... declared, that they would stand out by consent, and let you pick and choose a wife from among them' (II. 43). Of *her* Charles Jane Austen says, 'The singularity of his appearance, the beams which darted from his eyes, the brightness of his Wit, & the whole *tout ensemble* of his person had subdued the hearts of so many of the young Ladies, that of the six present at the Masquerade but five had returned uncaptivated'. Alice Johnson is the unhappy sixth, the Miss Simpsons having been 'defended from his Power by Ambition, Envy, & Selfadmiration'. 'Polite to all but partial to none', Jane Austen's hero remains 'the lovely, the lively, but insensible Charles Adams' (14–15). Of Sir Charles Grandison, whose marriage will break the hearts of half a score, Harriet had said bitterly, 'a man may afford to shew politeness to those he has resolved to keep at distance' (I. 291, 445).

This male love object acquires some of the passivity traditionally demanded of women, unfailingly attractive through no fault or effort of his own. Olivia, 'a woman of high qualities, nobly born, generous, amiable in her features, genteel in her person, and mistress of a great fortune in possession, which is entirely at her own disposal; having not father, mother, brother, or other near relations', actually pursues him round Italy and as far as England to renew her unconditional offer of herself. Sir Charles rejects her, and promptly leaves town (II. 117, 622). Charles Adams too is attacked by a lovely young woman who is 'fearfull that tho' possessed of Youth, Beauty, Wit & Merit, & tho' the probable Heiress of my Aunts House & business, he might think me deficient in Rank, & in being so, unworthy of his hand'. Deciding to make a bold push, she writes him 'a very kind letter, offering him with great tenderness my hand & heart. To this I received an angry & peremptory refusal, but thinking it might be rather the effect of his modesty than any thing else, I pressed him again on the subject. But he never answered any more of my Letters & very soon afterwards left the Country'. She pursues him to his estate in Pammydiddle, there to be caught in a gin-trap. 'Oh! cruel Charles to wound the hearts & legs of all the fair' (pp. 21–2), writes Jane Austen with a bathos Pope himself would have admired.

Harriet Byron loves Sir Charles from the first volume, but must seek out signs of love in his cryptic words and actions until the sixth, particularly in the library when he explains his involvement with the lovely Italian. 'His manner of *leaving* me – Was it not particular? – To break from me so *abruptly*, as I may say – And what he said with looks so earnest! Looks that seemed to carry more meaning than his words: And withdrawing without conducting me out, as he had led me in – and as if – I don't know how as if ... Why did he hesitate? Why did he tremble?', she puzzles (II. 133–4). Jane Austen satirically makes her Catherine muse,

... such was the power of his Address, & the Brilliancy of his Eyes, that when they parted for the Night, tho' Catherine had but a few hours before totally given up the idea, yet she felt almost convinced again that he was really in love with her. She reflected on their past Conversation, and tho' it had been on various & indifferent subjects, and she could not exactly recollect any speech on his side expressive of such a partiality, she was still however nearly certain of it's being so ...

She looks forward to their parting the next day, 'which she thought would infallibly explain his regard if any he had' (235), just as Sir Charles labours with the task of declaring love to Harriet while he is loyal to Clementina, on *his* departure. He owns a wish that 'while my honour has laid me under obligation to *one Lady* ... I should presume to hope, that *another*, no less worthy, would hold her favour for me suspended, till she saw what would be the issue of the first obligation' (II. 384). He would rather die, he says impressively, than offer such an indignity to them both. But he does suspend them both, and live. Jane Austen mocks him when her hero keeps up a similar option on Kitty: 'You were just the Girl to suit him, because you were so lively and good-natured, and he wished with all his heart that you might not be married before he came back ... Oh! you have no idea what fine things he said about you, till at last I fell asleep and he went away' (237).

Vicissitudes in Italy prolong Harriet's suspense until Clementina renounces Sir Charles for reasons of religion and country. As soon as Sir Charles reads her affecting letter, he falls 'astonished, perplexed, confounded' upon a 'soffa'. He clasps the fainting 'angel' Clementina to him, both kneeling, his cheek joined to hers and bathed with her tears. Camilla the servant calls out fervently, '*such* a scene! Hasten, hasten up. They will faint in each other's arms. Virtuous Love! how great is thy glory!' (II. 567–8). If Jane Austen found this as funny as I do, perhaps she used it for one of the best bits of slapstick in the juvenilia:

> Never did I see such an affecting Scene as was the meeting of Edward & Augustus.
> 'My Life! my Soul!' (exclaimed the former) 'My adorable Angel!' (replied the latter) as they flew into each other's arms. It was too pathetic for the feelings of Sophia and myself – We fainted alternately on a Sofa.   (86)

'Alternately' may well come from Sheridan's *The Critic*, as B.C. Southam points out in his edition of *Volume the Second* (p. 211), but the extraordinary expressions of sensibility, the extravagant epithets, and especially that sofa must come from *Grandison*. As Jane Austen knew, Richardson's characters habitually record detail even in emotional ecstacy. Sir Charles, at the very crisis of his amatory affairs, notes the convenient presence of a sofa, and Pamela, threatened by rape, notes Mr B.'s rich silk and silver morning gown.

If Jane Austen cast a sardonic eye on Richardson's serious scenes, she did not ignore his efforts to amuse. When for instance Sir Charles finally comes to propose to Harriet, Richardson ponderously tried to lighten the important event through Mrs Shirley's account of it:

> I gave orders for his admittance; and in came, to appearance, one of the handsomest men I ever saw in my life, in a riding-dress. It was a courteous Ghost: It saluted me; or at least I thought it did: For it answering to the description that you, my Harriet, had given me of that amiable man, I was surprised. But, contrary to the manner of ghosts, it spoke first – Venerable Lady, it called me; and said, its name was Grandison, in a voice – so like what I heard you speak of it, that I had no doubt but it was Sir Charles Grandison himself; and was ready to fall down to welcome him.
> It took its place by me: You, madam, said it, will forgive this intrusion: And it made several fine speeches, with an air *so* modest, *so* manly – It had almost all the talk to itself. I could only bow, and be pleased; for still I thought it was corporally, and indeed, Sir Charles Grandison.   (III. 15)

Jane Austen could not resist pointing out the folly of a man not telling his name. In her version the narrator is a rattle of a maid. 'Lord Ma'am! Here's a Gentleman in a Chaise and four come, and I cannot for my Life conceive who it is! ... And he is one of the handsomest young Men you could wish to see; I was almost ashamed of being seen in my Apron Ma'am, but however he is vastly handsome and did not seem to mind it at all'. 'Good Heavens!', says Kitty, 'what can all this mean! And who can it possibly be! Did you never see him before? And Did not he tell you his Name?' The maid gabbles out her inane conversation with the prodigious agreeable man, his name like his identity still remaining unknown. 'But he is as handsome as a Prince for all that, and has quite the look of one'. 'Perhaps he is come to rob the house – he comes in stile at least', guesses Kitty as she goes to meet the stranger. Like Sir Charles he greets her with an air of the most perfect ease and vivacity, immediately proving himself socially superior in a situation that makes her tremble. Kitty, 'who had been expecting him to tell his own name, instead of hers ... felt herself unable to ask it, tho' she had been planning her speech all the way down stairs, was so confused & distressed by this unexpected address that she could only return a slight curtesy to it, and accepted the chair he reached her, without knowing what she did'. The young man, far from proposing at the end of this ineffably Richardsonian episode, invites himself to a ball. As a last touch Jane Austen weaves in a detail from *Grandison* about Sir Charles returning to England on the melancholy event of his father's death. This young man hastens back to an equally 'shocking' and 'dreadful' affair, the illness of a favourite mare (213–22).

Before Sir Charles can even propose, Harriet's relatives press on him not only their child's hand, but meals and money too. Harriet's uncle Mr Reeves explains, 'An alliance more acceptable, were it with a prince, could not be proposed, than that which Sir Charles Grandison ... has proposed ... But as your spirit is princely, you ought to have something worthy of your own fortune with a wife'. He lists the sums accruing from her parents along with the sums he himself has laid up, hoping 'without promising for what this man will do further at his death, that you will accept of this Five or Six-and-twenty thousand Pounds, as the chearfullest given and best-bestowed money that ever was laid out'. Sir Charles, though mentioning that he is far richer, graciously accepts (III. 33–7).

Jane Austen exaggerates very little when, at the beginning of *Evelyn*, Mr and Mrs Webb greet the totally unknown Mr Gower. 'Welcome best of Men – Welcome to this House & to everything it contains'. They press on him chocolate, venison pasty, sandwiches, a basket of fruit, ices, soup, jellies, cake, and a purse full of money. 'Accept this my good Sir, – . Beleive me you are welcome to everything that is in my power to bestow. – I wish my purse were weightier, but Mr Webb must make up my deficiencies – . I know he has cash in the house to the amount of an hundred pounds, which he shall bring you immediately'. What else, they ask, can they do to 'contribute to your happiness and express the Affection we bear you. Tell us what you wish more to receive, and depend upon our gratitude for the communication of your wishes'. Mr Gower promptly asks for and gets 'your house & Grounds; I ask for nothing else'. On the entrance of three daughters this 'best of men' asks if they will 'complete their generosity by giving me their elder daughter in marriage with a handsome portion'. The parents are delighted. 'We bend under a weight of obligations to you which we can never repay. Take our girl, take our Maria, and on her must the difficult task fall, of endeavouring to make some return to so much Benefiscence' (182–3).

So much for the hero. The most elaborate praise of Richardson's heroine occurs in Volume I, letter ii, where an admirer states in terms often to be repeated that 'lovely as Miss Byron's person is, I defy the greatest Sensualist on earth not to admire her mind more than her person'. He proceeds however to list each physical perfection along with her accomplishments, all the time disavowing his ability so to do. To parody this account, Jane Austen once more transfers the character's praise into her own mouth: 'lovely as I was the Graces of my Person were the least of my Perfections. Of every accomplishment accustomary to my sex, I was Mistress. When in the Convent, my progress had always exceeded my instructions, my Acquirements had been wonderfull for my age, and I had shortly surpassed my Masters' (77–8). On another occasion too she calls Richardson's bluff about the irrelevance of personal charms:

Lovely & too charming Fair one, notwithstanding your forbidding Squint, your greasy tresses & your swelling Back, which are more frightfull than imagination can paint or pen describe, I cannot refrain from expressing my raptures, at the engaging Qualities of your Mind, which so amply atone for the Horror, with which your first appearance must ever inspire the unwary visitor. (6)

Jane Austen laughs at Richardson's excess when her heroine succumbs before quite ordinary events: 'Emma began to tremble ... Emma turned pale ... Emma sunk breathless on a Sopha ... her heart was too full to contain its afflictions' (31). And if Harriet's sensibility leads her to promise on her very first acquaintance with Clementina, 'you shall know all of me, and of my heart. Not a secret of it ... will I conceal from you. I hope we shall be true Sisters, and true Friends, to the end of our lives' (III. 355), Jane Austen accelerates the process only slightly: 'after having been deprived during the course of 3 weeks of a real friend ... imagine my transports at beholding one, most truly worthy of the Name ... She was all Sensibility and Feeling. We flew into each others arms and after having exchanged vows of mutual Freindship for the rest of our Lives, instantly unfolded to each other the most inward secrets of our Hearts' (85).

Such friendships do not however displace the plethora of kin for whom Harriet constantly expresses affection. 'Such an amiable woman is Miss Charlotte Grandison! ... Don't be jealous, Lucy! I hope I have a large heart. I hope there is room in it for half a dozen sweet female friends!' (I. 180). Jane Austen's Alice assures *her* Lucy very similarly that 'except her Father, Brother, Uncles, Aunts, Cousins & other relations, Lady Williams, Charles Adams & a few dozen more of particular freinds, she loved her better than almost any other person in the world' (23). Jane Austen also mimics Richardson's shifts to keep track of them all when her Emma asks after the Willmots. The mother replies, 'Our children are all extremely well but at present most of them from home. Amy is with my sister Clayton. Sam at Eton. David with his Uncle John. Jem & Will at Winchester. Kitty at Queen's Square. Ned with his Grandmother. Hetty and Patty in a Convent at Brussells. Edgar at college, Peter at Nurse, & all the rest (except the nine here) at home' (32–3).

Harriet is teased by the passionate proposals of several good men early in the novel, particularly by the aged Sir Rowland

Meredith on behalf of his nephew. Unfailingly kind, she keeps
them all in hope and in play. This too Jane Austen parodies. First
'an aged gentleman with a sallow face & old pink Coat, partly
by intention & partly thro' weakness was at the feet of the lovely
Charlotte, declaring his attachment to her & beseeching her pity
in the most moving manner'. Unable to make anyone miserable,
she consents, 'where upon the Gentleman left the room & all was
quiet'. Soon a second young man appears who wins her as fast
as the first. She accepts him too, but next morning the 'reflection
of her past folly, operated so strongly on her mind, that she
resolved to be guilty of a greater, & to that end threw herself into
a deep stream which ran thro' her Aunt's pleasure Grounds in
Portland Place' (8–9).

The question of first and second love in *Grandison* involves
not only Harriet but Clementina, Emily, Charlotte Grandison,
and the great Sir Charles himself. Lady Williams likewise warns
Alice against loving Charles Adams, in the juvenilia. 'Preserve
yourself from a first Love & you need not fear a second', she says
with the grandeur of generality (16). But when Alice gets drunk,
Lady Williams's story dissolves into farce, and first love with it.

Proposed to at last by Sir Charles, Harriet is asked to name the
day. Jane Austen must have found her modest scruples comical,
for she writes two separate versions in which the woman unfortunately names the wrong day. 'In a manner truly heroick, [she]
spluttered out to him her intention of being married the next
Day', to which comes the reply, 'Damme Elfrida *you* may be
married tomorrow but *I* wont' (11). Lady Percival, when pressed
by Sir William, unluckily names the first of September. 'Sir
William was a Shot & could not support the idea of losing such
a Day, even for such a Cause' (41). His delays enrage the lady,
who returns to London the next morning.

Anticipating and minutely recording the wedding day occupies
most of *Grandison*'s sixth volume. Jane Austen shows her
impatience with such longueurs when all the characters of one
story, after very cursory acquaintance, simply announce their
marriages in a newspaper (49). In her novels she is impatient
again, knowing that happiness depends not upon ceremony but
the establishment of a friendship to endure. 'The wedding was
very much like other weddings, where the parties have no taste
for finery or parade; and Mrs. Elton ... thought it all extremely

shabby ... "Very little white satin, very few lace veils; a most pitiful business!"' (*Emma*, 484). But the perfect happiness of the union between Emma and Mr Knightley fully answers the hopes of their true friends.

Jane Austen knew the characters of *Sir Charles Grandison* as if they had been living friends. But just as the true friends in her novels observe and correct those they love, so she admired Richardson and loved *Grandison*, but was blind to the lapses of neither. What she positively built on I have shown elsewhere, but in her juvenilia she uses parody to detect its extravagances of emotion, its falsities of tone, and its impossibilities of expression. She does so by checking *Grandison* against reality rather as Henry Tilney would advise Catherine on quite another occasion, 'Consult your understanding, your own sense of the probable, your own observation of what is passing around you'.

She tests Richardson's work by exaggeration, by transposition, by inversion, by incongruity, by alterations of register and tone, by all manner of comic devices subtle and not so subtle. This high-spirited tendency to farce modulates in the novel largely, but not entirely, to irony; Sir Thomas Bertram's hope for Fanny that the remaining cold pork bones and mustard in William's plate might but divide her feelings with the broken egg-shells in Mr Crawford's is a lovely flash of the old nonsense. But for the most part she calls upon a lesson she learnt from Richardson, something that Robert Penn Warren[3] says is crucial to the great work of art, that it should contain its own criticism. In every one of Richardson's novels the main characters are divided and self-questioning, with other characters specifically created to take up adversary stances. Anna Howe argues against the inflexible idealism of Clarissa, Charlotte Grandison subverts even the awfulness of Sir Charles's dilemma when he is torn between two women. 'Ass and two bundles of hay', she comments rudely, 'But my brother is a nobler animal: He won't starve. But I think, in my conscience, he should have you both' (III. 195).

Although Richardson could see the funny side of his work, he did not consistently dare to. Jane Austen's testing by laughter would be continuous. Even if she like Richardson could warn about wit's power to trivialise serious subjects, laughter was for her the test of absurdity and the touchstone of untruth. Truth remains when laughter dies away, for laughter alerts judgment.

That irresistible sudden effervescence of the spirit is a sign that something is up.

Jane Austen fooled to some purpose in her juvenilia. Here we see the artist as a young woman sharpening her perceptions, refining her techniques, and readying herself for the works of her maturity.

Notes

Preface

1 Henry Austen, 'Biographical Notice', p. 7. Margaret Anne Doody points out that Jane Austen makes virtually no reference to classical myth, story, or character, in 'Jane Austen's reading'. Bibliographical details will be found in the Bibliography, but I am indebted throughout to David Gilson's magisterial *A Bibliography of Jane Austen*.

2 *Jane Austen: The Critical Heritage*, p. 242; 'Criticism, 1939–83', p. 114. See also B. C. Southam, 'General Tilney's hot-houses: some recent Jane Austen studies and texts'.

3 See Virginia Woolf, 'Jane Austen at sixty'.

4 Leavis, 'A critical theory of Jane Austen's writings'; Chapman, *Jane Austen: Facts and Problems*; Southam, *Jane Austen's Literary Manuscripts: A Study of the Novelist's Development through the Surviving Papers*; Lascelles, *Jane Austen and her Art*; Thomson, *Jane Austen: A Survey*; Butler, *Jane Austen and the War of Ideas*; Moler, *Jane Austen's Art of Allusion*; Bradbrook, *Jane Austen and her Predecessors*; Ten Harmsel, *Jane Austen: A Study in Fictional Conventions*; De Rose, *Jane Austen and Samuel Johnson*; McMaster, *Jane Austen on Love*; Metcalfe, '*Sense and Sensibility*: a study of its similarity to *The History of Sir Charles Grandison*'; Fergus, *Jane Austen and the Didactic Novel: 'Northanger Abbey', 'Sense and Sensibility', and 'Pride and Prejudice'*; Barker, *Grandison's Heirs: The Paragon's Progress in the late Eighteenth-Century English Novel*; Duckworth, *The Improvement of the Estate: A Study of Jane Austen's Novels*; Kirkham, *Jane Austen, Feminism and Fiction*. LeRoy M. Smith, in *Jane Austen and the Drama of Women*, applies more modern feminist ideas to Jane Austen.

5 Gilbert and Gubar, *The Madwoman in the Attic: The Woman Writer and the Nineteenth Century Literary Imagination*; Bloom, *The Anxiety of Influence: A Theory of Poetry*; Spender, *Mothers of the Novel: 100 Good Women Writers before Jane Austen*; Spencer, *The Rise of the Woman Novelist from Aphra Behn to Jane Austen*.

To prevent the notes outstripping my text, I refer henceforth only to critics who have anticipated or helped me, or to mark departures from commonly held interpretations.

1   *Northanger Abbey*

1 The Gothic parallels noted by Chapman have convinced many people that the book is essentially Jane Austen's definitive comment on the history of late eighteenth-century fiction, as A. Walton Litz says, in *Jane Austen: A Study of her Artistic Development*, p. 19.

2 Chapter and section numbers refer to Locke's *An Essay Concerning Human Understanding*; section numbers alone refer to *Some Thoughts Concerning Education*.

3 De Rose, who believes that Jane Austen met Locke through Johnson, writes of 'the Lockean epistemology which underlines the literary burlesque in *Northanger Abbey*' (pp. 17, 15). Frederick M. Keener also argues, in *The Chain of Becoming: The Philosophical Tale, the Novel, and a Neglected Realism of the Enlightenment: Swift, Montesquieu, Voltaire, Johnson, and Austen*, that Jane Austen understood psychological philosophy.

4 See Maurice Cranston, *John Locke: A Biography*, pp. 365, 443 n. 2; and Kenneth MacLean, *John Locke and English Literature of the Eighteenth Century*, p. v. For Richardson's knowledge of Locke, see my *Samuel Richardson*.

5 D. D. Devlin, in *Jane Austen and Education*, believes that Jane Austen 'certainly knew [*Education*] well', but he is wrong I think to write of 'deficiencies' (pp. 7, 42) in an education so largely beneficial.

6 Numerical references to Jane Austen's works are found in brackets as here, and they refer to page numbers in the relevant text. These numbers correspond to the preceding sequence of quotations and, therefore, may not appear in numerical order.

7 Jane Austen used the same word in all seriousness when she wrote 'the loss of such a Parent must be felt, or we should be Brutes' (*Letters*, 21 January 1805).

8 See for instance Devlin, pp. 43–5; Litz's book, p. 69; John Odmark, *An Understanding of Jane Austen's Novels: Character, Value and Ironic Perspective*, p. 47.

9 Compare Gilbert and Gubar (p. 139).

10 Here I diverge sharply from those who agree with Lionel Trilling (see Butler, p. 178, n. 1) that the General proves as bad as Catherine first thought. The text says that the General does *not* belong at the extremity of evil, just as Henry does not belong at the extremity of

good. George Levine condemns General Tilney in 'Translating the monstrous: *Northanger Abbey*', but John Burrows, reviewing Barbara Hardy's *A Reading of Jane Austen*, sensibly remarks that the General's tyrannies 'consist, after all, in a domineering treatment of his children (and perhaps his wife); in a calculated and ill-informed attempt to find an heiress for his son; and in a gross breach of hospitality when his hopes are disappointed. Such "tyrannies" fall … far short of Montoni's'.

11 De Rose notes that the 'ray' is metaphorical (p. 27).

12 Juliet McMaster sees Catherine's ability to distinguish truth from artifice as a talent she must learn, in 'The continuity of Jane Austen's novels'. Park Honan argues that Catherine creates and liberates herself, in *Jane Austen: Her Life*, p. 141.

13 Such a thesis contradicts the generally held view that, as Lascelles says, Jane Austen's characters 'do not feel the impact of ideas' because of 'her want of a classical education' (pp. 132–3). Joel Weinsheimer accurately notes that 'the growth of Jane Austen's reputation has been impeded by nagging, often covert imputations that she is somehow "limited"'. But he himself attacks her 'absence of an impersonal frame of ideas', in 'Jane Austen's anthropocentrism'. Donald Greene demolishes 'The myth of limitation' once and for all.

14 Dorothy van Ghent remarks that Jane Austen herself was 'ambushed by imbecility', in *The English Novel: Form and Function*, p. 111. Katrin Ristkok Burlin, in ' "The pen of the contriver": the four fictions of *Northanger Abbey*', writes similarly of 'the battle for the heroine's understanding as well as her person, waged … with … distinctive linguistic weapons'. Stuart M. Tave writes in *Some Words of Jane Austen* that 'language is a given reality that presents choices and so tests the powers and the life of its users by their ability to make the right choices – as it tests those who hear what is conveyed by their ability to understand its meaning' (p. 21).

15 Tave notes how already in the nonsense of the juvenilia 'words begin to work against each other in self-contradiction' (p. 20), and Norman Page in *The Language of Jane Austen* remarks on the use in the minor works of such rhetorical devices as puns, zeugma, comic alliteration, similes, French words and phrases, parody of Johnsonian syntax, and colloquial words and idioms (p. 14).

16 Odmark points out (p. 193, n. 9), that the name probably comes from Richardson's Pamela Andrews, another woman notable, one might add, for needlework.

17 David Daiches, 'Jane Austen, Karl Marx, and the aristocratic dance'; Langdon Elsbree, 'Jane Austen and the dance of fidelity and complaisance'.

18 Page remarks in his book on the importance of openness in *Mansfield Park* and *Sense and Sensibility* as well (p. 69).

19 Michael Neill told me of this usage. See OED.

20 'The mind of Jane Austen', p. 116. Marvin Mudrick, in *Jane Austen: Irony as Defense and Discovery*, complains of Catherine's 'lightweight' mind (p. 40), while John Bayley asserts that Jane Austen was not, and never attempted to be, 'intellectually original, incisive, even profound', in his 'Characterization in Jane Austen', p. 25.

21 Jane Austen probably had in mind here the passage quoted in *Sir Charles Grandison* (III. 244) to prove that there is more than one kind of knowledge. Its 'hard words' all refer to Indian muslins. In both books a knowledge of muslins contributes to a debate about the abilities of women and men. The joke about deriving knowledge from the backs of books comes from Boswell's *Life of Johnson*, p. 267.

22 Obviously I disagree with those who view Catherine as passive, open to shaping by Henry. Ian Watt for instance thinks that Jane Austen's novels 'dramatize the process whereby feminine and adolescent values are painfully educated in the norms of the mature, rational and educated male world', in 'Serious reflections on *The Rise of the Novel*', while Joseph Wiesenfarth writes of *Northanger Abbey* that there 'the conserving voice is essentially male and recalls the would-be heroine from the chimeras of gothic fiction and romantic sensibility', in 'Austen and Apollo', p. 54. I agree neither with them nor with McMaster when she writes that Catherine is 'so apt and so docile a pupil', in her book (p. 48). As Butler observes, just about everyone assumes that Catherine is 'simple-minded' (p. 190).

23 Most critics cannot believe that Jane Austen means what she says. Kirkham (pp. 68–9) perceives it as a defence of a female art, but Litz writes more typically in his book of the passage's 'protective irony of overstatement' (p. 69).

24 Johnson in the *Dictionary* had used Swift's definition of 'style' as 'proper words in proper places', an idea picked up by Coleridge when he called prose 'proper words in their proper places' and poetry 'the most proper words in their proper places', 'Table Talk', p. 512.

25 See Ian Watt, *The Rise of the Novel: Studies in Defoe, Richardson, and Fielding*, for instance. F. R. Leavis remarks that Fielding 'is important not because he leads to Mr J. B. Priestley but because he leads to Jane Austen, to appreciate whose distinction is to feel that life isn't long enough to permit of one's giving much time to Fielding or any to Mr Priestley', *The Great Tradition*, p. 3.

26 See Ian Donaldson, 'Fielding, Richardson, and the Ends of the Novel'.

2   The return to Richardson

1 ' "Nice" and "sentimental": A parallel between *Northanger Abbey* and Richardson's *Correspondence*'.

2 Chapman summarises the evidence in his chapter v. See also B. C. Southam, in 'Jane Austen: a broken romance?', and Honan's biography.

3 William Austen-Leigh and Richard Arthur Austen-Leigh, *Jane Austen: Her Life and Letters. A Family Record*, pp. 95, 156.

4 *Life and Letters*, pp. 229, 235. P. B. S. Andrews suggests in 'The date of *Pride and Prejudice*' that the main conversion of that novel was done at Bath in 1802.

5 Joan Rees, in *Jane Austen: Woman and Writer*, pp. 41, 22.

6 See also Pat Rogers, 'Richardson and the Bluestockings'.

7 Jane Austen's much-criticised wish in a letter of 30 January 1809 that Sir John Moore 'had united something of the Christian with the Hero in his death' could refer to Young's praise of Addison as the Christian Hero in death. Compare Young's 'if all our men of genius had so breathed their last, – if all our men of genius, like him, had been men of genius for eternals, – then had we never been pained by the report of a latter end – O, how unlike to this!', *Edward Young's 'Conjectures' in England and Germany*, pp. 70–1. Richard Steele's phrase 'Christian Hero' in his treatise of that name (1701) was adopted by Richardson for his good man, Sir Charles Grandison (II. 293). Mrs Barbauld notes Richardson's love of death-beds, which were for him as for his friend Young 'a touch-stone of merit or demerit' (p. xcvii). For a fuller discussion of the Ancients and Moderns debate in Richardson and Young, see my 'Learning and genius in *Sir Charles Grandison*'. For Dodsley, see *Letters*, 21 May 1801.

8 Andrew H. Wright, *Jane Austen's Novels: A Study in Structure*, p. 3.

3   *Sense and Sensibility*

1 E. E. Duncan-Jones, in 'The Misses Selby and Steele' notes the allusion, together with similarities between Lucy and Nancy Steele and Harriet Byron's cousins, Lucy and Nancy Selby. D. C. Measham stresses the additional importance of Richardson's Indexes, in a letter.

2 *Jane Austen's 'Sir Charles Grandison'*, p. 10; Honan, p. 62. James Austen-Leigh wrote 'Lady L.' (p. 89), but the wedding day of Harriet Lady Grandison must be meant, as Thomson saw (p. 41). Elizabeth Jenkins, *Jane Austen: A Biography*, p. 34; *Jane Austen's 'Sir Charles Grandison'*, p. 90.

3 Metcalfe provides a useful summary of findings to 1967. See also *Jane Austen: The Critical Heritage* and Gilson's Index, throughout. Fergus and Honan (in his article) see similarities between *Pride and Prejudice* and *Grandison*.

4 In *The Daring Muse: Augustan Poetry Reconsidered*, Margaret Anne Doody argues from a dazzling array of examples that metamorphosis, change, charivari, disjunction, and recombination characterise the eighteenth-century poetry which is, of course, Jane Austen's nearest tradition.

5 J. M. S. Tompkins in '*Elinor and Marianne*: a note on Jane Austen', is an early supporter of Mrs West's *A Gossip's Story* (1796) as a starting-point for *Sense and Sensibility*; R. Brimley Johnson plumps for Fanny Burney in *Jane Austen: Her Life, her Work, her Family, and her Critics*, p. 133; and Ten Harmsel argues that Jane Austen drew upon the conventions. But as Metcalfe rightly points out, this 'theory rests on the acceptance of the a priori assumption that all of the juvenilia and the early novels were burlesques of the imitations: none was an imitation of the original' (p. 166).

6 Pat Rogers argues in 'The rise and fall of gout', that gout was a culturally approved malady, the mark of power, prosperity and a privileged situation in the social order. It regularly struck those of a robust constitution and was 'a mark of maturity, but not of senile imbecility'.

7 See my 'The reviser observed: the last volume of *Sir Charles Grandison*'.

8 Southam, 'Jane Austen and *Clarissa*'; Duncan-Jones, 'Jane Austen and *Clarissa*'; Bradbrook, p. 86; McKillop, 'The context of *Sense and Sensibility*'; Mudrick, 'Jane Austen's drawing-room'.

9 David Gilson, 'Jane Austen's books'; Christopher Gillie, *A Preface to Jane Austen*, p. 8. He cites Emma Austen-Leigh, *Jane Austen and Steventon*.

10 Tony Tanner, in his introduction to the Penguin edition of *Sense and Sensibility*, reprinted in Southam's *Casebook*, on the first three novels and with modifications in his own *Jane Austen*, recognises Marianne's madness, but works to his conclusion from Foucault rather than from Richardson. In his view Marianne's sickness is caused by societal restraints imaged in sheaths and screens, a reading very different from mine. Marianne's scream is not in any case 'muffled', as he says. 'Almost' screamed means surely OED's 'very nearly, well nigh, all but'. Marianne everywhere demonstrates that she represents *unrestrained* passions. Tanner also observes the Ophelia-like capacity for suicide in Marianne.

11 Butler remarks percipiently that another contemporary novelist

'would almost certainly have had Marianne seduced and killed off, after the errors of which she has been guilty' (p.189).

12 See Ian Donaldson, *The Rapes of Lucretia: A Myth and its Transformations*.

13 Jean Hagstrum writes that Willoughby 'rapes' Marianne's long lock, without exploring the matter more, in *Sex and Sensibility: Ideal and Erotic Love from Milton to Mozart*, p. 269. In her book, McMaster takes the 'rape of the lock' as 'an emblem of things possibly to come' (p. 69).

14 Hagstrum argues that 'back of the eighteenth-century union of sex and sensibility lay Milton's Eden' (p. 15), but he does not pursue the idea closely into *Sense and Sensibility*. He finds Clarissa's anguish under her father's curse 'almost incomprehensible' (p. 229). But the Miltonic analogy does, I think, explain it. See Gillian Beer, 'Richardson, Milton, and the status of evil', John Carroll, 'Lovelace as tragic hero', and my *Samuel Richardson*.

15 Griffin, pp. 166, 224, and 271, n. 92.

16 This interpretation might prevent such puzzlings as Tanner's, 'she is married off to Brandon to complete a pattern ... It is certainly hard to know how exactly to respond to the end' (p. 144). See Duckworth's book for the use of the *felix culpa* topos in eighteenth-century fiction, the return to 'the modified happiness that is proper to the mortal condition' (p. 12).

17 Andrew Wright expresses a more typical view than mine when in a Foreword to *Nineteenth Century Fiction* he writes that *Sense and Sensibility* 'may now be the most talked about of Austen's novels – perhaps because of the ways in which it tends to get out of control'.

18 See M. H. Abrams, 'A correspondent breeze: a romantic metaphor'. Although Joseph Wiesenfarth remarks in 'Austen and Apollo' that *Persuasion* is filled with the same invigorating breeze (p. 59), it is worth pointing out that Jane Austen was 'Romantic' in that way well before.

19 Compare Mary Crawford, 'a mind led astray and bewildered, and without any suspicion of being so; darkened, yet fancying itself light' (*MP*, 367). Tave shows in his book how imagination, fancy, and wit contrasted with judgment, understanding, and reason in the eighteenth century (pp. 206–11). Hagstrum explains that 'a nexus exists between love in any form and the imagination, whose tendency is to lead away from life'. He concludes that sensibility can 'lead to distortion of observation, and Marianne Dashwood ... sees life and nature through the skewing spectacles of fancy' (pp. 18, 270).

20 An acute reviewer in *The Critical Review* named her thus (see Southam's *Casebook*, p. 81), using an expression Richardson applied to Clementina.

4 *Pride and Prejudice*

1 For the controversy about the dating of the early novels see the appropriate sections in Gilson. In his article on the chronology Litz speaks of a radical revision of *Pride and Prejudice* in about 1812 based on almanacs for 1811–12, with extensive lopping and cropping before publication in January 1813. *Mansfield Park* was composed February 1811 to summer 1813.

2 Q. D. Leavis sees connections with Fanny Burney's *Cecilia*, but I prefer D. C. Measham's view in 'Sentiment and sentimental psychology' that Jane Austen did not necessarily require Fanny Burney as an intermediary to *Grandison*.

3 Richardson, being a successful business man and understandably sensitive to class snubs, wrote sarcastically, 'I live in the city; and my side of the Temple-Bar abounds with nuisances ... that upper life is low enough to despise the metropolis, which furnishes them with all their beloved luxury', *Selected Letters*, p. 219. A similar complaint is made in the *Correspondence* (V. 45) of a Mrs Palmer, a name perhaps noted for *Sense and Sensibility*.

4 Alistair M. Duckworth comments in 'Prospects and retrospects' that Lydia's immorality is marked not only by syntactical looseness, solecisms, and lexical exaggeration, but by 'immoderate mirth'.

5 Shunji Ebiike notes similarities with *Pamela* in his '*Pride and Prejudice* and *First Impressions*'. In this chapter I have used T. C. Duncan Eaves' and Ben D. Kimpel's edition of the first two volumes of *Pamela*, because *Pride and Prejudice* seems closer to the first edition, which they reprint, than to the 1801 edition. But Jane Austen may also have read *Pamela* in the second edition, if her unsuccessful attempt to find a portrait of Mrs Darcy (letter of 24 May 1813) is illuminated by Aaron Hill's comment printed there, 'I am so jealous ... in Behalf of our *inward* Idea of PAMELA's *Person*, that I dread *any* figur'd Pretence to Resemblance. For it will be a pity to look at an *Air*, and imagine it *Hers*, that does not carry some such elegant Perfection of Amiableness, as will be sure to find place in the *Fancy*' (p. 21).

6 Leapor had defied in 'Corydon. Phillario. Or, Mira's Picture. A Pastoral' the common eighteenth-century accusation that women poets were slatterns, when she wrote of two men criticising the solitary walking, soiled linen, sun-darkened skin, and eyes dim

with reading of that literary freak, herself. Jane Austen may have responded with her more optimistic picture of the healthy, bright-eyed reader Elizabeth, flushed and untidy from exercise, whose unconventionality only Darcy admires.

7 General Tilney, showing the beauties of Northanger Abbey to Catherine, commits the same fault (182–3).

8 *Pamela*, 86, 105, 118, 129–30.

9 Duckworth writes that 'the three classes of [Jane Austen's] fictional world – nobility, gentry, and trade – come together finally in the park at Pemberley' (p. 132). Jane Nardin, in *Those Elegant Decorums: The Concept of Propriety in Jane Austen's Novels*, identifies the concept of civility (p. 13) without showing how it expands into meaning.

10 See Reuben A. Brower, 'Light and bright and sparkling: irony and fiction in *Pride and Prejudice*'.

11 'The art of fiction', also quoted by Lascelles (p. 147). Q. D. Leavis's image of the 'kaleidoscope' is likewise too apt not to steal (p. 77).

5   *Mansfield Park*

1 This chapter first appeared in slightly different form under the title ' "As if they had been living friends": *Sir Charles Grandison* into *Mansfield Park*', in *Bulletin of Research in the Humanities*, 83:3 (Autumn, 1980), 360–405, copyright 1980 Readex Microprint Corporation. It is reprinted by generous permission of the editor, David Erdman.

2 *Letters*, 29 January 1813. R. W. Chapman puzzles in his book, 'we do not know what decided the choice of Northamptonshire' (p. 83), but this seems the likely explanation. Hedgerows figure largely in *Much Ado About Nothing*, which also lies behind *Pride and Prejudice*. Austen would realise a scene involving hedgerows in *Persuasion*.

3 When Walter Scott reviewed *Emma*, he used Richardson's abduction scene to show how Jane Austen differed from other novelists.

4 Fanny Burney wrote of her own suitor, 'In short, he does not *hit my fancy*', and added these lines. See Joyce Hemlow, *The History of Fanny Burney*, p. 59. Joseph Wiesenfarth compares Fanny Price's refusal with Harriet's in *The Errand of Form: An Assay of Jane Austen's Art*, ch. iv.

5 See E. E. Duncan-Jones, 'Notes on Jane Austen'. Bradbrook links the two fathers (p. 87). A briefer reincarnation is that of Mrs Eleanor Grandison in the 'Mrs. Eleanors' mentioned in the chapel (*MP*, 87).

6 See my 'The reviser observed'.

7　Avrom Fleischman uses this example to comment on the 'crescendo of meaning' produced in the novel 'when a word sounds repeatedly with constantly augmented force', in *A Reading of 'Mansfield Park': An Essay in Critical Synthesis*, p. 51.

8　The name probably derived from Crabbe. See E. E. Duncan-Jones, 'Jane Austen and Crabbe'. Sharon Footerman expands on the discovery in 'The first Fanny Price'. Edmund finds Crabbe's *Tales* of 1812 in Fanny's room (156).

9　Gilbert Ryle claims that Jane Austen's sense of 'mind' is curiously like Shaftesbury's or Pope's, being 'often used without the definite or indefinite article, to stand not just for intellect or intelligence, but for the whole complex unity of a conscious, thinking, feeling and acting person', in 'Jane Austen and the moralists', p. 121. Richardson's usage is often the same, as Phillips points out (p. 60).

10　Timothy G. A. Nelson suggests in *'Doubles-entendres* in the card game in Pope's *Rape of the Lock'* that games of cards were often seen as allegorical sexual encounters. Reuben A. Brower's 'From the *Iliad* to Jane Austen, via *The Rape of the Lock'* offers more general parallels with Pope.

11　Many people would agree with Joseph Wiesenfarth when he writes in *'Emma*: point counter point' that the Pygmalion myth in *Emma* is only 'the most delightful elaboration of a story that appears in *Northanger Abbey, Sense and Sensibility*, and *Mansfield Park* – in Henry Tilney's shaping of Catherine Morland, in Colonel Brandon's shaping of Marianne Dashwood [sic], and in Edmund Bertram's shaping of Fanny Price. The hard truth in these novels is that Pygmalion is inevitably male'. But as McMaster rightly points out in her book, the pattern is in fact the other way about. 'Elizabeth teaches Darcy as much as he teaches her; Anne and Fanny, in the main course of the novels' action, remain morally static while Wentworth and Edmund get the painful education; and Marianne, though she certainly has plenty to learn, learns from her sister'. Catherine and Emma also have for her 'a certain power whereby their Pygmalions find that Galatea has turned the tables on them' (p. 46). But even she thinks less highly of these two heroines than I do. Norman Page writes in 'Orders of merit', Jane Austen sets her women characters in a 'great tradition of liberated women, their intelligence and articulateness enabling them not merely to survive in a man's world ... but to show up their males as relatively dull and conventional'.

12　Jane Austen's cousin Elizabeth de Feuillide played the harp, but Mary's harp is symbolic rather than historical, as McMaster points out (p. 34).

13 Much has been made of Jane Austen's apparent identification of ordination as her topic in a letter of 29 January 1813. But as Hugh Brogan reminds us, it was simply mistranscribed.

14 See *Grandison* I. 340 and II. 30 for example, *Pamela* IV. 304, or *The Apprentice's Vade Mecum*.

15 See Lady Bradshaigh to Richardson, *Correspondence* VI. 113–4, *Spectator*, no. 104, and Mr Lovel's pretended aversion to Amazons, that is, to 'strength, either of body or mind, in a female', in *Evelina*, p. 361.

16 R. F. Brissenden also notes the similarity in '*Mansfield Park*: freedom and the family'. Duckworth remarks in his book on Henry's choice of Richard III, 'the supreme dissimulator, the diabolical shape-changer ... the usurper king' (p. 65).

17 See George A. Starr, *Defoe and Casuistry*.

18 Ellen Moers shows how for women the brother-sister relationship might actually substitute for adult sexuality, in *Literary Women: The Great Writers*, p. 160.

19 Phillipps describes various meanings of 'comfort' (p. 47). So does Page, whose 'key-words' include tranquillity and noise, in his book (pp. 38–42).

20 Hardy's article explores the significance of Fanny's books, and Stuart M. Tave, in 'Jane Austen and one of her contemporaries', explains why Fanny Price might cherish transparencies of Tintern Abbey and a moonlit lake in Cumberland.

21 Tave comments in his book on the importance of memory and history in the novel (pp. 195–204). In her article, Hardy compares Fanny's memory with that of the hero of the *Prelude*, David Copperfield, Henry Esmond, Maggie Tulliver, Stephen Dedalus, and Marcel Proust. Keener calls *Mansfield Park* 'the Book of Memory'. Memory, he says, is Fanny's personal identity, her lifeline (p. 279).

22 De Rose (p. 47) compares this passage to Locke, II. x. 5.

23 See C. J. Rawson, *Henry Fielding and the Augustan Ideal under Stress: Nature's Dance of Death and Other Studies*.

24 'The neighbourhood of Tombuctoo: conflicts in Jane Austen's novels', p. 185.

25 See my *Samuel Richardson*, and Griffin's book, which comes to the same conclusion. He sees that in Cowper's *The Task*, which Jane Austen seems to have remembered in *Sense and Sensibility* (p. 82 above), another garden is marked as Edenic by its Adamic gardener (pp. 129–33, 233). Barker notes (p. 149) that when Austen mocked the god-like man in the juvenilia, she called him Charles Adams!

26 Many critics believe that Jane Austen's work is neither symbolic nor metaphorical. Nikolaus Pevsner for instance, seeking originals for her houses, complains that 'she is without exception vague', in 'The

architectural setting of Jane Austen's novels'. Fleischman perceives that Mansfield Park is paradisal without calling it Miltonic. His reading of 'the evil which brought such good to her!' (p. 443) supports mine, however. Devlin remarks that Henry at the altar whispers in Maria's ear like Satan (p. 93), and Butler writes that the Crawfords appear 'like Satan in the Garden of Eden' (p. 229). Duckworth sees in his book that 'there are vestigial suggestions of the expulsion from the Garden theme, as when in *Mansfield Park* Maria Bertram breaks out of the gate into the park with Crawford at Sotherton' (p. 25), and Brissenden's article also sees the Bertram family 'in the context of the Edenic myth'. Tanner reads the episode in a more generally allegorical way, remarking in his book that this is a version of the Renaissance *topos* of the wood of love, 'a dark maze in which one loses one's way' (p. 160).

27 Richardson repeats here his praise of Ralph Allen at Prior Park in Defoe's *A Tour Thro' the Whole Island of Great Britain*, the third edition of which he revised and printed in 1742. Richardson, who knew Allen, dined with him in 1752 around the time that he was writing this part of *Grandison*. Aspects of Prior Park appear at Grandison Hall, as Benjamin Boyce points out in *The Benevolent Man: A Life of Ralph Allen of Bath*, pp. 210, n. 45, and 114. In *Tom Jones*, Fielding called his own compliment to Prior Park 'Paradise Hall'.

Morris Brownell, who reprints the Defoe quotation, argues convincingly in *Alexander Pope and the Arts of Georgian England* for Pope's influence at Prior Park and elsewhere. Pope's principle of use justifying expense must have sustained Jane Austen in her attack on the Timon's villa that is Sotherton, or on Henry's plans to raise the functionally unpretentious farm at Thornton Lacey to a *place* showing forth the grandeur of its owner (244).

28 Samuel Kliger's 'Jane Austen's *Pride and Prejudice* in the eighteenth-century mode', discusses the opposition in a more political sense. Douglas Bush notes in *Jane Austen* some connections between *Grandison* and Jane Austen's novels, and remarks 'it would not be altogether fanciful to think of Fanny, Edmund, and Mary Crawford as descendants of a trio perhaps unknown to Jane Austen – Spenser's Una, Red Cross Knight, and Duessa' (p. 132). In her book, McMaster also believes that Jane Austen means us to read the wilderness scene symbolically. 'It was Mary who led the way into this wood, with its "serpentining" pathways, and Edmund enters it much as the Redcrosse Knight, accompanied by his Una, enters the Wandering Wood in which he encounters the female monster, Error' (p. 34).

29 *Selected Letters*, p. 296. 'Carvers', or choosers, is the correct reading.

30 Brower remarks similarly of *Pride and Prejudice* in 'Light and bright and sparkling', 'Though we are always being led to make double interpretations, we are never in confusion about what the alternatives are' (p. 71).

31 See Trilling's article, and Robert A. Colby, *Fiction with a Purpose: Major and Minor Nineteenth-Century Novels*, ch. 3.

32 Norman Page shows in 'Categories of speech in *Persuasion*' how a sentence from that novel creates 'the illusion of social relationships being worked out through discussion, but simultaneously presents the author's judgment on the generous behaviour of the Harvilles'. In *The Daring Muse*, Doody speaks of 'the Augustan poetic ideal, that every utterance should speak twice at the same time. A language should be enriched by another counter-language, a voice by a counter-voice' (p. 231).

33 Denis Donaghue, in 'A view of *Mansfield Park*', argues that we must receive it in the ethical idiom in which it is cast, approaching it 'by way of the eighteenth-century moralists'. I agree, if 'novelist' and 'moralist' may be allowed to be often similar. Duckworth's book exemplifies the historical method used sympathetically for Jane Austen, while Tave's conclusions, based on historical study of words actually used by Jane Austen, resolve many critical difficulties.

34 *Selected Letters*, p. 89.

6 *Emma*

1 For what she might have worked up from *The Watsons*, the *Letters*, and life, see Q. D. Leavis, pp. 61–81. McMaster's book links the romantic comedies of Shakespeare and Jane Austen, and the Index entry under Shakespeare in the *Jane Austen Companion* gathers up other references. John Halperin, in 'The worlds of *Emma*: Jane Austen and Cowper', writes of the connections between those two authors, that 'even a single chance phrase remembered suggests a substantial intellectual or philosophical imprint beneath, upon which it rests'. Mr Knightley's 'faultless in spite of all her faults' (433) derives from Congreve's *The Way of the World*, in which the poet Suckling features *in absentia*, like the Sucklings of Maple Grove.

2 See Tave on imagination and truth in *Emma*.

3 This analogy bears out John Burrow's careful investigation of Mr Knightley as 'a leading but not oracular participant' in the novel, *Jane Austen's 'Emma'*, p. 13, rather than (say) Litz's opinion that Jane Austen's 'authority is quickly vested in Mr Knightley, and by the end of the fifth chapter we have complete faith in his judgment' (p. 148).

4 Lloyd W. Brown remarks in *Bits of Ivory: Narrative Techniques in Jane Austen's Fiction* how 'the weather is generally used as a barometer of the emotional crises of the narrative' (p. 98).

5 Griffin shows, for example, how John Philips and John Dyer in *Cyder* (1708) and *The Fleece* (1757) celebrated England's orchards, pastures, and political order in a context of Virgil and Milton (pp. 115–124, 270).

6 The Austen-Leighs' *Life*, p. 307, n. 1.

7 Persuasion

1 Gilbert and Gubar anticipated me in identifying the allusion (p. 11). Caroline Spurgeon's 'Two masters of comedy' offers suggestive parallels between Jane Austen and Chaucer without going so far as to say that she might have read him. This chapter originally appeared as 'Anne Elliot, the Wife of Bath, and other friends', in *Jane Austen: New Perspectives*, ed. Janet Todd, *Women and Literature*, n.s. 3 (1983), pp. 273–93. It is reprinted here, with changes, by kind permission of the editor.

2 Compare Griffin on Cowper's Miltonic allusions, which, he writes, are all 'slight but unmistakable. Taken one at a time, each is perhaps negligible. Cumulatively, they help establish the mock-heroic note of the poem and associate Cowper with the Miltonic narrator of *Paradise Lost*' (p. 222).

3 See Peter J. Dorman, 'Chaucer's reputation in the Restoration and eighteenth century'. The anthologising of Tyrwhitt's *Tales* by John Bell in 1776–83 and Robert Anderson in 1793–5 ensured even wider distribution. I am grateful to Reg Berry for this information.

4 *Complete Writings*, pp. 572–4.

5 A reference to Sonnet 104 seems likely when it is said of Elizabeth Elliot that 'thirteen winters' revolving frosts had seen her opening every ball of credit which a scanty neighbourhood afforded; and thirteen springs shewn their blossoms, as she travelled up to London with her father' (7).

6 Most people think *Persuasion*, and by implication the author, 'autumnal'. But Jane Austen surely stresses *renewal* in her book. Griffin, who explores connections between Thomson and *Il Penseroso*, argues that in *The Seasons* Paradise is 'unlost'. Thomson moves from innocent golden age to paradisal spring without any intervening Fall (pp. 192–4).

7 See G. S. Rousseau, 'Science', p. 189.

8 This sounds like Thomson, who, says Griffin (p. 195), 'makes Milton's Edenic day a metaphor for a whole lifetime of happiness':

Enamour'd more, as more Remembrance swells
With many a Proof of recollected Love.

(*The Seasons*, ll. 1173–4)

9 Litz writes, 'more than has been generally realized or acknowledged, she was influenced by the Romantic poetry of the early nineteenth century' (p. 153). McMaster adds in her article that 'Critics have been fond of saying that Jane Austen was virtually oblivious of the romantic revolution'. Alethea Hayter anticipated me in her 'Xanadu at Lyme Regis'. In the next issue of the same journal, B. S. Southam replies, I think mistakenly, that Jane Austen's description of the scene is only realistic.

10 Dryden had pointed to his translation of Boccaccio's *Sigismonda and Guiscardo* as being similar in theme to the Wife's Tale. Here as in *Persuasion*, a tyrant father separates his noble daughter from a 'Plebian Mate' (*Poems*, l. 489). See also Crabbe's tale in *The Parish Register* about a proud miller who refuses to let his daughter marry a bold sailor, a tale which is also the source for Fanny Price's name. Again the similarities with *Persuasion* are marked.

11 Jane Austen had already used *Lear* for the start of *Sense and Sensibility*, when the John Dashwoods blandly reduce the amount they will give their poor relations. See Cecil C. Seronsy, 'Jane Austen's technique'. Chapman remarks, 'call [Anne] Cordelia, and Miss Elliot assumes the proportions of Goneril, if Mary Musgrove is an inadequate Regan' (p. 190). Kirkham sees Fanny as Cordelia and Edmund as the younger dispossessed son (p. 113).

12 Nora Crook finds suggestions of 'the weaker vessel' and 'corruption' in the name 'Clay' to support her discovery that Gowland's Lotion was used to treat venereal disease. Mrs Clay's use of it, together with her symbolically flawing freckles and her ready flight to William Elliot, link her discreditably to the decadence of Regency Bath.

13 Malcolm Bradbury in '*Persuasion* again' makes the same point. He sees the book as morally radical.

14 Garrick, who supplied Mr Woodhouse with his riddle about Kitty, a fair but frozen maid (see Chapman's note to *Emma*, p. 70), may here be assisting Admiral Croft. See his prologue to Goldsmith's *She Stoops to Conquer* (1773), 'I've that within – for which there are no plaisters'.

15 Anne's sportings with pretty musings of high-wrought love and eternal constancy, 'almost enough to spread purification and perfume all the way', are something like Richardson's rewriting of *Hudibras* for Harriet,

Where-e'er she treads, her feet shall set
The primrose, and the violet:

All spices, perfumes, and sweet powders,
Shall borrow from her breath their odours.

(Grandison, I. 71)

16 Byron wrote in *Don Juan* shortly after *Persuasion* was published,
'Man's love is of man's life a thing apart, / 'Tis woman's whole
existence' (I. cxiv). Was he returning Benwick's compliment to his
Turkish Tales?

17 Richard Simpson, in *Jane Austen: The Critical Heritage*, anticipated
me in seeing that Anne is 'Shakespeare's Viola translated into an
English girl of the nineteenth century'. He says that 'the chapters
which she wrote during the last months of her life are directly
founded upon Shakespeare' (p. 256). Lloyd W. Brown, in 'Jane Austen
and the feminist tradition', argues that Jane Austen found her ideas
in writers such as Mary Wollstonecraft. But feminism is older than
that.

18 Jane Austen's list must include Constance in Benwick's favourite
Marmion, a woman of 'matchless constancy' in a 'form so soft and
fair' (II. xxi, xxvi). The dashing young Lochinvar, 'so faithful in love
and so dauntless in war', who plucks fair Ellen from the heart of her
family at Netherby Hall (Canto V) contains more than a hint of
Captain Wentworth. Captain Harville for his part could point to
Scott's lines, quoted in *Sanditon* (397),

O Woman! in our hours of ease,
Uncertain, coy and hard to please.
And variable ...   (VI. xxx)

For the importance of constancy in Shakespeare, see Germaine
Greer, *Shakespeare*, pp. 109–13.

19 Mudrick writes in his article that '(Anne almost says, glorying in her
exemplary role) no book, until this one, has ever told the truth about
me'.

Conclusion   'Nothing can come of nothing'

1 Norman Page's 'The Great Tradition revisited' perceptively recon-
structs the book that the Leavises never wrote.

2 'The second discourse', *Discourses Delivered to the Students of the
Royal Academy*, pp. 20–1.

3 In his article, Brissenden notes the 'parallel between the exposure
of the grease and dirt in the Portsmouth parlour and the exposure
[of Maria's elopement]'.

4 *Structuralism in Literature: An Introduction*, p. 30. See also Jonathan
Culler, *Structuralist Poetics: Structuralism, Linguistics, and the
Study of Literature*, pp. 90, 30.

5 'The lesson of Balzac' and 'Gustave Flaubert', pp. 62–3, 207. Culler remarks that 'the line between the conscious and the unconscious is highly variable, impossible to identify, and supremely uninteresting' (p. 118).

6 *The Formal Strain: Studies in Augustan Imitation and Satire*, p. 4. His first chapter is a particularly full guide to the theory.

7 In his book, and especially in the valuable afterword, 'Notes toward an eighteenth-century theory of literary influence', Griffin arrives at some of the same conclusions about eighteenth-century poets as I do about Jane Austen: deliberate and companionable challenging of predecessors, rewriting of other authors, creation as re-creation, ideas of imitation, translation, and improvement, and an absence of anxiety. His paradoxical description for their poetry, 'free-standing imitative originals', applies perfectly to Jane Austen's novels.

Appendix 2   *Sir Charles Grandison* in the juvenilia

1 This appendix appeared in slightly different form as 'All the impassioned, & most exceptionable parts of Richardson: Jane Austen's juvenilia', in *The Interpretative Power: Essays on Literature in Honour of Margaret Dalziel*, ed. C. A. Gibson (University of Otago, 1980), pp. 59–68. It is reprinted by kind permission of the editor.

2 Duncan-Jones sees the similarity in 'Notes on Jane Austen'.

3 *Selected Essays* (New York: Vintage Books, 1966), pp. 85–104.

Bibliography

General

Abrams, M.H., 'A correspondent breeze: a romantic metaphor', in *English Romantic Poets: Modern Essays in Criticism*, ed. M.H. Abrams (New York: Oxford University Press, 1960), pp. 25–43

Anon., 'Western wind', cited in *The Oxford Dictionary of Quotations* (London: Oxford University Press, repr. 1972), 11:14

Bacon, Francis, *The Advancement of Learning* (1605), in *English Critical Essays (Sixteenth, Seventeenth and Eighteenth Centuries)*, ed. E.D. Jones (London: Oxford University Press, 1922, repr. 1956)

Barker, Gerard A., *Grandison's Heirs: The Paragon's Progress in the late Eighteenth-Century English Novel* (Newark: University of Delaware Press, 1985)

Bayley, John, 'Life-enhancing world-views', a review of Angus Wilson's *Diversity and Depth in Fiction: Selected Critical Writings* (London: Secker and Warburg, 1983), *TLS* (16 September 1983), 978

Beer, Gillian, 'Richardson, Milton, and the status of evil', *Review of English Studies*, n.s. 19 (1968), 261–70

Blake, William, *Complete Writings*, ed. Geoffrey Keynes (London: Nonesuch Press, 1957, repr. Oxford University Press, 1972)

Bloom, Harold, *The Anxiety of Influence: A Theory of Poetry* (New York: Oxford University Press, 1973)

Bloom, Harold, and Pat Rogers, debate on plagiarism, *TLS* (9 April 1982)

Boswell, James, *Life of Johnson*, edd. R.W. Chapman and J.D. Fleeman (Oxford: Oxford University Press, 1953, repr. 1970)

Boyce, Benjamin, *The Benevolent Man: A Life of Ralph Allen of Bath* (Cambridge, Mass.: Harvard University Press, 1967)

Brownell, Morris, *Alexander Pope and the Arts of Georgian England* (Oxford: Clarendon Press, 1978)

Burney, Fanny, *Evelina*, ed. Edward A. Bloom (London: Oxford University Press, 1968)

Byron, Lord George Gordon, *The Poetical Works of Lord Byron* (London: Oxford University Press, repr. 1957)

Carroll, John, 'Lovelace as tragic hero', *University of Toronto Quarterly*, 42 (1972), 14–25

Chaucer, Geoffrey, *Complete Works*, ed. F.N. Robinson (London: Oxford University Press, 1957)

Colby, Robert A., *Fiction with a Purpose: Major and Minor Nineteenth-Century Novels* (Bloomington: Indiana University Press, 1968)

Coleridge, Samuel Taylor, 'Table Talk', in *Coleridge: Select Poetry and Prose*, ed. Stephen Potter (London: Nonesuch Press, 1950)

Crabbe, George, *The Poems of George Crabbe*, ed. Adolphus Ward, 3 vols. (Cambridge: Cambridge University Press, 1905–7)

Cranston, Maurice, *John Locke: A Biography* (London: Longmans, Green & Co., 1957)

Culler, Jonathan, *Structuralist Poetics: Structuralism, Linguistics, and the Study of Literature* (London: Routledge and Kegan Paul, 1975)

Dodsley, Robert, *A Collection of Poems by Several Hands* or, *Dodsley's Miscellany* (1745 and often reprinted)

Donaldson, Ian, 'Fielding, Richardson, and the ends of the novel', *Essays in Criticism*, 32:1 (January 1982), 26–47

    The Rapes of Lucretia: A Myth and its Transformations (Oxford: Clarendon Press, 1982)

Doody, Margaret Anne, *The Daring Muse: Augustan Poetry Reconsidered* (Cambridge: Cambridge University Press, 1985)

Dorman, Peter J., 'Chaucer's reputation in the Restoration and eighteenth century', unpublished doctoral dissertation (New York University, 1971)

Dryden, John, *The Poems of John Dryden*, ed. James Kinsley (Oxford: Clarendon Press, 1958)

    Of Dramatick Poesie: An Essay, ed. James T. Boulton (London: Oxford University Press, 1964)

Duncombe, John, '*The Feminiad*. A poem', ed. Jocelyn Harris, Augustan Reprint Society, no. 207 (Los Angeles: William Andrews Clark Memorial Library, 1981)

Eliot, T.S., 'Tradition and the individual talent', *Selected Essays* (London: Faber, 1932, repr. 1958)

Fielding, Henry, *The History of Tom Jones*, edd. Martin C. Battestin and Fredson Bowers (Oxford: Clarendon Press, 1974)

Gilbert, Susan, and Sandra Gubar, *The Madwoman in the Attic: The Woman Writer and the Nineteenth-Century Literary Imagination* (New Haven and London: Yale University Press, 1979)

Greer, Germaine, *Shakespeare* (Oxford: Oxford University Press, 1986)

Griffin, Dustin, *Regaining Paradise: Milton and the Eighteenth Century* (Cambridge: Cambridge University Press, 1986)

Hagstrum, Jean, *Sex and Sensibility: Ideal and Erotic Love from Milton to Mozart* (Chicago: University of Chicago Press, 1980)

Harris, Jocelyn, 'The reviser observed: the last volume of *Sir Charles Grandison*', *Studies in Bibliography*, 29 (1976), 1–31

'Learning and genius in *Sir Charles Grandison*', *Studies in the Eighteenth Century*, IV, edd. R.F. Brissenden and J.C. Eade (Canberra, 1979), pp. 167–91

Samuel Richardson (Cambridge: Cambridge University Press, 1987)

Hemlow, Joyce, *The History of Fanny Burney* (Oxford: Clarendon Press, 1958)

James, Henry, 'The art of fiction', 'The lesson of Balzac', and 'Gustave Flaubert', reprinted in *The House of Fiction: Essays on the Novel by Henry James*, ed. Leon Edel (London: Rupert Hart-Davis, 1957)

Johnson, Samuel, *A Dictionary of the English Language*, 10th edition (London, 1810)

The History of Rasselas Prince of Abissinia, edd. Geoffrey Tillotson and Brian Jenkins (London: Oxford University Press, 1971)

Leapor, Mary, 'Corydon. Phillario. Or, Mira's Picture. A Pastoral', in *Poems by the Most Eminent Ladies of Great Britain*, edd. Bonnell Thornton and George Colman (1755), II, 123–6

Leavis, F.R., *The Great Tradition* (London: Chatto and Windus, 1948, repr. 1960)

Lichtenberg, Georg Christian, *Lichtenberg: Aphorisms and Letters*, edd. Franz Mautner and Henry Hatfield (London: Jonathan Cape, 1969)

Locke, John, *An Essay Concerning Human Understanding* (1690), ed. Peter H. Nidditch (Oxford: Clarendon Press, 1975)

Some Thoughts Concerning Education (1693) in *The Educational Writings of John Locke. A Critical Edition*, ed. James L. Axtell (Cambridge: Cambridge University Press, 1968)

On the Conduct of the Understanding, in *The Posthumous Works of Mr John Locke* (1706)

MacLean, Kenneth, *John Locke and English Literature of the Eighteenth Century* (New York: Russell, 1962)

Pope, Alexander, *The Poems of Alexander Pope*, ed. John Butt (London: Methuen, 1965)

Rawson, C.J., *Henry Fielding and the Augustan Ideal under Stress: Nature's Dance of Death and Other Studies* (London: Routledge and Kegan Paul, 1972)

Reynolds, Sir Joshua, 'The second discourse', *Discourses Delivered to the Students of the Royal Academy*, ed. Roger Fry (London: Seeley, 1905)

Richardson, Samuel, *The Apprentice's Vade Mecum* (1739), ed. Alan Dugald McKillop, Augustan Society Reprint, nos. 169–70 (Los Angeles: William Andrews Clark Memorial Library, 1975)

    Pamela [1740], edd. T. C. Duncan Eaves and Ben D. Kimpel (Boston: Houghton Miflin, 1971)

    Pamela, 4 vols. (New York and London: Garland, 1974)

    Pamela, ed. Peter Sabor with an introduction by Margaret Anne Doody (Harmondsworth: Penguin, 1980)

    Clarissa (1748–9), 1st edition copy in the de Beer Collection, University of Otago Library

    '*Clarissa*: preface, hints of prefaces, and postscript', ed. R. F. Brissenden, Augustan Society Reprint, no. 103 (Los Angeles: William Andrews Clark Memorial Library, 1964)

    The Correspondence of Samuel Richardson, ed. Anna Laetitia Barbauld, 6 vols. (London: 1804, repr. AMS Press, 1966)

    Selected Letters of Samuel Richardson, ed. John Carroll (Oxford: Clarendon Press, 1964)

    The History of Sir Charles Grandison ed. Jocelyn Harris, 3 parts (London: Oxford University Press, 1972, repr. 1986)

Rogers, Pat, 'The rise and fall of gout' *TLS* (20 March 1980), 315–16

    'Richardson and the Bluestockings', in *Samuel Richardson: Passion and Prudence*, ed. Valerie Grosvenor Myer (London and Totowa, N. J.: Vision and Barnes & Noble, 1986), pp. 147–64

Rousseau, G. S., 'Science', in *The Eighteenth Century*, ed. Pat Rogers (London: Methuen, 1978) pp. 153–207

Said, Edward W., *Beginnings: Intention and Method* (New York: Basic Books, 1975)

Scholes, Robert, *Structuralism in Literature: An Introduction* (London and New Haven: Yale University Press, 1974)

Shakespeare, William, *The Complete Works*, ed. Peter Alexander (London and Glasgow: Collins, 1951, repr. 1978)

Sidney, Sir Philip, 'Apology for Poetry' (1595), see Bacon

Starr, George A., *Defoe and Casuistry* (Princeton, New Jersey: Princeton University Press, 1971)

Steele, Richard, *The Christian Hero* (1701), ed. R. Blanchard (Oxford: Oxford University Press, 1932)

Thomson, James, *The Seasons*, ed. James Sambrook (Oxford: Clarendon Press, 1981)

Trilling, Lionel, *Sincerity and Authenticity* (London and Cambridge, Mass.: Oxford University Press, 1972)

van Ghent, Dorothy, *The English Novel: Form and Function* (New York: Harper and Row, 1953)

Warren, Robert Penn, *Selected Essays* (New York: Vintage Books, 1966)

Watt, Ian, *The Rise of the Novel: Studies in Defoe, Richardson, and Fielding* (London: Chatto and Windus, 1957, repr. Penguin, 1963)
  'Serious reflections on *The Rise of the Novel*', *Novel*, 1 (1968), 205–17

Weinbrot, Howard, *The Formal Strain: Studies in Augustan Imitation and Satire* (Chicago and London: University of Chicago Press, 1969)

Young, Edward, *Conjectures on Original Composition* (1759)
  Edward Young's 'Conjectures' in England and Germany, ed. M. W. Steinke (New York: Folcroft Press (1917), repr. 1970)

Jane Austen

R. W. Chapman's edition of the novels (Oxford and London: Oxford University Press, 1923, reissued 1965–6), the *Minor Works* (Oxford: Oxford University Press, 1954), and *Jane Austen's Letters to her Sister Cassandra and Others* (London, New York, Toronto: Oxford University Press, second edition 1952, repr. 1979); *Volume the Second*, ed. B. C. Southam (Oxford: Clarendon Press, 1963)

Collections of essays on Jane Austen

Critical Essays on Jane Austen, ed. B. C. Southam (London and New York: Routledge and Kegan Paul, 1968)

Jane Austen's Achievement, ed. Juliet McMaster (London: MacMillan, 1976)

Jane Austen: Bicentenary Essays, ed. John Halperin (Cambridge: Cambridge University Press, 1975)

The Jane Austen Companion, edd. J. David Grey, A. Walton Litz, and Brian Southam (London: MacMillan, 1986)

Jane Austen: The Critical Heritage, ed. B. C. Southam (London and New York: Routledge and Kegan Paul, 1968)

Jane Austen Today, ed. Joel Weinsheimer (Athens, Georgia: University of Georgia Press, 1975)

'Sense and Sensibility', 'Pride and Prejudice', and 'Mansfield Park': A Casebook, ed. B. C. Southam (London: MacMillan, 1976)

Books and articles about Jane Austen

Andrews, P. B. S., 'The date of *Pride and Prejudice*', *N & Q*, 213 (1968), 338–42

Austen, Henry, 'Biographical notice', printed with *Northanger Abbey* and *Persuasion* (1818)

Austen-Leigh, Emma, *Jane Austen and Steventon* (London: Spottis-woode, Ballantyne, & Co., 1937)

Austen-Leigh, James Edward, *A Memoir of Jane Austen* (Oxford: Clarendon Press, 1926, repr. 1951)

Austen-Leigh, William, and Richard Arthur, *Jane Austen: Her Life and Letters. A Family Record* (London, 1913, reissued New York: Russell, 1965)

Bayley, John, 'Characterization in Jane Austen', *The Jane Austen Companion*, pp. 24–34

Bradbrook, Frank W., *Jane Austen and her Predecessors* (Cambridge: Cambridge University Press, 1966)

Bradbury, Malcolm, '*Persuasion* again', *Essays in Criticism*, 18 (1968), 383–96

Brissenden, R. F., '*Mansfield Park*: freedom and the family', in *Jane Austen: Bicentenary Essays*, pp. 172–9

Brogan, Hugh, letter on 'ordination', *TLS* (19 December 1968), 1440

Brower, Reuben A., 'Light and bright and sparkling: irony and fiction in *Pride and Prejudice*', in *The Fields of Light: An Experiment in Critical Reading* (New York: Oxford University Press, 1951), pp. 164–81

'From the *Iliad* to Jane Austen, via *The Rape of the Lock*', *Jane Austen: Bicentenary Essays*, pp. 43–60

Brown, Lloyd W., *Bits of Ivory: Narrative Techniques in Jane Austen's Fiction* (Baton Rouge: Louisiana State University Press, 1973)

'Jane Austen and the feminist tradition', *Nineteenth-Century Fiction* 28 (1973–4), 321–38

Burlin, Katrin Ristkok, ' "The pen of the contriver": the four fictions of *Northanger Abbey*', in *Jane Austen: Bicentenary Essays*, pp. 89–111

Burrows, John, *Jane Austen's 'Emma'* (Sydney: Sydney University Press, 1968)

review of Barbara Hardy, *A Reading of Jane Austen* (London: Peter Owen, 1979), *Journal of the Australasian Universities' Modern Languages Association*, 54 (1980), pp. 251–4

Bush, Douglas, *Jane Austen* (New York and London: MacMillan, 1975)

Butler, Marilyn, *Jane Austen and the War of Ideas* (Oxford: Clarendon Press, 1975)

Chapman, R. W., *Jane Austen: Facts and Problems* (Oxford: Clarendon Press, 1948, repr. 1961)

Critical Essays on Jane Austen, ed. B. C. Southam (London and New York: Routledge and Kegan Paul, 1968)

Crook, Nora, 'Gowland's Lotion', *TLS* (7 October 1983), 1089

Daiches, David, 'Jane Austen, Karl Marx, and the aristocratic dance', *American Scholar*, 17 (1947–8), 289–96

De Rose, Peter L., *Jane Austen and Samuel Johnson* (Washington: University Press of Washington, 1980)

Devlin, D. D., *Jane Austen and Education* (London: MacMillan, 1975)

Donaghue, Denis, 'A view of *Mansfield Park*', *Critical Essays on Jane Austen*, pp. 39–59

Donovan, Robert Alan, 'The mind of Jane Austen', in *Jane Austen Today*, pp. 109–27

Doody, Margaret Anne, 'Jane Austen's reading', in *The Jane Austen Companion*, pp. 347–63

Duckworth, Alistair M., *The Improvement of the Estate: A Study of Jane Austen's Novels* (Baltimore and London: Johns Hopkins Press, 1971)

'Prospects and retrospects', *Jane Austen Today*, pp. 1–32

Duncan-Jones, E. E., 'Notes on Jane Austen', *N & Q*, 196 (1951), 14–16

'Jane Austen and Crabbe', *RES*, n.s. 5 (1954), 174

'Proposals of marriage in *Pride and Prejudice* and *Pamela*', *N & Q*, 202 (1957), 76

'Jane Austen and *Clarissa*', *N & Q*, 208 (1963), 350

'The Misses Selby and Steele', *TLS*, 10 September 1964, 845

Ebiike, Shunji, '*Pride and Prejudice* and *First Impressions*', *Studies in English Literature* (Tokyo, 1965), 31–45

Elsbree, Langdon, 'Jane Austen and the dance of fidelity and complaisance', *Nineteenth-Century Fiction*, 15 (1960–1), 113–36

Farrer, Reginald, 'Jane Austen, *ob.* July 18 1817', *Quarterly Review*, 228 (1917), 1–30

Fergus, Jan, *Jane Austen and the Didactic Novel: 'Northanger Abbey', 'Sense and Sensibility' and 'Pride and Prejudice'* (London: MacMillan, 1983)

Fleischman, Avrom, *A Reading of 'Mansfield Park': An Essay in Critical Synthesis* (Minneapolis: University of Minnesota Press, 1967)

Footerman, Sharon, 'The first Fanny Price', *N & Q*, 223 (1978), 217–19

Gillie, Christopher, *A Preface to Jane Austen* (London: Longman, 1974)

Gilson, David, 'Jane Austen's books', *Book Collector*, 23 (1974), 27–39

A Bibliography of Jane Austen (Oxford: Clarendon Press, 1982)

Greene, Donald, 'The myth of limitation', in *Jane Austen Today*, pp. 142–75

Grierson, H. J. C., in *TLS* (8 December 1921), 827

Halperin, John, 'The worlds of *Emma*: Jane Austen and Cowper', in *Jane Austen: Bicentenary Essays*, pp. 197–206

Hardy, Barbara, 'The objects in *Mansfield Park*', in *Jane Austen: Bicentenary Essays*, pp. 180–96

Harris, Jocelyn, '"As if they had been living friends": *Sir Charles Grandison into Mansfield Park*', in *Bulletin of Research in the Humanities*, 83:3 (Autumn, 1980), 360–405

'All the impassioned, & most exceptionable parts of Richardson: Jane Austen's juvenilia', *The Interpretative Power: Essays on Literature in Honour of Margaret Dalziel*, ed. C.A. Gibson (University of Otago, 1980), pp. 59–68

'Anne Elliot, the Wife of Bath, and other friends', in *Jane Austen: New Perspectives, Women and Literature*, ed. Janet Todd, n.s. 3 (1983), 273–93

Hayter, Alethea, 'Xanadu at Lyme Regis', *Ariel*, 1:1 (1970), 61–4

Honan, Park, *Jane Austen: Her Life* (London: Weidenfeld and Nicholson, 1987)

'Richardson's influence on Jane Austen (some notes on the biographical and critical problems of an "influence")', in *Samuel Richardson: Passion and Prudence*, ed. Myer, pp. 165–77

Hough, Graham, 'Narrative and dialogue in Jane Austen', *Critical Quarterly*, 12 (1970), 201–30

Jenkins, Elizabeth, *Jane Austen: A Biography* (London: Victor Gollancz, 1938)

Johnson, R. Brimley, *Jane Austen: Her Life, her Work, her Family, and her Critics* (London, Toronto, and New York: Dent, 1930)

Keener, Frederick M., *The Chain of Becoming: The Philosophical Tale, the Novel, and a Neglected Realism of the Enlightenment: Swift, Montesquieu, Voltaire, Johnson, and Austen* (New York: Columbia University Press, 1983)

Kirkham, Margaret, *Jane Austen, Feminism and Fiction* (Brighton and New Jersey: Harvester Press, 1983)

Kliger, Samuel, 'Jane Austen's *Pride and Prejudice* in the eighteenth-century mode', *University of Toronto Quarterly*, 16 (1946–7), 357–70

Lascelles, Mary, *Jane Austen and her Art* (London: Oxford University Press, 1939)

Leavis, Q.D., 'A critical theory of Jane Austen's writings', *Scrutiny*, 10 (1941–2), 61–87, 114–42, 272–94; 12 (1944–5), 104–19

Levine, George, 'Translating the monstrous: *Northanger Abbey*', *Nineteenth-Century Fiction*, 30:3 (December 1975), 335–50

Litz, A. Walton, *Jane Austen: A Study of her Artistic Development* (London and New York: Chatto and Windus, 1965)

'Chronology of composition', in *The Jane Austen Companion*, pp. 47–52

'Criticism, 1939–83', in *The Jane Austen Companion*, pp. 110–17

Lodge, David, 'The vocabulary of *Mansfield Park*', in *Language of*

Fiction: Essays in Criticism and Verbal Analysis of the English Novel (New York: Columbia University Press, 1966, repr. 1967), pp. 94–113

McKillop, A. D., 'The context of *Sense and Sensibility*', *Rice Institute Pamphlets*, 44:1 (April 1957), pp. 65–78

McMaster, Juliet, 'The continuity of Jane Austen's novels', *Studies in English Literature 1500–1900*, 10 (1970), 723–39

Jane Austen on Love (Victoria: University of Victoria Press, 1978)

Measham, D. C., 'Sentiment and sentimental psychology', *Renaissance and Modern Studies*, 16 (1972), 61–85

Letter in *TLS* (17 April 1981), 437

Metcalfe, Alvin C., '*Sense and Sensibility*: a study of its similarity to *The History of Sir Charles Grandison*', unpublished doctoral dissertation (Kent State, 1970)

Modert, Jo, 'Chronology within the novels', in *The Jane Austen Companion*, pp. 53–9

Moers, Ellen, *Literary Women: The Great Writers* (Garden City, N.Y.: Doubleday, 1976, repr. 1977)

Moler, Kenneth M., *Jane Austen's Art of Allusion* (Lincoln, Nebraska: University of Nebraska Press, 1968)

Mudrick, Marvin, *Jane Austen: Irony as Defense and Discovery* (Princeton, N.J., and London: Princeton University Press, 1952)

'Jane Austen's drawing-room', in *Jane Austen: Bicentenary Essays*, pp. 247–61

Nardin, Jane, *Those Elegant Decorums: The Concept of Propriety in Jane Austen's Novels* (Albany: State University of New York Press, 1973)

Nelson, Timothy G. A., '*Doubles-entendres* in the card game in Pope's *Rape of the Lock*', *PQ*, 59:2 (Spring 1980), 234–7

Odmark, John, *An Understanding of Jane Austen's Novels: Character, Value and Ironic Perspective* (Oxford: Basil Blackwell, 1981)

Page, Norman, 'Categories of speech in *Persuasion*', *Modern Language Review*, 64 (1969), 734–41

The Language of Jane Austen (Oxford: Basil Blackwell, 1972)

'Orders of merit', in *Jane Austen Today*, pp. 92–108

'The Great Tradition revisited', in *Jane Austen's Achievement*, pp. 44–63

Pevsner, Nikolaus, 'The architectural setting of Jane Austen's novels', *Journal of the Warburg and Courtauld Institutes*, 31 (1968), 404–22

Phillipps, K. C., *Jane Austen's English* (London: Andre Deutsch, 1970)

Rawson, C. R., ' "Nice" and "sentimental": A parallel between *Northanger Abbey* and Richardson's *Correspondence*', *N & Q*, 209 (1964), 180

Rees, Joan, *Jane Austen: Women and Writer* (New York and London: St Martin's Press, 1976)

Ryle, Gilbert, 'Jane Austen and the moralists', in *Critical Essays on Jane Austen*, pp. 106–22

Scott, Walter, review of *Emma*, *Quarterly Review*, 14:27 (October, 1815 [March, 1816]), 188–201

Seronsy, Cecil C., 'Jane Austen's technique', *N & Q*, 200 (1956), 303–5

Simpson, Richard, unsigned review of the *Memoir*, *North British Review* (April 1870), reprinted in *Jane Austen: The Critical Heritage*, pp. 241–65

Smith, LeRoy M., *Jane Austen and the Drama of Women* (London and Basingstoke: MacMillan, 1983)

Southam, B. C., 'Jane Austen: a broken romance?', *N & Q*, 206 (1961), 464–5

'Jane Austen and *Clarissa*', *N & Q*, 208 (1963), 191–2

Jane Austen's Literary Manuscripts: A Study of the Novelist's Development through the Surviving Papers (London: Oxford University Press, 1964)

'General Tilney's hot-houses: some recent Jane Austen studies and texts', *Ariel*, 2:4 (1971), 52–62

Southam, B. C., ed., *Jane Austen's 'Sir Charles Grandison'*, with an introduction by Lord David Cecil (Oxford: Clarendon Press, 1980)

'Sense and Sensibility', 'Pride and Prejudice', and 'Mansfield Park': A Casebook (London, MacMillan, 1976)

Spencer, Jane, *The Rise of the Woman Novelist from Aphra Behn to Jane Austen* (Oxford and New York: Basil Blackwell, 1986)

Spender, Dale, *Mothers of the Novel: 100 Good Women Writers before Jane Austen* (London and New York: Pandora, 1986)

Spurgeon, Caroline, 'Two masters of comedy', *TLS* (25 August 1927), 565–6

Tanner, Tony, introduction to *Sense and Sensibility* (Harmondsworth: Penguin, 1969)

Jane Austen (Basingstoke and London: MacMillan, 1986)

Tave, Stuart M., *Some Words of Jane Austen* (Chicago: University of Chicago Press, 1973)

'Jane Austen and one of her contemporaries', in *Jane Austen: Bicentenary Essays*, pp. 61–74

Ten Harmsel, Henrietta, *Jane Austen: A Study in Fictional Conventions* (The Hague: Mouton, 1964)

Thomson, C. L., *Jane Austen: A Survey* (London: Horace Marshall & Son, 1929)

Todd, Janet, ed., *Jane Austen: New Perspectives, Women and Literature*, n.s. 3 (New York: Holmes & Meier, 1983)

Tompkins, J. M. S., '*Elinor and Marianne*: a note on Jane Austen', *RES*, 16 (1940), 33–43

Trilling, Lionel, '*Mansfield Park*', in *The Opposing Self: Nine Essays in Criticism* (London and New York: Viking Press, 1955)

Tucker, George Holbert, *A Goodly Heritage: A History of Jane Austen's Family* (Manchester: Carcanet Press, 1983)

van Ghent, Dorothy, *The English Novel: Form and Function* (New York: Harper and Row, 1953)

Weinsheimer, Joel, 'Jane Austen's anthropocentrism', in *Jane Austen Today*, pp. 128–41

Whalley, George, 'Jane Austen: poet', in *Jane Austen's Achievement*, pp. 106–33

Wiesenfarth, Joseph, *The Errand of Form: An Assay of Jane Austen's Art* (New York: Fordham University Press, 1967)

'Austen and Apollo', in *Jane Austen Today*, pp. 46–63

'*Emma*: point counter point', in *Jane Austen: Bicentenary Essays*, pp. 207–20

Wilson, Angus, 'The neighbourhood of Tombuctoo: conflicts in Jane Austen's novels', *Critical Essays on Jane Austen*, pp. 182–99

Woolf, Virginia, 'Jane Austen at sixty', *Nation and Athenaeum*, 34 (1923), 433–4

Wright, Andrew H., *Jane Austen's Novels: A Study in Structure* (Harmondsworth: Penguin, 1963)

Foreword to the Jane Austen issue of *Nineteenth-Century Fiction*, 30: 3 (December 1975)

Index